GREAT AMERICAN GOLF STORIES

Lyons Press Classics

Great American Golf Stories

Edited by Jeff Silverman

Essex, Connecticut

An imprint of Globe Pequot, the trade division of The Rowman & Littlefield Publishing Group, Inc.
4501 Forbes Blvd., Ste. 200
Lanham, MD 20706
www.rowman.com

Distributed by NATIONAL BOOK NETWORK

British Library Cataloguing in Publication Information available

Library of Congress Cataloging-in-Publication Data
ISBN 978-1-4930-7191-3 (paperback)
ISBN 978-1-4930-7345-0 (e-book)

♾™ The paper used in this publication meets the minimum requirements of American National Standard for Information Sciences—Permanence of Paper for Printed Library Materials, ANSI/ NISO Z39.48-1992.

In memory of Guy Cary

A great American golf story without question

Contents

CONTENTS

Acknowledgments

With thanks to the crew at Lyons Press for making an excursion like this possible, and, as ever, to Abby Van Pelt, for simply staying the course.

Why Golf is Art and Art is Golf
We have not far to seek —
So much depends upon the lie,
So much upon the cleek.

     —RUDYARD KIPLING, *THE ALMANAC OF SPORTS*

Introduction

ESSENTIALLY, EVERY TIME WE SET OUT TO PLAY GOLF, WE SET OUT IN search of new stories to tell. Not every story will be great, of course, unless we can expand our fairways—real and imagined, external and internal—to simultaneously include absurdity, burlesque, misadventure, disaster, tragedy, and all the other insanely hysterical things we human beings are capable of inflicting on a golf ball . . . and on ourselves. Yet, whatever the quality of our games, a round of golf is plot in a nutshell with a urethane cover attached. It begins, as stories do, with infinite possibilities and the hope of a happy ending. Then, along the way, all hell's likely to break loose. Nature taunts us. Luck rewards—or kills—us, the difference determined by silly millimeters. Hazards await. Penalties are imposed. Despair moves in. Elation moves it out. Despair moves back in again. Character is tested. True character is revealed.

I remember all those college literature lectures in which professors would proudly march out the idea that "in literature, as in life . . ." and I'd zone out immediately. The two are pretty much the same, I thought; after all, what's literature if not life—or at least a few pieces of it—recorded on a page in the symbols we use to communicate? What's golf, then, if not one of life and literature's ideally twined settings. I mean, how could the most maddening endeavor ever devised by evil Druids to play out everything existence can throw at us over eighteen holes of varying length and difficulty not be?

Golf and literature go hand in hand. It's the very nature of the game—golf's leisurely, thoughtful pace; the dilemmas the game presents; its inherent mysteries and mind games and how we go about solving them—that's led so many superb writers over so long a time to wade into it and retrieve so many splendid tales, both fact and fiction. Some of them—to suit the demands of the title of this collection—are truly "great." All date back to the first decades of golf in America. All still speak clearly to us through the portals of time.

So, what makes these golf stories great ones? A number of things, really, but, ultimately, I think, it comes down to this: Even if the language is a bit thick or floral by contemporary standards, even if certain aspects of the game seem a little arcane, even if some manners are as dead as the dodo, the atmosphere seems somewhat out of whack with ours, and not everything passes the politically correct smell test, they nonetheless hold up a mirror that offers a true reflection of who we are—as men, as women, and as golfers. In short, they stand the test of time—all tales in this volume have been standing for a century or more. Some dispatch insights on how to play better, how to comport ourselves better, or how to simply enjoy the overall experience more. Some capture the drama. Some expose the folly. All show us something about ourselves.

According to the Oxford English Dictionary, the word golf was originally teed up in our written language back in 1457 when Scotland's King James II ordered Parliament to issue an act that deemed the undertaking verboten. The ban was problematic, but it was by no means a game killer, and its devotees played on. By the mid-seventeenth century, golf had bounced back fully into the open salt air of Scottish linksland; it had also bounced its way into poetry. The game's first appearance in fiction came in 1771, with a brief aside on the diversion "called Golf" in "the fields called the Links" of Edinburgh in Tobias Smollett's novel *The Expedition of Humphry Clinker*. By the second half of the nineteenth century, as the game took off through the British Isles, and sports became more fit subject matter for popular journals directed toward the moneyed leisure class, golf, quite naturally, began developing a distinctive literature all its own. The game, and writing about the game, were growing up together.

With the planting of golf's permanent flag on American shores in the 1880s—there had been fleeting forays earlier—American writers began getting in on the fun. As they took to the game, so did their typewriters.

And so did transplanted brethren with the foresight to alight on these shores with niblicks and mashies and stories to tell and verses to craft. Take Rudyard Kipling, for example. He arrived in Vermont in 1892 with balls and sticks—one handcrafted by Old Tom Morris himself— but, alas, had no place to play. Undeterred, Kipling purchased an estate in Brattleboro with a fine meadow overlooking the Connecticut River and established a wee intimation of a golf course on the property. Summer and winter alike, he'd take his whacks on the makeshift layout that began just beyond his front door, often with the local minister, and at least once with Arthur Conan Doyle, his visiting golf-mad fellow scribbler from back home. The Nobel Prize winner's four-year sojourn in the Green Mountain State turned out to be wonderfully productive. Not only did Kipling write *Captains Courageous*, the *Jungle Books*, and the magnificent short-story collection *The Day's Work in Vermont*, he also thought up the idea of the red golf ball, thus facilitating his ability to keep whacking away at with his passion—and keep track of his shots—even through the North American snow cover. In my book, such ingenuity warrants enough honorary American status to earn his four lines of poetry the right to kick off this volume.

Not every writer in this book can join Kipling in the ranks of the Nobel anointed, though Sinclair Lewis can. He incorporated a whiff of golf into his timeless novel, *Babbitt*. Perhaps, if F. Scott Fitzgerald, represented in these pages by the elegiac "Winter Dreams," had drunk a little less and lived a little longer, the Swedes might have recognized him, too. Fitzgerald, by the way, based the character of Jordan Baker in *The Great Gatsby* on his acquaintance Edith Cummings, the golfer victorious in the national Women's Amateur two years before.

A few notes follow about the other contributors to this volume, because they, too, have their own stories even if most of their names are no longer as familiar as they once were. For me, just knowing a little about the writer always adds an extra layer of enjoyment to the reading. So, please, feel free to jump in and out of the next paragraphs as you jump in and out of the stories these writers tell.

If the bylines belonging to Damon Runyon, Grantland Rice, Ring Lardner, and Hugh Fullerton don't ring a bell, Google them. Like four horsemen, their insights once ran across sports pages from coast to coast. Rice, the golfiest of them all, also edited the *American Golfer*, the game's must-read weekly magazine for the first third of the last century. Their contemporary, Heywood Broun, was another powerful voice in the sporting press of the time, but he left a larger legacy beyond that arena as a critic, pundit, correspondent, and gregarious member of the famed Algonquin Round Table. Atlanta columnist O. B. Keeler was more of a one-trick pony, a reliable chronicler of the game who found his fame as hagiographer of all things Bobby Jones.

Before Rice became the rare editor with his handle planted on his magazine's cover, W. G. Van Tassel Sutphen's had been stamped on *Golf*, the monthly bulletin of the United States Golf Association, across most of its first decade. Beyond his memorable moniker, Sutphen was a compendium of merits. His 1898 book *The Golficide and Other Tales of the Fair Green* was the first collection of golf fiction written and published in this country. That same year, Sutphen published "The Tantalus Loving-Cup." Even then, the purist in him was calling the game's purity into question. Beyond that, Sutphen coined the term "Nineteenth Hole"; wrote exhaustively about other sports, especially football, which he starred in at Princeton; penned several novels; reviewed books; played golf competitively at a high level; and was eventually ordained an Episcopal priest, presiding over a New Jersey congregation blessedly close to the golfing grounds on his beloved Morris County Golf Club.

Two other masters of early golf fiction, with excellent names of their own, have come down to us. Charles E. Van Loan was an immensely popular interpreter of the sporting scene, particularly of baseball, and was widely published in the leading magazines of the day. He also happened to chase deadlines at the same Los Angeles newspaper that I once did. Holworthy Hall, born Harold Everett Porter, appropriated the name of his Harvard residence as his *nom de plume*. His short story "Dormie One" is every bit as insightful an exploration of the golfer's mind today as it was when first published in 1917.

And then there's the Ivy Leaguer who perfected the Western: Zane Grey. If you've never associated him with golf, you're in good company; nobody else has either. Baseball was his game. He pitched and played outfield at Penn, then spent four years in the minors, compiling a collection of fine short stories about the sport. Golf found its way naturally into his 1914 novel *The Light of Western Stars*, widely considered one of his best. Its central theme is the east-meets-west culture clash with which he was so familiar. For some context, Grey built the tale around a debutante named Madeline Majesty Hammond and her trip to New Mexico to visit her brother Alfred in cattle country, where he's quickly made his fortune. As the two ride his ranch together one morning, Majesty—astride her horse, also named Majesty—eyes a vast swath of land that she suggests would make a perfect golf course, "the finest links in the world," in fact. Alfred agrees, but with a caveat: "Could anybody," he asks her, "stop looking at the scenery long enough to hit the ball?" Her wish was his command anyway; it resulted in the episode called "Cowboy Golf," and a tradition, as one contemporary sports announcer might describe it, unlike any other.

Grey's contemporary George Ade was a beloved humorist, dubbed "The Aesop of Indiana" for his fable-like tales of the Midwest, and he, too, builds a golf course—in "Forty Miles From Nowhere." Unfortunately, his land is nowhere near as memorable as the Hammond land in New Mexico. Fortunately for us, Ade adhered to the unvarnished demands of nonfiction to avoid improving the landscape he was given. As readers, we're the better for it.

Just as golf continues to provide fertile landscape for writers and readers both, many fine golfers from the game's first American decades were adept at wielding pens as impressively as their brassies. A. W. Tillinghast and Max Behr were both championship golfers. They were also superb craftsmen of the game's playing fields. Tilly famously coaxed Winged Foot, Baltusrol, Bethpage, and San Francisco Golf Club from the terrain; Behr, a US Amateur finalist, left his imprint on one of Los Angeles's most exquisite layouts—Lakeside, the golfing home of Bing Crosby and Bob Hope. Both Behr and Tillinghast also were sophisticated voices in print on every aspect of the game; each served a stint as editor of the influential monthly *Golf Illustrated*.

Alexa Stirling was one of the famed "Dixie Kids," along with her great friend Bobby Jones. She ascended golf's heights in the early twentieth century when she won the first of her three consecutive US Women's Amateurs (1916, 1919, and 1920—no tournaments were held during the US's involvement in World War I). Though she could play with the men—and beat most of them—her plea to incorporate the women's game into course design would go largely unheeded for decades.

Back one hundred years ago, the majority of America's best golfers were either college-educated amateurs, such as Bobby Jones, or graduates of the caddie yard, such as Francis Ouimet. While Ouimet has some words of his own to offer in these pages, both he and Jones feature prominently in the reminiscences of two other fine golfers, John G. Anderson, an Amherst grad with more than fifty sectional titles and a pair of runner-up finishes in the National Amateur, and Chick Evans, who, amazingly, qualified for every US Amateur from 1907 to 1962. Finances forced Evans to drop out of Northwestern after his freshman season on the golf team. Four years later, he became the first golfer to win both the US Open and Amateur in the same campaign. But he never forgot his roots in the caddie yard; to help ensure that caddies had access to the college scholarships he hadn't, he seeded a fund that became, in 1930, the Evans Scholars Foundation. It's still going strong.

A golfer growing up, Reinette Douglas didn't need financial help to enroll at the University of Wisconsin. She was not yet twenty when she wrote her delightful essay on the "Magic" of the game for a journalism class; it not only won a university award, Grantland Rice swooped it up for the pages of the *American Golfer*.

Walter Hagen, the finest American professional of his time, was, well, a force of nature, and as colorful and unrestrained a competitor as the game has ever known. What makes his observations so trenchant in his essay comparing American pros to their British and Irish counterparts is his envisioning of the Ryder Cup, the biennial matches he would become so much a part of. In all honesty, though, Hagen's byline generally appeared atop sentences set down by his marvelous ghostwriter, H. B. Martin. Beneath his own signature, Martin was an admired New York columnist, cartoonist, and a true man-about-golf: writer, editor, promoter, and co-founder of the Professional Golfers' Association (PGA) in 1917. He was a pretty good player, too. His best known book, *Fifty Years of American Golf*, published in 1936, remains a cornerstone of the game's history.

New Yorker Eddie Loos learned his golf at Van Cortlandt Park in the Bronx, America's first public layout; by nineteen, he'd won the Eastern Open. Blessed with a buttery swing, he later found himself in great demand as both an instructor and a communicator. He relied on those skills throughout a long career as a club professional on each coast.

A few quick words about the rest of the line-up:

Charles Quincy Turner (writing as "Albion") was the editor of *Outing*, the most ubiquitous sporting journal of its time. Published in its pages in 1890, his "Golf for Women"—which really isn't about golf for women—is the first important magazine piece devoted to the royal and ancient endeavor published on these shores.

Richard Harlan, an Episcopal priest, and president of Lake Forest College, wrote affectionately about his father's late and complete embrace of the game, which would be of no interest had his father not been Supreme Court Justice John Marshall Harlan. Known as "The Great Dissenter," Harlan cast the court's only nay vote in Plessy v. Ferguson, insisting, in his loud but lonely protest, that the Constitution "is color-blind." Sadly, the game he so loved hasn't always agreed.

Edwin L. Sabin was a Midwestern newspaperman who achieved wide acclaim as a short-story writer in the late nineteenth century. He went on to publish dozens of well-received adventure books for young boys.

A. E. Thomas spent almost two decades as a reporter and editor on several New York papers. He then found his true calling: the theater. More than a dozen of his plays were produced on Broadway.

Richard Florance was the early pseudonym of author Robert Nathan. His two best-known novels, *The Bishop's Wife* and *Portrait of Jennie*, were turned into hit movies in the 1940s.

John Montgomery Ward's sporting acclaim came late to golf—long after it first blossomed on the baseball diamond. His accomplishments as a player (he pitched the second perfect game in Major League history), manager, and executive are deservedly enshrined in Cooperstown. For all who hate slow play, Ward's plea for foursomes deserves a plaque, too.

Attorney turned man-of-letters Marrion Wilcox wrote extensively on South and Central America, edited *Harper's Weekly* and the *Encyclopedia Americana*, taught English at Yale, published verse for a gaggle of journals, critiqued architecture—and occasionally turned his eye to golf. His daughter was a writer, too; she crafted the tale that Hollywood adapted into *The Mummy* for Boris Karloff.

After Adele Howells left her native Utah, she lived in New York—hence golf on the roof—then served as a foreign correspondent for the *New York Morning Telegram*. She eventually returned to Utah and became the highest-ranking woman in the Mormon church.

William Almon Wolff, another veteran of New York's newspapers, contributed both short stories and articles to the major monthlies of the day before rolling out a series of well-received Manhattan-based detective novels.

Better known as Rube Goldberg, R. L. Goldberg possessed one of the wildest imaginations in American history. His name became synonymous with the unimaginably complicated chain-reaction contraptions with which he filled his cartoons. Those cartoons, which appeared from coast to coast, made him an eponym in *Webster's Dictionary* and won him a Pulitzer Prize. Fortunately, he also loved golf and was always searching for ways to improve it.

Like Eddie Loos, Walt Lantz played his early golf at Van Cortlandt Park. He began his career as a newspaper cartoonist in New York before hearing the call of the new world: animated movies. In Hollywood, he changed his name to Walter—as cartoonists went, the name Walt had already been locked up by Disney—and created a menagerie of memorable characters, most famously Woody Woodpecker, an avid, if not entirely astute, golfing birdie.

Marjorie Trumbull's penchant for travel, history, and sports all found their way into her 1920 fashion statement. Thirteen years later, a stylish young British golfer named Gloria Minoprio caused a sensation when she arrived on the first tee at Royal North Devon for the English Ladies Championship in a pair of tailored black trousers, thus becoming the first female to play a sanctioned round of championship golf in pants.

Attorney Alvin R. Springer was one of those pillars of the community—in his case, Manhattan, Kansas—whose death warranted salutes on both the front and editorial pages of the day's paper. Among the legacies he left was the Manhattan Country Club; he was a founder, played in the inaugural foursome, and chaired the green committee for years. His obituary hailed his golf and his writing style, both on display in his lyrical essay, "The Joy of Golf."

Two stories come down to us with no writers designated. One, on gambling on the golf course, purportedly penned by a prominent player of his day, carries equal resonance in ours. The other is an unbylined excerpt from the *New York Times* report on the third-round matches of the 1916 US Amateur at Merion. What makes the story timeless isn't the way the writer detailed fourteen-year-old Bobby Jones's loss to eventual runner-up Robert Gardner, it was the writer's ability to recognize—on deadline—the birth of a legend.

Finally, let me introduce you to John Kendrick Bangs, an all-purpose writer pretty new to me. As celebrated as any humorist of the fin-de-ciecle, he was a high-brow editor; a back-breakingly prolific novelist; a losing candidate for mayor of New York; and, though among the first members of Saint Andrews Golf Club in Yonkers, the nation's oldest in continuous operation, he was, self-admittedly, a thoroughly awful practitioner of the art. That didn't stop him from writing about it, and despite his contribution's title, "Golf in Hades" isn't about him. It's the final chapter of his engaging 1899 fantasy, *The Enchanted Type-Writer*. The conceit is simple. One morning, as our narrator prepares to sit down to work, the keys on his machine start tapping on their own and words begin to appear on paper. They've been banged out by James Boswell, Dr. Johnson's biographer, who has returned, incorporeally, to report and converse on various aspects of life—or, more appropriately, death—on the Other Side. Bangs saves his best—golf—for last.

In golf, past is always prologue, and what's so enjoyable for me about reencountering so many of the old friends in these pages, is how they all, in their own ways, mine the same veins of emotion, the same frustrations, and even the same occasional joys we still encounter whenever we see nothing but open fairway ahead. Sure, clubs now come in space-age metals, and the new balls have nuclear reactors in their cores, but what brings us to the game, what we take from the game, and even what we give back to it, remains—refreshingly—akin to what our long line of forebears on the links experienced in their plus fours and tweed jackets. Then, as now, the game finds fascinating ways to reel us in, instruct us, cajole us, tease us, entertain us, enrage us, defeat us, and, in the end, bless us.

Which is why we keep coming back for more.

We golfers, we marchers in the long and glorious parade of the game's foot soldiers, are a gluttonous bunch—on the course, and on the page. And as I trust the stories that follow make clear, we've been that way for longer than any golfer now alive can remember.

The Other Lure of Golf

Grantland Rice

THE LURE OF THE AVERAGE SPORT LIES SOLELY IN THE KEEN COMPETI-
tion that awaits. The appeal here is all human, even unto the mighty
crowds who pack the Yale Bowl or file into Madison Square Garden
for some fight. It is all man and man or the gathering of many men and
many women.

But in all these forms of competition, the ruggedness and beauty
of the vast outdoors play little part. Dempsey and Carpentier will meet
within the confines of some twenty-four-foot ring, where most of the
surrounding scenery is a blur of human faces, well enough in their way,
but hardly novel and not too often picturesque. The ball player and the
fan are surrounded by a combination of stands and fences. The stadium
and the bowl shut in the gridiron stars and the accompanying spectators.
The tennis player knows only the confines of the court.

But what about golf?

First, of course, there is the thrill of keen competition, the burning
desire to wallop the ball a mile down the fairway, flick a high mashie shot
to the green, and then gently but firmly tap in the twelve-foot putt.

ENOUGH COMPETITION

There is plenty of competition in the game and all the nerve strain any
hardy soul could desire. Those who don't believe this should have followed Chick Evans and Reggie Lewis through the last eight or nine
holes of their forty-one-hole struggle, where a national championship
swung upon every turn.

The yearning to step forth and remove the scalp of Bill Jones or Bob Smith or Augustus Whipple has, of course, its direct appeal. But this is not the only reason the game grew from five-thousand players in 1895 to nearly two million in 1920. For golf erects formidable barriers against all entrants. It isn't convenient, it isn't easy, and it isn't cheap.

Yet the rush into its fold has come with all the pell-mell clatter of the dash to the goldfields. For golf happens to be the one competitive sport for the public at large that offers the lure of the open spaces where the vision is unbound and where the feet can follow league after league of open ground.

THE CALL OF THE OPEN
Golf is the one competitive sport that comes with the call of the open. Hills and valleys; mountain ranges and ravines; rivers and lakes; plains, moors, and meadows; field and forest all figure in its makeup. And no two of the two thousand courses that comprise two hundred thousand acres of our soil are alike.

There is, for one example, Pine Valley, just outside of Philadelphia. This great course was carved out of a pine forest where, in addition to pines, each fairway winds through guarding columns of maple and oaks. Here the golfer is shut off from any view of man's handiwork. No smokestack tells him that some factory is at work. No houses meet his view to show that human habitation is near. There are no roads or trains or passing cars. He might be out beyond the last frontier for all that he can see or hear from the outside world.

His way moves through an ancient solitude that is only broken by the slash of the iron blade and the muttered and melancholy curse of the brooding devotee who has hooked, topped, or sliced. Pine Valley is the greatest inland course in America and one of the greatest in the world. It is not only a wonderful test of golf, but its natural scenic effect is unsurpassed.

It may be that you don't care as much for the inland view as you do for the sweep of water. In that case at Lido or at The National, among other great courses, you can inhale the salt air and follow the bleaker beauty of the treeless spaces that echo and re-echo with the rush of young gales that are either on their way to sea or headed in for shore.

Here you get merely another view of nature beyond the city walls—sand and surf—the far horizon—that make it hard to keep your eye on the ball if the open places and open spaces of the outdoors have any message for your soul.

ANOTHER VIEW

If golf courses carved through the forests or built along the dunes and headlands of the sea may not happen to suit your fancy, there are still great courses winding beneath over-shadowing mountains, such as Shawnee at the Delaware Water Gap; Ekwanok at Manchester, Vermont; Bretton Woods, where the human eye is soon replete with all the majestic scenery it can carry.

At Shawnee and Ekwanok there are not only championship courses, but the mountains seem to lean above you, almost close enough to be reached by a well-pitched niblick that can carry a mile or so in the air.

One doesn't even have to play with the mountains overhead. There is the Bald Peak course recently built by Thomas G. Plant above the shores of Lake Winnepesaukee in New Hampshire. This course rambles along high above the world, unsurpassed for the magnificence of its scenic wonder. Or there is Banff amid the Canadian Rockies, a mile above the plains below where one can follow the elusive sphere.

Golf has now fought its way through every form of nature. If anyone had told the greenkeepers who came over with Ponce de Leon that grass would one day flourish in the Floridian sand, his mangled remains would have been tossed in the Everglades. But the miracle has happened. The maples and oaks of Florida with their ancient moss that "stand like Druids of old," now overshadow some of the finest turf greens to be found anywhere in the realm.

There is a softness and a gentleness to the scenic beauties of Florida widely differing from the more rugged types of courses farther north. But it is still all part of the great outdoors with its far breath of the open, unbounded, and limitless, holding froth the eternal lure to those who can see something else in life beyond the massed rush of the cities.

In the spring, the golfer wanders through apple orchards in full blossom or by dogwood drifts that upon some courses are massed along the borders of the fairway. But if he is a wanderer, no season of the year can stop him, from Banff in summer to Cuba and Florida or California in winter.

For those who are willing to cultivate a closer look at all this scenic wonder along the way, there is always an antidote for the fluffed mashie or the topped brassie or the missed putt. There is plenty of recompense for any mistake you may make if you will only take time to look around and observe the wonders about you.

Golf for Women

"Albion"

ARCHERY AND CROQUET WERE THE PIONEERS THAT MADE A BREACH IN the walls that that awful personage Mrs. Grundy had raised up to separate the sexes in outdoor games; lawn tennis came with a rush, and, taking the fortress by storm, the colors of the stern and gentle sex now mingle in friendly contests on the netted courts and tented fields. The advent of this popular and health-giving pastime has created a new era in the lives of "our girls," and certainly has done "our boys" no harm. Baseball, cricket, and even football, have been lately tried by the fair sex, but never can become popular with womanly women. For those who object to the "slowness" of archery of croquet, or the fatigue that a hard-fought tennis battle entails, a splendid medium will be found in the grand old game of golf. Like the thistle, golf was but a few years ago considered indigenous to the soil of Scotland, but, thistle-like, the "down" has been wafted to many a fresh field and has opened up pastures new.

The main point that distinguishes golf from all other outdoor games is that it is a game of competition only and not of antagonism. Each player's object is to reach the goal with fewer strokes than the other competitors, and no effort is made to balk or delay them. It is a race of skill, in fact, and not an antagonistic struggle. The means of indulgence in golf are quite easily available in most parts of the United States.

The only condition that may in some cases create a difficulty is the extent of the field of operations, known to the golfer as the "links," for these fields must be of considerable area. In England, the provision near most large cities and villages of commons or greens obviates this difficulty in inland cities, while the seaside of both countries affords an easy way of overcoming it for all the great centres of population bordering it. Indeed, the broad beach is a favorite resort of the golfer.

In the neighborhood of a city there are, however, pretty sure to be available rough pastures that, with little alteration, will make capital links. With such a ground provided, all the golfer's real difficulties have disappeared. The remainder is but to learn the few simple rules that govern the game, or better still, secure the cooperation and instruction of some son of Scotia, of whom there must be many who possess at least an elementary knowledge of a pastime so common in the land of their birth. These secured, a little ball for each player, and a few light, easily handled clubs, and the golfer's outfit and field of operations are complete.

The game is to send a ball set on a slight elevation in such a direction and with such force and judgment as will best enable you by following it up and striking it again and again to take it, in the fewest strokes, into each of a circle of holes cut entirely round the links, as the playing grounds are called, and finally home into the last hole. The holes, which vary in number from seven to eighteen, according to the capaciousness of the ground, are about four hundred yards apart and are two or three inches in diameter; the ball is of hard, compressed gutta-percha, about half the size of an ordinary lawn-tennis ball; the clubs are of ash, about three and a half feet long, tapering from the handle down very fine to the club head, which forms an obtuse handle and is weighted with lead and faced with horn. There is great elasticity in one of those "drivers," and a ball can be sent a long distance by an expert. "Cleeks" and "irons" are used if the ball gets into sand or scrub, and the "putter" when making fine strokes near the holes. The object is to go from hole to hole with the smallest number of strokes, and the party who makes the round with the lowest score is the victor.

It will naturally occur to the mind of the novice that in traversing the complete round of the links, a ball, hit even with the best judgment, must, of necessity, meet with numberless obstructions, and at times get into difficult positions, from which it must be extricated by the blow of the club alone. These varying circumstances call for the use of clubs of differing shapes and fashioned for different effects. To go backward and forward to a given point for the particular club required would entail an endless tramp, and to obviate this, a lad, technically called a caddie, follows each player with the reserve clubs.

When the intervening obstructions between each hole have been successfully overcome and the ball is brought into position near a hole, the interest in the game intensifies. To facilitate the play at these points the ground has, for a certain distance round each hole, been artificially or by the aggregation of footsteps, leveled. This area is the "putting green," and it is here, simple though it seems, the greatest nicety in play is requisite. Too little momentum and the ball is still short; too much momentum and it skips the hole, like vaulting ambition, "falls o' the other side."

At last the joyful moment of success is reached; the little ball disappears and a "hole" is scored. Then the struggle begins again; the ball is taken out and mounted on a slight artificial elevation; a driving club is again selected, and with a swish away it flies on its course toward the next hole, and so on and on until the whole round is successfully accomplished. And all this time the zest of rivalry animates the players. Sometimes one's opponent has forged far ahead; sometimes a few fortunate strokes have left him, or her, far behind, and over all blows the health-giving breeze and through all there is just that moderate exercise and play of wit and judgment that enervates without exhaustion and distracts the mind without absorbing it.

That the game is admirably adapted for a ladies' pastime there can be no doubt, and it has the advantage of being an amusement in which the fair sex are not so heavily handicapped as in other games.

Lady golfers are taking quite a prominent part in the game both in England and Scotland. Warwickshire, in the former country, and North Berwick and Saint Andrews, in the latter, have ladies' clubs that have lately held very successful meetings, as many as forty competitors taking part in some of the contests.

At the West Cornwall meeting, we find two ladies competing in the handicap, and one of them, Mrs. W. N. Harvey, made an excellent score, beating a number of her male competitors. At many of the summer resorts, and in close proximity to the great cities, excellent fields for the game, which would bear favorable comparison with the famous Scottish "links," are in daily use. As a game for ladies, there can be no doubt that it must become a favorite and popular one. It has the advantage of giving plenty of moderate and healthful exercise, without any of that over exertion that tennis may call forth and which every young lady is not equal to.

Even if the fair golfer does not become very expert, the mere indulgence in the game will ensure a return more commensurate with the effect than almost any other pastime. It will ensure at least one health-giving exertion of the most valuable nature, for the necessities of the locality will, in most cases, ensure the links being placed at a distance from the residential centers.

A pastime that proves an incentive to taking a brisk walk of a mile or two, over the fine breezy "downs," cannot be overestimated, while the pleasurable excitement of the changes and chances of the game keeps the mind from every thought of fatigue, and it is a game that can be very quickly learned.

The Supersensitive Golf Ball

Edwin L. Sabin

BEETHOVEN WATKINS, ORDINARILY AS MILD A MANNERED INDIVIDUAL as ever endured with equanimity a crowded streetcar, swore dreadfully on the golf links.

Off the links, Watkins never had been known to use improper language. He was absolutely a gentleman—suave in demeanor, precise in deportment, and blameless in speech. That on the links he should be able to extemporize so fluently may be adduced as a proof of the tremendous mental strain that the individual pursuit of golf imposes upon its worshippers.

The passion that causes golfiacs to leave home, friends, and business in order to follow the ball is based upon two human characteristics—ambition and combativeness. The ambition may be social or athletic. The combativeness has only one objective point—that of subduing the little sphere, which, as all golfists know, is at times a living, breathing, devilish nucleus of malignity.

Now many a man forgets himself while playing golf, but as a rule golf swears are not considered genuinely abhorrent parts of speech. Rather are they condoned, if used in moderation—of course always in moderation. But the language of Watkins when he made a particularly bad stroke, or had a particularly bad lie, was so hearty, so blood-curdling, and bore such evidence of sincerity that hearers blushed. Watkins did not blush, because doubtless more than half the time he did not comprehend the import of his words.

After he had been in the golf club long enough for his peculiarity to become generally known, the other people avoided, if possible, playing with him. Everybody liked Watkins, and realized he was not vicious, but only weak. Men who were glad to have him at their houses for dinner, and who felt perfectly safe in allowing him to enter at will into their families, drew the line at golf. When a twosome or a foursome was proposed, and Watkins indicated a desire to be of the number, the others hastily hatched excuses, and the match dwindled down to him and the Colonel. So day after day he went the rounds alone, or accompanied by a faithful caddie who had grown callous. At first, quite a retinue of unemployed caddies attended Watkins from hole to hole, with delighted awe at his vocabulary. They furnished a breakwater to his overflow of irritation, until even they gave way, and were seen no more in his neighborhood. When it is stated that Watkins really was not conscious of the frequency and liberality with which he swore, it will readily be understood that reformation, in such a case, is hard to accomplish.

It was one afternoon early in November, and he was playing, as usual, by himself, and indulging in his customary soliloquies. A light snow had fallen the day before, and, drifting over the field, had collected in little patches. Watkins had been unwise enough to attempt to use white balls, with the consequences that already he had lost three, the spots of snow making it a difficult matter to locate the spheres.

His feelings gained in warmth, until the expressions to which he was giving vent actually melted nearby bits of snow. Then, when he lost his fourth, and last, ball, his words were shocking—simply shocking.

Back and forth through the fair green he walked, covering the area within which he judged the ball must be lying. With his eyes feverishly taking in every inch of the ground he marked his rapid nervous steps by fervent objurgations. But it was a choice of finding the ball or of going home, and the combativeness that made of Watkins an acute business-man and an ardent golfer kept him to his quest long after weaker natures would have abandoned the task.

Suddenly and unexpectedly, he found a ball. It was not the one he had lost, for when he picked it up it gleamed with frost. Also, it bore a strange trademark, almost effaced, but still showing a few letters. As in the instance of many a golf ball lost and found, it was lying right in the open, so that when once seen one marveled how it ever could have been overlooked. With a sense of great satisfaction, Watkins stooped and grasped it. Probably there is no purer pleasure in life than that of finding a golf ball that someone else has lost. By the laws of golf, finders are keepers.

Watkins's irritation vanished instantly. This was a good ball—better than the one for which he had been seeking. It was about where his own lost ball should be, and therefore he was content to play it from where it had been lying. With care he replaced it, and drawing a mashie from his bag, he prepared to atone for wasted time by an accurate approach shot.

"Now, [blank] you!" he ejaculated, menacingly, taking his stance, and, in a double significance, addressing the ball. Forthwith he did a thing that had not happened to him in months—he swung right over the globe, missing it entirely! His ephemeral good nature yielded to a startling reaction. A distinct odor of brimstone pervaded the atmosphere.

When, at the next attempt, he ploughed into the turf, his language increased in force; and when in quick succession he committed every fault that attends the merest novice, and ended by slicing the ball far off the course, into the rough, he was thoroughly aroused. Never in all his previous playing had he perpetrated such a series of outrageous blunders. And yet as he walked to where his last stroke had landed the sphere, his frenzy settled to a stony calmness. His long, angry strides shortened, becoming less pronounced as he proceeded, and when he reached the ball, lying there with its cunning, shining countenance staring up at him so blandly, he did not even stamp on it. With exceeding coolness he surveyed the position—a bad one, amid the ragweed—and deliberately selected a club from his bag. He forced a pleasant smile to his face, and whistled a popular melody.

"My little man," he mildly said to the ball, "we'll have to get out of here."

Thus speaking, he carefully measured with his eye the distance, paid close attention to his stance, and drawing a deep breath, struck, civilly, skillfully. It was a beautiful stroke. The ball sailed over the weeds, down the course, and stopped on the green about four feet from the hole.

Watkins smiled—naturally this time. Then picking up his bag, he walked after the ball.

But in the glow of pleasure that crowned his victory, he forgot the courtesy due to the conquered. As, putter in hand, he arrived on the green, he hailed his antagonist with the open menace of old.

"Now, [blank] you!" he said.

If there was one department of golf in which, above all others, Watkins thought he excelled, it was putting. This was an easy putt, too. The hole was a scant four feet away, and the green level as a billiard table. Nevertheless, either Watkins was overconfident, or he took his eye off the ball, or—or something else must have happened; at any rate, he missed the hole by eight inches, and went five feet on the farther side.

Watkins swore plainly, unreservedly, and vehemently.

Again he over putted, this time jumping the hole, and going on and on until it seemed to him that the ball had legs. Already he had run up to twelve strokes. Was he never going to make that hole?

Another fruitless essay, but Watkins, by a strong effort, repressed his righteous indignation. For the second time this day he calmly approached the ball, calmly prepared for the stroke, calmly and sweetly smiled, and with the gentle admonition, "We'll see if we cannot do better this trial," putted.

The ball tumbled snugly into the hole. Watkins, picking out the sphere, examined it with attention. Solemnly he teed it, and not having uttered another syllable, by a clean drive he sent it flying for hole No. 5.

During ensuing days the club members noted a curious irregularity in Watkin's scores. He did the course in as low as 43 (it was a nine-hole course), and in as high as 80. The one surprised his friends as much as did the other, for Watkins was not a crack, even when on his game, but then neither was he in the duffer class.

He grew extremely irritable, and his uncertain temper was noted with sorrowful surprise by his business associates. It is true that he did not swear nearly so much on the links, but as an offset, a number of persons averred that they had heard him using unparliamentary language when not on the course. The truly moral pointed to Watkins as an example of the insidious nature of profanity.

"He acquired the dreadful habit playing golf, and now he can't control himself at all," they asserted, pityingly.

The day of the last club match of the season was at hand. When the qualifying scores were posted Watkin's read: 72, 41, 53. The handicap committee was, in consequence, somewhat puzzled as to the proper handicap, if any—for this affair was a free-for-all, with generous allowances.

What could be done with a man who might make the course in 40, but who was just as likely to make it in 70 or 80?

When Watkins teed his ball, a little murmur of astonishment swept through the spectators. It was not a new clean ball, such as is usually preferred for important contests. It was a wretched, dissipated-looking globe, scarred by cuts, and mottled with black where the paint had been worn from the gutta-percha.

"Watkins must have manufactured it from an old rubber boot," sarcastically observed De Lancey.

But no one ventured to suggest or to protest. Watkins, wholly indifferent to public opinion, drove for two hundred yards, and left the crowd behind.

Through the testimony of his caddie, we know that Watkins started by playing the best amateur game ever seen on the course of the Upland Golf Club. He made hole No. 1 in 5, No. 2 in 4, Nos. 3 and 4 in 6, No. 5 in 3, No. 6 in 4—so far only 1 over—and then—and then—ah!

The caddie has laid especial stress on the wonderful, unprecedented calmness that characterized Watkin's progress up to this spot. The caddie, in a measure, blames himself for what then occurred. He says that by mistake he handed his employer a driving mashie when the cleik had been called for, and that while Watkins did not offer any objection, and the lie was adapted for either club, nevertheless the stroke proved a miserable effort—quite the worse Watkins had made that day.

Although everyone is at times liable to make a misplay, Watkins instantly turned on the luckless caddie and swept him with a storm of upbraiding. The caddie would not repeat the language but is of the firm conviction that it more than made up his employer's general average of things one would have wished to have left unsaid.

The ball had moved only a few feet, and now was in a nasty bunker. Watkins stood over the place and swore vigorously. He appeared to revel in his freedom. Finally he endeavored to extricate the ball. Four times he struck at it and succeeded only in forcing it deeper into the sand. At last he lifted it partly out. The bunker was at the bottom of a slight declivity, and halfway up this the ball stopped. The lie was fair, although rather ticklish. Watkins, blaspheming joyously at this deliverance, hastened to the ball, anxious to regain lost ground. Whether he jarred the earth or not the caddie does not know; but he does know that just as Watkins swung his club the ball rolled—back, ten yards, plump into the bunker.

The caddie says that the stillness was awful. Watkin's jaws came together with a snap, the masseter muscles—the bunch at the point of the jaw on either cheek—knotting and hardening convulsively. He dropped his club, walked resolutely to the bunker, grabbed the ball, continued to the edge of the pond near hole No. 6, and with great force threw the offender far into the midst of the waters.

Of course Watkins lost the medal—he had lost it, anyway, by the disaster at the bunker. But from that day to this no one has heard him swear. For some weeks, it is true, he was very irritable, as is anybody who suddenly abandons smoking or drinking or other stimulating habit, but that quickly passed. Unruffled, imperturbable, serene, he does his daily round, a moral high-minded gentleman whose fiercest indignation never goes beyond a "tut! tut!" And it is excellent golf that he plays. Indeed Watkins is now rated as a crack, and plays at two behind scratch.

Today, somewhere in the mud in the center of hole No. 6 pond, and despised by the resident community of other whiter balls exported there by the clubs of various players, is this potted, disfigured old rounder of a ball, secure from the heat and cold, bunker and whins, brassie, cleik, and niblick. Perhaps in its odd little heart it is conscious that it has not lived in vain.

The Humorous Side of Golf

A. W. Tillinghast

GOLF HAS BEEN DESCRIBED AS A SERIOUS GAME, AND INDEED THERE ARE players who regard it so seriously that the casual observer of some melancholy match well might wonder if these solemn visaged ones really find enjoyment in it. Some become so absorbed that anything other than their strokes and the match is exiled from their thoughts. Frequently there are happenings that are absurdly funny, but the actors are unable to see that side of it.

For example the man in the bunker, crashing vainly away until finally he fairly explodes with wrath cannot understand why others are forced to laugh at his torrid and original remarks. You see it depends entirely on the viewpoint. Possibly we may find a laugh here and there as we regard the game from the humorous side. Every man who golfs generally has a golf story to tell—the observation of a caddie, one of the oft-repeated Scotch anecdotes of old vintage, and the like. It is not any of these that shall be recorded here, but rather actual occurrences in serious golf wherein tragedy goes arm in arm with comedy.

There is an old story of two players who visited old Saint Andrew's one day for a double round. At the finish of the first eighteen they were on even terms, and they were still level when the home green was reached in the evening. Consequently they decided to play on through the village streets to the railway station, and the first to hole out in the box by the stove was to be the winner. Unfortunately one of them sliced through the second story window of one of the little gray houses, and their discussion of the rules has been the topic of considerable embellishment and humorous narrative. Surely, the situation was one that would spread a smile over the most dour countenance, but to the two players it was serious business. As a matter of fact this is not fable, for the men were humble clerks in an Edinburgh countinghouse. They had one holiday each year, and for months they had been preparing for this match that was to decide supremacy. Not a day passed without bantering each other, for the great match was serious business with them, and when at last they were forced to take the train on the run, haggling over the rules but with the question of supremacy still unsettled, they surely gave no thought to the ridiculously funny finale, which has served to amuse thousands of golfers since.

Determined men have scrambled to rooftops to play lodged balls, climbed trees, waded into water, and there is recorded the story of one whose ball went down a chimney, but, undismayed, he played out through the open door from the fireplace. Yet, probably, at the time not one of them cracked a smile.

One of the most amusing situations imaginable resulted from the misunderstood directions of a caddie. His employer started his round over an entirely strange course. He was a terrific slicer, and to keep on the course at all, it was necessary for him to face many degrees to the left of the true line.

"What is my line, lad?" he asked.

"Bear on your steeple, sir," the boy answered.

But there were two steeples in the distance, one far to the right of the other, which was on line. Seeing but one (and the wrong one), the player took his stance. Thinking that his man was standing for a pull the boy held his tongue but was startled by the weirdest slice he had ever seen. The ball came to rest far in the rough, almost at right angles to the line to the hole and from which point it required a number of strokes to regain the fairway, not far from the original starting place. It would have been suicide to have laughed at the unfortunate at the time, although the occurrence has given him much amusement since.

A number of years ago, a delegation waited on a certain English nobleman, who was the owner of vast estates. They represented a newly organized golf club and they craved permission to lay out a small course on his lordship's land. His consent was obtained and in due time the links were completed.

Again the delegation came, hats in hands to ask another favor, a very great one. Would his lordship graciously consent to be present for the opening ceremonies—and drive the first ball.

"But, my friends, I have never struck a ball in my life, and I am much too old to attempt it now," he expostulated.

However, when it was explained that he would not be expected to knock it very far—"Just a tap, Sir! It is an honor that will be greatly appreciated, for you see, Sir, we want to keep that ball as a constant reminder of your lordship's generosity."

Finally, pleased with the thought, the venerable gentleman gave his consent, and when the eventful day arrived the whole village in their Sunday clothes and smartest frocks assembled around the first teeing ground.

A murmur waved through the gathering as the great man drew near, and amid cheers and applause he stepped with dignity to the tee on which rested a glistening white ball. A great silence fell over them as a new driver was put into his hands and with uncovered heads they watched him waggle it. But after all he was only a man, and suddenly there was born in his breast the overwhelming desire to hit that ball. No gentle tap could satisfy his intense longing to—(only a vulgar term can express it) "soak it."

Walking deliberately to the ball, he poised the club high in the air and looked out over the fairway. Every eye hung on each moment and the crowd held its breath, for history was in the making. Suddenly he swung with might and main, but sad to relate he missed the ball completely, whirled around like a top and, losing his feet, suddenly sat down on the ball. Thus was the course opened, for the great man had broken his collarbone. The story is a sad one, but it has its funny side, too.

At Newport, there used to be a blind drive to a green that could be reached with an iron. During one of their tournaments the field found great congestion here because nearly everyone had lost his ball. They were sure that the drives had been straight on the pin, but not a ball was in sight. While the search was on, a loud snore attracted one of the players to a tree close by the green. There in the shade reposed one who had passed quietly out of the tournament after a very hard night with the cups that cheer. Someone happened to turn him over, and there under him were the missing balls. For a while he had amused himself by craftily gathering each ball as it rolled onto the green, and after arranging his nest to his entire satisfaction, he had gone to sleep.

One of the most laughable sights of any tournament was that of a well-known player seated on a campstool, calmly reading while his opponent was playing. It happened in this way. In the tournament was one whose dilatory tactics worried his rivals to defeat. He had won several matches against admittedly better players because his obviously studied slowness had angered them. However, he of the campstool outwitted him.

"Let him take all the time he wants," campstool observed, "I am in no hurry." So he took three caddies: one for his bag; another to bear the seat, an umbrella, and reading matter; while the third carried a bucket of iced drinks. The match was speedily ended.

Advice to the Young Golfer

Max Behr

THERE IS A THING IN THE GAME THAT SEEMS TO BE ENTIRELY HIDDEN to the young golfer, and that is its technic. Perhaps it is better to say that he does not realize its importance and hence is uninterested. And this lack of appreciation proceeds from two causes: first, the natural desire to hit the ball as far as possible, and second, the detrimental effects that the striving for immediate success entails.

The young golfer very naturally endeavors to emulate his elders. Whenever he hears them talking golf, it is usually of some extraordinary drive, or of a green reached in one or two shots with clubs that were only meant to be used for half the distance. The effect is only to stimulate an ambition that must stand in the way of any education toward the true and only art values in the game. It is only another phase of that worship of quantity over quality that is destructive of all values in any art. Achievement is one thing, but to those who know, it is the manner in which a thing is done that counts. Even to the uninitiated, the playing of Vardon must be a delight to watch; and this pleasure does not proceed from any exhibition of physical power, but rather from a restraint of it that has the faculty of adding grace to his style. It is the perfect ease with which he accomplishes everything that distinguishes his methods. In the young golfer, however, we are immediately conscious of a worship of distance. Every shot is a full shot. Continual pressing from the tee establishes a habit of hard hitting with the irons with the inevitable result of overplaying every club. Some, with these unwarranted methods, have been very successful, thanks to supple muscles, natural ability, and a keen eye.

But what, in the long run, can such a method of play lead to but a coarsening of style and the establishing of bad habits that eventually must be overcome.

As soon as the young golfer plays any sort of game, he starts to play in competitions. There is nothing better in the world than the experience of tournament play, but unfortunately keen competition has the tendency of making the golfer play safe. His repertoire of shots is reduced to those he has confidence in, and instead of dominating the situations that present themselves, he is dominated by them—he takes the safest road. This mental attitude in itself becomes a habit, and all real progress is stultified by it.

What the young golfer should therefore be made to realize is that immediate success is the last thing he should seek. Instead, he should strive to so cultivate his style that in the end he would never have to compromise over a shot. How many of us can approach a green in all the possible ways that a full set of clubs will allow. There is a young golfer we know of who has had considerable success and who only, until recently, used his mashie-niblick exclusively to approach anywhere from 150 yards down to the little chip off the green. He played most remarkable shots with it, but after all is said and done, can this be called golf? What he should now do is discard his niblick altogether and play his approaches with a mid-iron. Let him master that club so he can play a shot of any length with it, and not only that, but of any height as well. A true master of the game knows by experience the smallest and greatest value of a club, and it is just that that the young golfer should strive to learn.

We remember a golfer who, when young, learned his game upon a course where the high mashie pitch was the usual approach shot to the greens. He never played anything else and became tolerably proficient at it. Later he became a member of the Garden City Golf Club, and he very soon became aware of the fact that in the high winds that usually blow over the Hempstead Plains his approach shots were completely ruined. So he set himself the task of learning the run approach with a rather straight-faced mid-iron. It was two years before he had in any way mastered it, for the simple reason that the shot demanded a different swing from the cut shot with a Taylor mashie. He did not lose his command over his mashie, he could still cut across his ball and sky it, but he had in the bargain now a much safer shot to play, a shot that is needed more than any other when the ground becomes hard and baked.

If then the right ambition of a younger golfer should be to broaden his technic and make himself as versatile as possible, what course should he follow when he plays in tournament? Tournament play can be the greatest of all educative forces, for under stress the natural tendency is always to exaggerate conditions, not by making them actually more difficult, but by heightening the consciousness of them. If the young player will never compromise, will always play every shot as his judgment dictates and not as his weaknesses force him to, it will not be long before he will find his game strengthening on all sides. For it must be remembered that it is only under trying situations that we gain confidence. We may practice a shot a hundred times, but it does not really belong to us until it has gone through the baptism of fire. It may not succeed the first time, it may not succeed the second, but eventually it will, and the confidence that real success inspires will make it ours forever after.

And the learning of all the various shots and when they should be played can best be gained by watching our best amateurs and professionals, Jerome Travers is exceedingly versatile with his irons, as is Francis Ouimet, and Charles Evans Jr. Travers's usual shot is a more or less push iron shot. He always takes a big divot. But he is just as capable with a mashie or a mashie-niblick. He can send the ball very nearly straight in the air if he wishes, a shot that is not always found in the bag of a golfer who habitually plays all his shots low with a run at the end of them. In fact, this high mashie-niblick pitch, which is mandatory at times, is the possession of a very few.

Summing up, one might advise the young golfer as follows. Never press; always keep a little power in reserve. One can only learn to hit hard by learning to hit easy first. With the exception of a cleik, never play an iron club to its full distance value. If a green can be reached with a full mashie, play a half mid-iron. It is only in restraint that accuracy can be cultivated. Above all else, play the shot demanded whether the outcome of a match depends upon it or not. Never allow any situation to dominate right judgment. A compromise is a sign of weakness. And last of all, always keep the larger ambition of future success above the immediate needs of the present.

Dormie One

Holworthy Hall

It was five o'clock and rapidly shading into dusk. The September sun, which earlier had set the air to simmering in tremulous heat-waves, now moved reluctant to ambush behind the hills, and, as though sullen at the exigency of its time, gave warning by its bloodshot eye of pitiless heat to be renewed with tomorrow's dawn. From the curving line of trees—thin elms and maples, bordering upon the hard-packed road—long, soothing shadows edged out into the fresh green of the fairway, measuring with their deeper green the flight of hours and the peaceful ebbing of the afternoon.

From the distant Sound, a transient breeze, shy as a maiden in the manner of its coming, ventured out from the protection of the ridge, hesitated, wavered, and passed across the sward so fleetingly that almost before it seemed assured a fact, it was a memory.

Then, from the trees at the roadside, and from the trees beyond, and from the little brook dawdling along from east to west, and from the reeded lake far over to the right, a breath of evening crept out upon the lawns, and there was silence.

In a squared clearing at the southern end of the sinuous line of maples there was a trim plateau, close-shorn of grass, and sharply defined by boundaries of sedge and stubble. From this spot forward an expansive belt of untrimmed land stretched northward for a hundred yards, to merge presently with the more aristocratic turf of the fairway. Thereafter, narrowing between the trees and a long alignment of arid pits, the trail of adventure ran through rolling country, skirted a grove of locusts, dipped down to ford the brook, climbed past a pair of shallow trenches that glistened with coarse sand, and finally found refuge on a terraced green protected by towering chestnuts and flanked by the arm of a colonial house that rested comfortably beneath the trees.

From clearing to terrace, the crow, flying as crows are popularly supposed to fly, would have accomplished five hundred and twenty yards. It was the eighteenth hole at Kenilworth.

The trim plateau, which was the eighteenth tee, now marked the apex of a human letter, a V of which a thousand men and women formed each stroke. Converging sharply toward that rectangle in the sedge, two thousand men and women—twin lines of white slashed here and there with vivid, burning color—restrained and held in check by twisted ropes, leaned out and gaped and wondered, breathless; now standing hushed by things already seen, now vibrant to the future, uneasy, murmuring. And as in recompense for toiling through the humid afternoon, two thousand men and women held this privilege: to stand, and wait, and watch until a boy—a sturdy, laughing boy—and then a man—a grayed and quiet man—played, stroke by stroke, the eighteenth hole at Kenilworth.

And silhouetted in the background, nervous on the tee, stood man and boy, paired finalists for the Amateur Championship; two wizards of the links whose faces had gone rigid, whose palms were suddenly wet and cold, whose souls were newly strung upon the natural laws that govern flying objects. Each of them had reason for his agitation; their mutual loss of equilibrium was mutual in its cause; for of these two, the man—Hargrave, the present champion—was dormie one.

He was fifty-five, this Hargrave; in commercial life he had known bankruptcy at forty. Golf, which had been heretofore diversion, he made the solace of his penury; it had then constituted itself his religion. Within a decade he had snatched the national title for his keepsake; subsequently he had lost it, struggled for it desperately, regained, and twice defended it. The gold medal meant infinitely more to him than a mere visible token of success at golf; it was suggestive of success elsewhere; it was the embodiment of conquests he had never made, of victories he never might accomplish. In other years wealth had eluded him, power had been alien to him, social distinction was to be classed among the impossibilities; but when he stepped morosely out upon the course, he vaunted in his heart that he was highborn to the purple.

Granted that he was poor indeed in purse, he knew no multimillionaire in all the world who could undertake to meet him on equal terms; he could concede six strokes, and still administer a beating to the finest gentleman and the finest golfer in the Social Register. And so, while golf was his theology, and the arbitrary standard of par his creed, he played the Scottish game as though it symbolized the life he had proved incapable of mastering—and he mastered the game instead. It was his single virtue; it was the hyphen that allied him to the rest of civilization.

To win was the wine of his existence; to surmount obstacles was the evidence of his regeneration; to come from behind, to turn impending downfall into disconcerting triumph, was his acrid compensation for the days and months and years when the man in him had cried out for recognition, and the weakling in him had earned his failure. And he was dormie one—and it was Stoddard's honor at the last hole.

The man stiffened perceptibly as Stoddard, nodding to the referee, took a pinch of sand from the box, and teed for the final drive. Then, in accordance with the grimmest of his grim theories of golf, he abruptly turned his back on his opponent, and stared fixedly at the ground. He had trained himself to this practice for two unrelated reasons: the moral effect upon his adversary, and the opportunity to detach himself from the mechanics of his surroundings and to visualize himself in the act of playing his next stroke.

Habitually he conjured up a vision of the ball, the club, himself in the address, the swing, the attack, the aftermath. He compelled his faculties to rivet upon a superb ideal. And it was largely by virtue of this preliminary concentration that he was enabled to bring off his shots with such startling absence of delay: the orders were transmitted to his muscles in advance; his swing was often started when, to the openmouthed observer, he had hardly reached the ball. And it was by virtue of his utter disregard of his opponent that he was never discouraged, never unnerved, never disheartened. He was neither cheered by the disaster of the enemy, nor cast down by the enemy's good fortune. He was contemptuous not only of the personality of the opponent, but also of his entity. He played his own game, and his best game, ironically ignoring the fact that it was competitive. To all intents and purposes, Hargrave in contest was the only man on the course; he even disregarded his caddie, and expected the proper club, as he demanded it, to be placed in his hand extended backward.

But as now he formally prepared to shut Stoddard out of his consciousness, and as he exerted his stern determination to picture himself in yet another perfect illustration of golfing form, he discovered that his will, though resolute, was curiously languid. It missed of its usual persistence. The ideal came and went, as though reflected on a motion film at lowered speed. There was no continuity; there was no welding of motor impulses. According to his theory, Hargrave should have been purely mechanical. On the contrary, he was thinking.

He entertained no sense of actual antagonism toward Stoddard. Indeed, from the inception of the finals, at ten o'clock this morning, the boy had shown himself considerate and generous, quick of applause and slow of alibi, a dashing, brilliant, dangerous golfer with the fire of an adventurer and the grace of a cavalier. He was confident yet modest, and he had performed a score of feats for which his modesty was none of that inverted conceit of mediocrity in luck, but literal modesty, sheer lack of self-aggrandizement. He was dogged while he smiled; he was still smiling with his lips when his eyes betrayed his chastened mood; and the smile faded and vanished only when he saw that Hargrave was in difficulty. The gallery, nine tenths of it, was with him boisterously. The gallery was frankly on the side of youth and spontaneity. The mass, unresponsive to the neutral tints of Hargrave's character, thrilled to the juvenile star ascendant.

The gray-haired champion, introspective on the tee, frowned and grimaced, and toyed with his dread-naught driver. Early in the morning he had confessed guiltily to himself that Stoddard was the sort of lad he should have liked to call his son. And yet he knew that if he had ever married, if he had ever glowed to the possession of an heir, the boy couldn't conceivably have been in the least like Stoddard. Too many generations forbade the miracle. The mold of ancestry would have stamped out another failure, another charge upon the good opinion of the world.

The child would have been the father of the man. And Stoddard—witness his behavior and his generosity—was of no varnished metal. He was without alloy. He was a gentleman because his great-grandfathers had been gentlemen. He was rich because they had made him so. But Hargrave had allowed himself to experience an anomalous and paternal emotion toward Stoddard—Stoddard who at twenty was higher in rank, higher in quality, higher in the affection of the people than Hargrave at fifty-five. He had nourished this emotion by trying to imagine what he could have made of himself if, at his majority, he had been of the type of Stoddard.

And now, recalling this quondam sentiment, he shuddered in a spasm of self-pity; and simultaneously, in one of those racking bursts of humanity that come to men unloving and unloved, he longed to whirl about, to stride toward Stoddard, to grip his hand and say—well, one of the common platitudes. "May the best man win"—something of that sort; anything to show that he, too, was living rapidly in the crisis.

In another moment he might have yielded; he might have bridged the fearful chasm of self-imposed restraint. But he was slothful to the impulse. Behind him there was the sharp, pistol-like crack of a clean and powerful drive; and before him, brought clear by reflex and by the will that had been lagging, the ghostly mirage of a ball, and of himself swinging steadily and hard, and of the joy of impact, and a tremendous carry and run, true to the flag. The champion had remembered he was dormie one. A voice, low but distinct, came to him through a volume of incoherent sound: "Mr. Hargrave!"

The man turned slowly. He saw neither the referee, who had spoken to him, nor Stoddard, who had stepped aside; he saw no caddies; he saw no fairway. Both lines of the V were weaving, undulating; on the faces of the men and women nearest him he perceived beatific, partisan delight. The thousand-tongued shout that had gone up in praise of Stoddard was dwindling by degrees to a pleasant hum, which throbbed mercilessly in Hargrave's ears and challenged him. He knew, as he had known for hours, how earnestly the public hoped for his defeat. He knew that if he bettered Stoddard's drive his sole reward would be a trifling ripple of applause, smirched by a universal prayer that ineptly he might spoil his second shot.

He grinned sardonically at the throng. He rubbed his palms together, drying them. He teed a ball, and took his stance; glanced down the course, took back the club a dozen inches, carried it ahead, and rested for the fraction of a second; then, accurate, machinelike to the tiniest detail, swung up, hit down, and felt his body carried forward in the full, strong finish of a master drive.

"Good ball!" said Stoddard in a voice that trembled slightly. From the V—sporadic hand clapping. Hargrave, the national champion, had driven two hundred and sixty yards.

Ahead of him, as he walked defiantly through the rough, the fairway bobbed with men and women who, as they chattered busily, stumbled over the irregularities of the turf. Now and then a straggler threw a look of admiration over his shoulder, and, meeting the expressionless mask of the amateur champion, insouciantly shrugged that shoulder and resumed his march.

Hargrave's caddie, dour and uncommunicative as the champion himself, stalked abreast, the clubs rattling synchronously to his stride. Hargrave was studying the contour of the land in front; he glowered at the marshals who had suffered the gallery to break formation and overflow the course; and he was tempted to ask his caddie how, when the entire middle distance was blocked by gabbling spectators, the Golf Association thought a finalist could judge the hole. But he denied himself the question; it was seven years since he had condescended to complain of, or to criticize, the conditions of any tournament. Nevertheless he was annoyed; he was certain the ground sloped off just where his second shot should properly be placed; his memory was positive. Blindfold, he could have aimed correctly to a surveyor's minute.

Still, he was impatient, irritated. He wanted to verify his scheme of play. He wanted to do it instantly. The muscles of his neck twitched spasmodically; and without warning, even to himself, his canker flared into red hate. His eyes flashed venomously; and when it seemed that unless that crowd dispersed and gave him room, his nerves would shatter in a burst of rage, he saw the marshals tautening their lines, the gallery billowing out into a wide and spacious funnel, and felt the caddie's timid touch upon his sleeve.

"Look out, Mr. Hargrave! Stoddard's away!"

The champion halted, and without a glance toward Stoddard, stared at his own ball. It was an excellent lie; he nodded imperceptibly and took a brassie that the caddie, without instructions, placed in his outstretched hand. His fingers closed around the smooth-worn grip; he tested the spring of the shaft and focused his whole attention upon the ball. He strove to summon that mental cinema of Hargrave, cool, collected, playing a full brassie to the green. But Stoddard again intruded.

In the morning round, Hargrave had won the first three holes in a row, and he had held the advantage, and brought in his man three down. He had made a seventy-four, one over par, and Stoddard had scored a creditable seventy-eight—doubly creditable in view of his ragged getaway. And in the afternoon Hargrave had won the first two holes, and stood five up with sixteen more to play, when Stoddard had begun an unexpected spurt. Hargrave scowled at the toe of his brassie as he recounted errors that, if they could have been eliminated from his total, would have erased five needless strokes, and ended the match long since. Cruelly, three of those errors were on successive holes. On the fifteenth he had missed a simple putt for the win; on the sixteenth he had overapproached and thrown away a half; on the seventeenth he had topped an iron and still accomplished a par four—but Stoddard had made a three.

The champion felt his heart flutter and his knees yield a trifle as he reflected what havoc one more ineffectual shot would work upon his nerves. He was surely, steadily slipping, and he knew it. The bulk of his vitality was gone; and he was drawing heavily upon his light reserve. He realized, not in cowardice but in truth and in fact, that if the match should go to an extra hole, he, and not Stoddard, would be the loser. His customary command of his muscles was satisfactory, but his control of his nerves was waning. He was overgolfed; overstrained; stale. He could bear the strain of this hole, but that was all. His stamina had touched its limit; his fortitude could stand no more. He could gage it to a nicety; he had a debilitating intuition that told him if he had to drive again from the first tee, he should founder wretchedly; and he believed this message from his soul, because he had never before received it.

If Stoddard won the eighteenth, it would be the fourth consecutive godsend for Stoddard, and Stoddard's game was improving, not deteriorating; he had moral courage behind him, he had the savage exhilaration of metamorphosing a forlorn chance into a delirious certainty, he had the stimulus and the impetus of his grand onrush, he had the responsive gallery to cheer him on. It was inevitable that Stoddard, if he won the eighteenth, would win the next; so that the champion, who was dormie one, must have a half—he must divide this hole with Stoddard. He must!

The champion grew restive. He needed the supreme effort of his career to force himself to inertia, to refrain from wheeling swiftly, and shrieking aloud to Stoddard, to demand why he didn't play! Was the boy asleep? Dead? Dreaming? Had he succumbed to paralysis? Was he gloating over his triumph? Hargrave wet his lips and swallowed dustily.

A tremor ran through his limbs, and his wrists tightened in palsied fear. His eyes pained him; they reminded him of a doll's eyes, turning inward; he was aware that his face was drawn. He wondered stupidly whether the spoon would be safer than the brassie. He liked the spoon—but was the cleik surer yet? He caught his breath in a gasp, and at the same moment his spine was chilled in a paroxysm of futile terror. He essayed once more to swallow and thought he was strangling. His soul cried heartbreakingly out to Stoddard: "Shoot! For God's sake, shoot!"

The tension snapped. A roar of jubilance went up from twice a thousand throats, a roar which, dying momentarily, swelled up in glory, and hung, and splintered into a thousand reverberations against the hills. Hargrave shivered and cleared his throat. For the life of him he couldn't maintain his principles; his nature revolted; and jerking his head toward the north, he was gazing at a tiny fleck of white ten feet to the side of the terrace, which was the eighteenth green. Stoddard was hole high in two! A lucky ricochet from the stones of the brook! Five hundred and twenty yards in two! Hargrave went sickly white and looked despairingly at his caddie.

He needed a half, and Stoddard was hole high. There was an outside possibility, then, that Stoddard could make a four—one under par. And

Hargrave was nearly three hundred yards away. Could he, too, make a four—for the half?

The champion, with two alternatives looming bold before him, shuddered in exquisite incertitude. He could attempt a heroic stroke with the brassie, sacrificing accuracy for distance, or he could play his normal shot, which was practically sure to clear the brook, but still would leave him at a critical disadvantage. In the latter instance he could guarantee himself a five, but already Stoddard was assured of four. And that four, if he achieved it, meant a squared match for Stoddard, and a resultant victory. Hargrave would halve the hole only if Stoddard blundered; and for an hour and more Stoddard's golf had been flawless. There was no blunder in him.

But if Hargrave should risk his own crown on a mighty endeavor to equal Stoddard's titanic brassie shot, he would have the odds of war alarmingly against him. The trajectory must be perfect to a ruled, undeviating line. The ball must either fall short of the brook by ten yards, or clear it by ten, and bounding neither to the left, among the trees, nor to the right, among the sand pits, surmount the grade. An unfortunate angle of consequence, a mere rub of the green, would be doubly fatal. The ball might even be unplayable. There would yet be a hazardous last chance for a five; but again, there was no reason to expect that Stoddard would need so many. Stoddard had been deadly, uncannily deadly, on those short running approaches. Stoddard would make his four, and Hargrave knew it. He closed and unclosed his fingers around the grip of his brassie. A rim of ice, pressing inward, surrounded his heart. His brain was delicately clouded, as though he had just awakened out of the slumber of exhaustion, and looked upon the world without comprehending it, sensed it without perceiving its physiology. He passed a hand over his forehead, and found it damp with perspiration.

A year ago he had promised himself that, as champion, he would withdraw from competition. It was his dream to retire at the height of his prowess, to go down in the history of games as one of that rare company who have known when to file their resignations. Indeed, as late as February he had vowed not to defend his title this year. But when he had once sniffed the intoxicant atmosphere of a club grill, and after he had proved his strength in a practice round or two, he had diffidently entered for the Atlantic City tournament, and won it. Infectiously, the old ardor had throbbed in his veins. He was keenly alive to his dominant tenure; his nostrils dilated, his jaw set.

He would add one consummating honor to those who had gone before; he would take his third successive championship with him into exile. And so, at Deal, at Apawamis, at Sleepy Hollow and at Garden City, at Montclair and Wykagyl and Piping Rock, he had groomed himself, thoroughly and deliberately, for the fitting climax. The metropolitan supremacy was his for the fifth occasion; he had finished fourth in the Metropolitan Open, third in the National Open. In the handicap list of the great central association, he stood proudly aloof at scratch. He was invincible.

And now, with six days of irreproachable golf behind him; with the greatest prize of a lifetime shining in his very eyes, he looked at a distant red flag, drooping on its staff, and looked at a ball lying in tempting prominence on the fairway, and felt his chin quiver in the excess of his passionate longing, and felt a white-hot band searing his forehead, and penetrating deep.

He kept the brassie. And as he took his stance, and struggled to centralize his wishes upon the problem of combining vast length with absolute precision, his mind became so acutely receptive to impression, so marvelously subjective, that he found himself repeating over and over to himself the series of simple maxims he had learned painfully by heart when he was a novice, striving to break through the dread barrier that divides those who play over and those who play under a hundred strokes for the single round.

He experienced, for the first time in years, a subtle premonition of ineptitude. He was again a tyro, whose margin of error was 95 percent. Where was the ball going? It was incredibly small, that sphere in the fairway; it was incredible that he should smite it so truly and so forcibly that it would fly even so far as a welcome furlong. Suppose he, a champion, with a champion's record, should slice, or pull, or top—or miss the ball completely?

Hargrave's teeth came grindingly together. His eyes dulled and contracted. He took the club back for a scant foot, raised it, took it forward, past the ball in the line of the hole, brought it to its original position, pressed it gently into the velvet turf with infinitesimal exertion of the left wrist, and swung. Wrists, forearms, shoulders, and hips—his whole anatomy coordinated in that terrible assault. The click of the wood against the ball hadn't yet reached his ears when he knew, with exultation so stupendous that it nauseated him, that the shot had come off. His eager eyes picked up the ball in flight; and as he paused momentarily at the finish of his terrific drive, he was filled with a soft and yet incongruously fierce content. Again he had foiled the gallery, and Stoddard! He saw the ball drop, across the brook; saw it leap prodigiously high in air, and fall again, and bound, and roll, slower and slower, and cease to roll—a good club's length from the lower pit, twenty yards from the green.

The champion and the challenger were on even terms.

Unlike the average man of gregarious instincts, Hargrave never sought proximity to his opponent during a match. His procedure was exactly as though, instead of playing against a flesh-and-blood antagonist, he was going around alone. He went his independent way, kept his peace, and entertained no thought of conversation or courtesy. If fortuitously he had to walk a course parallel to that of his opponent, and even if the interval between them was a matter of a scant rod or so, the champion was invariably thin-lipped, reflective, incommunicative.

He observed with a little flicker of amusement that Stoddard was eyeing him sidewise, and he felt that Stoddard was not a little affected by that enormous brassie, as well as by Hargrave's outward indifference toward it. Hargrave, however, appraised his own flinty exterior as one of his championship assets. He never praised the other man; and if the other man chose to burst into fervid eulogy, the champion's manner was so arctic, so repelling, that not infrequently he gained a point on the very next shot through the adversary's dazed inefficiency, and even one stroke in match play is worth saving.

He knew he was unpopular, he knew he was affirmatively disliked; he knew the public, the good-natured and friendly public, yearned for Stoddard's triumph rather as a vindication of gentility than as a proof of might. But as he observed that Stoddard showed premonitory symptoms of increased nervousness, and that Stoddard was impelled to speak and yet held his tongue to save himself from sure rebuff, the champion's breast expanded with golden hope.

Stoddard, after all, was a mere boy: a veteran golfer—yes, but immature in the mentality of golf. And Hargrave sometimes won his matches, especially from younger men, in the locker room before he put on his shoes. If Stoddard congratulated him now, he could send Stoddard into catastrophe with one glowing sentence. But Stoddard didn't speak.

In addition to his other reasons, he was anxious to beat Stoddard because of his very youth. It had galled Hargrave to be called, by the luck of the draw, to meet five of the youngest experts of the country in this tournament; it had galled him, not because he was loath to win from younger men, but because the public naturally discounted his victories over them.

On Tuesday he had overwhelmed a Western prodigy, a freckled schoolboy who had blushingly donned full-length trousers for this great event. On Wednesday he had won, three up and two to go, from a Harvard freshman, a clubable youngster who had capitulated to Hargrave primarily because his optimism had slowly been destroyed by Hargrave's rude acerbity. On Thursday he had met, and easily defeated, the junior champion of Westchester—defeated him by the psychology of the locker room, by knocking him off-balance at the outset, much as the gladiator Corbett once shook the poise of the gladiator Sullivan. In the semifinals yesterday he had beaten his man—browbeaten him—by diligently creating an atmosphere of such electric stress that a too-little-hardened Southron, as sensitive as could be, had gone to pieces at the ninth, surrendered at the twenty-seventh hole.

And Hargrave, whose bitterness toward the golfing world had progressed arithmetically through these earlier rounds, had come up to the finals in a mood of acid which, in the true analysis, was a form of specious envy and regret. He realized that in comparison with any of the men he had removed from brackets, he was unattractive, aged, cynical, repugnant. He envied youth—but how could he regain his own? How could he crystallize at fifty-five the secret ambitions of a boy too young to vote? He couldn't stand before this fashionable gallery and, indicating Stoddard, cry out to them: "But I want to be like him! I want to be! And it's too late! It's too late!"

A great wave of self-glorification swept over him, and left him calmer, more pragmatic. After all, he was Hargrave, phenomenon of the links, the man who, beginning serious golf at the age of forty, unaided by professional tutoring, unschooled by previous experience in the realm of sports, had wrenched three amateur championships and unnumbered lesser prizes from keen fields. He was the unconquerable Hargrave; the man who had victoriously invaded France, England, Austria, Canada, Scotland. He had averaged below seventy-five for the previous three years on all courses and at all seasons. He had been six down with nine to play in the finals of the English Amateur, and come romping home to triumph, four under par. It was said of him that he was never beaten until the last putt on the last hole. Better than that, it was true.

By this time the gallery was massed rows deep around the eighteenth green. Hargrave crossed the little footbridge over the brook and permitted the vestige of a smile to temper the severity of his face. They hoped to see him lose, did they? Well, he had often disappointed them in the past; he could disappoint them now! All he required was a half, and he was barely off the green in two.

But even in the vanity that somewhat relieved the strain upon him, he was conscious of a burdening weariness that wasn't solely physical. He was impatient, not only to end the hole, and the match, but also to end his tournament golf forever. He was sure now that, winner or loser, he should never enter an important contest again. His nerves were disintegrating. He was losing that essential balance without which no man, however skillful in the academics of the game, may be renowned for his examples.

Next year he should unquestionably play with less surety, less vigor. Some unknown duffer would catch him unawares and vanquish him; and after that the descent from scratch would be rapid—headlong. It had been so with the greatest golfers of old; it would be so with Hargrave. Great as he was, he wasn't immune to the calendar. But to retire as merely a runner-up—that was unthinkable! To retire in favor of a slim boy whose Bachelorhood of Arts was yet a fond delusion—that was impossible! He must win—and on the eighteenth green, after he had holed out, he would break his putter over his knee, and he would say to the gallery—and it ought to be dramatic . . .

He brought himself to a standstill. His heart pounded suffocatingly. A lump rose in his throat, and choked him, and his whole intellect seemed to melt into confusion and feeble horror; there was a crushing weight on his chest. A slow, insistent cacophony poured through his brain, and for an instant his universe went black. The ball, which had appeared to carry so magnificently, and roll so well, had found a bowl-shaped depression in the turf, a wicked concavity an inch and a half in depth, two in diameter; and there it lay, part in the sunlight, part nestling under the shelter of a dry leaf, a ball accursed and sinister.

Blindly, and apprehensive, the champion turned to look at Stoddard. The boy was struggling to conceal the manifestation of his hopes; the muscles of his lower face were flexed and unrelenting. Between him and the flag was level turf, untroubled by the slightest taint of trickery or unevenness. He knew, and Hargrave knew, that nothing short of superhuman skill could bring the like to Hargrave. He knew, and Hargrave knew, that at the play-off of a tie the champion was doomed. The champion had faltered on the last few holes; his game was destined to collapse as surely as Stoddard's game was destined to rise supreme. As Hargrave paused, aghast, there came a rustle and a murmur from the gallery. A clear voice—a woman's voice—said ecstatically, "Then Bobby'll win—won't he?"

Hargrave glared in the direction of that voice. The veil of horror had gradually dissolved, but Hargrave, as he weighed the enigma of the shot, was visited by a cold apathy that staggered him. It wasn't a phlegmatic calm that sat upon him; it was inappetency—as though he had just been roused to a sense of proportionate values.

The matter of coaxing a golf ball out of a casual depression—what significance had it? Tomorrow would yet be tomorrow; with breakfast, and the newspapers, and all the immaterial details of living and breathing. Why all this bother and heartache about it? What was golf, that it should stir a man to the otherwise unprobed depths of his soul? Why should he care, why should he squander so much mental torture as could be computed by one tick of a clock, why should he tremble at this ridiculous experiment with a little white ball and a bit of iron on the end of a shaft of hickory?

For one elemental moment he was almost irresistibly impelled to pick that ball out of its lie, and dash it in the face of the gallery, hurl his clubs after it, and empty himself of the accumulated passion of fifty-five years. Sulfurous phrases crowded to his lips. . . .

And then he realized that all this time he had been glaring in the direction of a woman's voice. He exhaled fully and held his hand out backward to the caddie.

"Niblick!" said Hargrave thickly.

The distance to the hole was greater than he had fancied. The lie of the ball was worse than he had feared. His calculation intimated that he must strike hard, and stiffly, with a pronounced up-and-down swing to get at the back of the ball. The force of the extricating stroke must be considerable; the green, however, was too fast, too fine, to permit liberty in the manner of approaching it. The ball, if it were to carry the full thirty yards to the pin, couldn't possibly receive sufficient reverse power to fall dead. It must, therefore, be played to reach the nearer rim of the green, and to drift gently on to the hole.

Hargrave caught his breath. The knowledge that he distrusted himself was infinitely more demoralizing than any other factor in the personal equation; he was shocked and baffled by his own uncertainty. Through his brain ran unceasingly the first tenets of the kindergarten of golf. He didn't imagine himself playing this shot: he speculated as to how Braid, or Vardon, or Ray or Duncan would play it. He was strangely convinced that for anyone else on earth it would be the simplest of recoveries, the easiest of pitches to the green.

He glanced at his caddie, and in that glance there was hidden an appeal that bespoke genuine pathos. Hargrave wasn't merely disturbed and distressed: he was palpitatingly afraid. He was afraid to strike, and he was afraid not to strike. His mind had lost its jurisdictive functions; he felt that his thews and sinews were in process of revolt against his will.

He was excruciatingly perceptive of people watching him; of Stoddard regarding him humorously.

The collective enmity of the gallery oppressed and befuddled him. He was crazily in dread that when he swung the niblick upright, someone would snatch at it and divert its orbit. His ears strained for a crashing sound from the void; his overloaded nerves expected thunder. He knew the fall of an oak leaf would reverberate through his aching head like an explosion of maximite and make him strike awry. His vitals seemed suddenly to slip away from his body, leaving merely a febrile husk of clammy skin to hold his heartbeats. The throbbing of the veins in his wrists was agony.

The niblick turned in his perspiring hands. He gripped more firmly, and as his wrists reacted to the weight of the club head, he was automatic. The niblick rose, and descended, smashing down the hinder edge of the bowl-like cavity, and tearing the ball free. A spray of dust sprang up, and bits of sod and dirt. The ball shot forward, overrunning the hole by a dozen feet. Almost before it came to rest, Stoddard played carefully with a jigger, and landed ten inches from the hole.

Hargrave's sensation was that he was encompassed with walls that were closing in to stifle and crush him. That they were living walls was evident by the continuous whisper of respiration, and by the cross-motion of the sides. He was buried under the tremendous weight of thousands of personalities in conflict with his own. He tottered on the verge of hysteria. He was nervously exhausted, and yet he was upheld, and compelled to go on, to play, to putt, by nervous energy that by its very goad was unendurable. Hargrave looked at the green under his feet and fought back a mad impulse to throw himself prone upon it, to scream at the top of his lungs, and writhe, to curse and blaspheme, and claw the grass with his nails. Each breath he drew was cousin to a sob.

He stood behind the ball to trace the line and recognized that he was seeing neither the ball nor the hole. He couldn't see clearly the grass itself. He was stricken, as far as his environment was concerned, with utter ophthalmia. And although the boy Stoddard was outside the scope of Hargrave's vision, the champion saw Stoddard's face, as he had seen it just now, before Stoddard turned away. He despised Stoddard; unreasonably but implacably he despised him, because of the light he had seen in Stoddard's eyes. The boy wasn't a philosopher, like Hargrave: he was a baby, a whining infant grasping for the moon. He had no sense of proportion. That expression in his eyes had convicted him. This tournament was to him the horizon of his life. It was his life!

Hargrave's mouth was parched and bitter. He tried to moisten his lips. Details of the green began to develop in his consciousness as in a photographic negative. He saw the zinc-lined hole twelve feet away. His eye traced an imaginary line, starting from his ball and leading, not straight to the cup, but perceptibly to the left, then curving in along the briefest of undulations, swerving past a tiny spot where the grass was sun-scorched, and so to the haven of the hole.

If he could sink that curling putt, nothing could deprive him of his victory. He would be down in four, and Stoddard now lay three. He would have a half—and the match by one up in thirty-six holes. He would be the Amateur Champion of the United States—and he could quit! He could quit as the only man who ever won in three successive years. And if he missed, and Stoddard took the hole in four to five, Hargrave knew that even if his legs would support him to the first tee, his arms would fall at the next trial. He doubted if sanity itself would stay with him for another hole.

The murmur of the gallery appalled him with its vehemence. The noise was as the rushing of the falls of Niagara. Hargrave stood wearily erect and eyed that section of the crowd before him. He was puzzled by the excitement, the anxiety of that crowd. He was violently angered that no smile of encouragement, of good fellowship, met his inquiring gaze. The misanthrope in him surged to the surface, and he was supercilious— just for a second!—and then that sense of impotence, of futility, of shaken poise fell upon him once more, and his throat filled.

He needed the half. He must hole this putt. He was thinking now not so much of the result of holing it as of the result of missing it. He could fancy the wretched spectacle he would make of himself on the play-off; he could fancy the explosive, tumultuous joy of the gallery; he could picture the dumb, stunned radiance of Stoddard. And Stoddard was so young. Hargrave wouldn't have minded defeat at the hands of an older man, he told himself fiercely—but at the hands of a boy! Hargrave, the man who had made more whirlwind finishes than any other two players of the game, beaten by a stripling who had come from behind!

On the sixteenth and seventeenth holes the champion had reviled himself, scourged himself, between shots. He had clenched his teeth and sworn to achieve perfection. He had persuaded himself that each of his mishaps had been due to carelessness; and he had known in his heart that each of them was due to a fault, a palpable fault of execution. On the eighteenth hole he had reverted to sincerity with himself. He was harrowed and upset, and in confessing his culpability he had removed at least the crime of overconfidence. But this was far worse! He was doubting his own judgment now: he had determined upon the line of his putt, and he was reconsidering it.

He peered again and, blinking, discovered there were tears in his eyes. The hole seemed farther away than ever, the green less true, the bare spot more prominent, the cup smaller. He wondered dully if he hadn't better putt straight for the hole. He braced himself, and, trembling, addressed the ball with his putter. This was the shot that would take stomach! This was the end!

He had a vision of tomorrow, and the day after, and the day after that. If he missed this putt, and lost the match, how could he exonerate himself? He had no other pleasure in life, he had no other recreation, no other balm for his wasted years. If he tried again next season, he would lose in the first round. He knew it. And he might live to be seventy—or eighty—always with this gloomy pall of failure hanging over him. Another failure—another Waterloo! And this time he would be to himself the apotheosis of failure! Why—Hargrave's heart stopped beating—he wouldn't be champion!

With a final hum, which was somehow different from those that had preceded it, the gallery faded from his consciousness. Stoddard was as though he had never existed. Hargrave bent over the putter, and a curious echo rang not unpleasantly in his ears. He saw a white ball in the sunlight, a stretch of lawn, a zinc-lined hole in shadow. There was no longer an objective world in which he lived; there were no longer men and women. He himself was not corporeal. His brain, his rationality, were lost in the abysmal gulf of nothingness. He was merely a part of geometric space; he was an atom of that hypothetical line between two points. His whole being was, for the moment, the essence of the linear standard.

In a blank detachment—for he had no recollection of having putted—he saw the ball spinning on a course to the left of the hole. A terrible agony seized him, and for the second time a black curtain shut him off from actuality. It lifted, leaving him on the brink of apoplexy, and he saw that the ball had curved correctly to the fraction of an inch, and was just dropping solidly and unerringly into the cup.

And from the morning paper:

Hargrave was dormie one. Both men drove two hundred and fifty yards straight down the course. Stoddard banged away with his brassie, and nearly got home when the ball caromed off a stone in the brook. Hargrave, playing with that marvelous rapidity that characterizes his game, wouldn't be downed, and promptly sent off a screaming brassie that found a bad lie just off the green, but after studying it fully ten seconds—twice his usual allowance—he chipped out prettily with a niblick. Stoddard ran up, dead. Hardly glancing at the line of his fifteen-footer, Hargrave confidently ran down the putt for a birdie four, and the match. Probably no man living would have played the hole under similar conditions, with such absence of nerves and such abnormal assurance. From tee to green, Hargrave barely addressed the ball at all. And certainly in the United States, if not in the world, there is no player who can compete with Hargrave when the champion happens to be in a fighting mood.

To our reporter, Hargrave stated positively after the match that he will defend his title next year.

The Revenge that Went Astray

A. E. Thomas

THERE WAS NOT THE LEAST DOUBT OF IT—NOT THE LEAST IN THE world. Skaggs was an excessively unpleasant person to have about a golf club; and as he was seldom anywhere else, outside of the hours unwillingly snatched for business and sleep, Skaggs was unanimously elected president of the Disagreeable Association. His chief claim to this distinction was his assumption of a knowledge of the theory and practice of the royal and ancient game of golf so impeccable and flawless that to possess it one must have been the golfing heir of all the experts who ever swung a driver.

The worst of it was that there was no escaping him. If Skaggs came out of the clubhouse for his daily round and spied a pair of duffers practicing putting on the green, down he would swoop upon them, upset about what little form they had already acquired, and insist that there would never be hope for them until they threw aside their heresies and set themselves to learn his peculiar style, which was, to tell the truth, somewhat successful in his hands, although nobody else used it. Nobody *would* have used it even if it had ensured a round in bogie figures, just because it *was* Skagg's.

Again, if Skaggs was pursuing his own ball through the fair green and observed that another man had fallen short or overrun on his approach to an adjacent green, he would at once abandon his own affairs, and, with an altruistic smile, approach his unfortunate victim in this wise:

"I say, my dear fellow, tough luck there, I notice. I thought, though, that you did not follow through—yes, you seemed to check the stroke just before the iron reached the ball—fatal to the back spin, you know; thought you might like to know."

Nobody was ever grateful for this advice, unless it might be a new member, and he soon got over his gratitude. But that did not deter Skaggs. His advice was like the rain. It fell alike upon the grateful and the reverse. Unfortunately, there are no umbrellas that are proof against advice.

It can easily be seen that by strict attention to business, Skaggs soon achieved the reputation of being a very choice article in the line of nuisance. What aggravated the case to the last point of endurance was the incontrovertible fact that the man could play golf. It was not merely the unremitting industry and devotion to the game that he displayed, for any laborious duffer knows—alas, how well!—that these things will not make an able golfer. Skaggs had golfing talent of no mean order, which made the situation all the more heart-rending. Things went from bad to worse, and finally to the worst possible when the handicap committee posted an announcement that Skaggs had been placed at scratch along with Belden, the club champion.

It is not to be supposed that Skaggs knew how unpopular he was. Indeed, it is doubtful if he bestowed the least thought upon the subject. All he wanted was to golf and give advice. The non-golfing reader may suppose that Skaggs had difficulty in securing partners. But the golfer will not fall into this error. He knows what a balm to wounded sensibilities it is to beat a man like Skaggs. But this is what was seldom accomplished. Occasionally one of the Best Ones would catch him napping, but for the most part Skaggs played with balls and clubs won from the opposition, which included the rest of the club, and ate dinners paid for by the same, punctuating the courses thereof with insults in the shape of more advice. Of course when a man has beaten you, you can't get profane if he offers a few comments upon your game and how it differs from his.

When Skaggs won the club championship from Belden, gloom and melancholy settled upon all hands, and it came to be a question of Skaggs or the club. A council of war was held, at which plans were devised for self-protection. As a result, all sorts of things began to happen to Skaggs's locker. One day he found that somebody had emptied a pail of water into it and ruined his clothes. Whenever he left a sweater out to dry, it promptly disappeared. On another occasion the tires of his automobile were punctured where it had been left standing while its owner played a round. The very night he gave his pet driver to the club's professional to refurbish the handle, somebody broke into the shop and stole it. All these and sundry other forms of petty persecution were wasted upon him. Skaggs never appeared to notice them.

At last, however, fate presented an opportunity for revenge. One July evening when Skaggs and Belden and Cassell, of the green committee, were smoking on the clubhouse porch, Belden chanced to say that he understood some English professional of reputation played his wooden clubs with his thumbs running down the shaft instead of curled around it. This enraged Skaggs exceedingly.

"Nonsense," he snorted. "Perfectly absurd." And he proceeded in stentorian tones to demonstrate the impossibility of making an effective stroke in that fashion, illustrating his argument by action.

"Why, see here," he shouted, seizing his stick as if it were a driver, and taking an imaginary stance. "Don't you see how it hampers and confines the action of the wrists?" and so on, while Belden and Cassell yawned and looked at their watches.

When he had exhausted his rhetoric, Cassell remarked, "See here, Skaggs, I know a chap who plays that way who can beat you to death."

Skaggs grinned in a superior way and said he would be glad to see the man. So he should, Cassell said, on certain conditions, and the upshot of it was that they arranged an eighteen-hole match between Cassell's friend, who, Cassell said, was a chap named Bally, and Skaggs. Bally was to drive with this thumbs down the shaft in the fashion derided by Skaggs. Cassell, however, exacted a promise that if Skaggs were beaten, he should forever and always renounce all claims to authority on any point of the game of golf.

At first Skaggs balked at this.

"It's such dodgasted nonsense, you know," he complained.

"Oh, I thought you were sure of winning!" sneered Cassell.

"And I am," insisted Skaggs. "Why, nobody can play his stroke in that fool way. It's against all the canons of golf—and common sense, too."

"Well, then, what are you afraid of?" said Cassell, craftily.

"Afraid nothing!" retorted Skaggs, angrily. "Bring him on."

So they made the match for the following Saturday.

Now Bally, it appears, was no less a person than Knox, the celebrated English professional, who had just arrived in this country, and so had been seen by very few on this side. And of those few Skaggs was not one. As everybody knows now, Knox actually does play his wooden clubs in the manner described, and great was the hubbub caused by the discovery of that fact. But at that time, Cassell was one of only three persons on this side of the water who were aware of this peculiarity.

On the given Saturday the match took place, and before it was half over the identity of the supposed Bally had leaked out, until pretty nearly everybody knew it but Skaggs. The latter was attending strictly to golf, and the most unfriendly person in that exceedingly hostile gallery had to admit that the nuisance was playing the game of his life. His courage, skill, and aplomb were admirable, and he advised Bally only once in the eighteen holes. The latter was somewhat handicapped by his entire unfamiliarity with the course, and had bad luck with 1 or 2 putts; and this, taken with Skagg's really magnificent golf, brought it about that when the two players faced the home green they were all square.

"The luck of the devil," snarled Cassell to Belden as he bit his fingernails in exasperation.

It was Skagg's honor, and he got off a good ball. Bally, however, outdrove him several yards. A brassie and an approach brought each to the green in three, but Bally's ball was practically dead to the hole, while Skaggs had a putt of some fifteen feet. Cassell shook hands with himself, and a smile of delight ran around the gallery.

Skaggs looked cheerful, however, and picking up his favorite putter, played the stroke. He missed, but rimmed the cup, laying his opponent a full stymie. The best the professional could do was to halve the hole, and, consequently, the match.

Skaggs congratulated Bally; said he couldn't see how any man could play that well in such an ungainly fashion, referring to the disposition of his thumbs.

After that Skaggs was more of a pest than ever. He even went so far as to explain, with careful elaboration, how Bally might have beaten him—an error of judgment at the "Willow Burn" and "over-approach at the third hole," and so on.

Meantime Cassell gave himself up to dark thought and meditated revenge. At length it ran, so it seemed to him, to meet him.

There came to visit his sister a girl by the name of Angelina Dewsnap—a girl who played the piano. Whether she played it well or ill does not matter. But she played it much and often, and more, too. Aside from this habit, however, she was a charmer. Now Cassell remembered that Skaggs hated the piano as violently as he adored golf, and that he had the reputation of being susceptible to the charms of the fair sex. On the other hand, Angelina abominated golf. All her eight brothers played it, and she played the piano to get even. They said she did, too.

So, then, to Angelina the fair, Cassell brought Skaggs the "golfiac," having informed the lady of Skagg's aversion to the piano and having likewise warned the innocent Skaggs to be mum on the subject of golf. The devilish design of the inhuman Cassell will at once appear.

His plan worked beautifully—so beautifully that for one whole delirious week Skaggs did not appear at the club, while Cassell used to sit on the porch at home and warn Angelina to turn off the piano when Skaggs approached. Cassell took time from his office hours to do this.

The eagerness with which he pursued his diabolical revenge brought its own punishment, however, for as the days went by without tangible result the overstrained system gave way, and Cassell took to his bed. The family doctor was called in. He was a member of the club, and as he knew Skaggs, he immediately divined the truth. He lost no time in ordering Cassell's removal to a sanitarium. Skaggs called it the Nerve Institute. The doctor declared he would not be responsible for the consequences if he were disobeyed. Cassell had never heard of a doctor being answerable for any but good consequences, whatever happened, but, as he was very tired of Skaggs, he consented to go, cheered by the hope that in his absence grim retribution and Angelina might overtake the unregenerate Skaggs simultaneously.

Cassell was immured at the Nerve Institute for six long months, during which time all news of outside doings was prevented from reaching him, lest the Skaggs-shattered system should be retarded in its progress toward recovery. At length, however, he was allowed to return to the world he had known, and it was with a heart full of hope that he again set foot in his native town.

The first person he beheld was Skaggs, who greeted him warmly. That looked bad in itself. Cassell was on his guard.

"Come to the house and see us," said Skaggs, effusively. "Angelina will be glad . . ."

"Angelina, eh?" said Cassell, but still he was not overwhelmed with glee. Skaggs was too genial.

"You hadn't heard?" said Skaggs, "Well, anyhow, come up," and off he trotted.

Cassell went with all speed to the club and sought out Belden. That worthy took a gloomy view of the future. He supposed Cassell meant well enough, but his revenges were not of the first grade—a trifle rancid, as it were.

"You see, he explained, "Skaggs listens to Angelina's piano playing by the hour—says he never really heard the piano played before."

"Ah! But how about his golf?" demanded Cassell, hopefully.

"Oh, as to that," said Belden, "Angelina follows the beast about the course as if he were a Vardon; declares she never knew what a royal game it was."

Cassell gave a gasp and fainted gently away. That same night, kind friends bore him back to the Nerve Institute. When Skaggs heard of it the next day, he sent Cassell a jar of currant jelly that his aunt Sophia had given him when he had the grip in 1893.

There is such a thing as the personal equation.

The Greatest Golf Finish I Ever Saw

John G. Anderson

THERE HAVE BEEN THRILLING MOMENTS ON THE GOLF LINKS SINCE Willie Park won the first championship belt at Musselburgh in 1860. There have been legends of wonderful, unexpected victories, vastly improved with age no doubt, which we like to hear again and again, with the sum total of exciting features piled mountain high and steeped in golfing history and tradition.

We would like especially to witness the staging for the second time of the amateur championship at Holyoke, where this year's title play will be held, and once more follow a grandfather. Mr. Charles Hutchings, to see him win the amateur title of Great Britain at the age of fifty-three. Or as happened two years later cheer Walter J. Travis as he putted to victory in the amateur championship at Sandwich.

Could anything be more interesting to golfers than to watch a replay between Mr. C. A. Palmer and Lionel Munn in the British amateur championship of 1908 when they halved in par nine successive extra holes with the older man Palmer winner at the tenth extra? And for variety sake, applaud unsparingly that foursome match in 1906 at Musselburgh where was beaten by a stalwart crew of players including Mr. R. D. Thomson, eighty-nine years young, Mr. John Doleman, a mere kitten at eighty, playing most seriously within sight of the links eighty-six years before partnered by a lifelong friend in Mr. James Bennet who was but eighty-five.

We ourselves cannot go farther back than 1895 for golfing recollections. We are mindful that since Blackheath was first started in 1608, the

Edinburgh Burgess Golfing Society in 1735, the Honourable Company of Edinburgh Golfers in 1744, and the Royal and Ancient at Saint Andrews in 1754, that momentous drives and putts, recoveries kaleidoscopic, have startled the attention of golfers. But out of the hundreds and thousands of contests and medal play rounds that we have read about or seen, nine holes stand out as preeminent, distancing by a full mashie shot all other thrillers.

THE JOUST AT BROOKLINE
The year 1913, the player Ouimet, the situation desperate for America's chances for a win as blurred as the vision on that rainy day.

Reams have been written in verse and prose about the open championship victory of the Brookline boy still in his teens, but stress has always been laid on the remarkable 72 he scored in the play-off against his formidable opponents, Harry Vardon and Edward Ray. But just as a battery warmed up recharges itself, so was Ouimet surcharged with strength and hope for the morrow by his display of golf on the Friday afternoon.

The setting was after this wise. The internationalists Vardon, Ray, Reid, and Tellier had set the pace early in the play, had been caught at the various times by at least half a dozen American golfers, but, starting out on the last round were in a tie at 225 only with Ouimet who was expected to fade from the picture. When Ray went to the turn in 43 and Vardon in 42 there was little hope left in them. An opportunity as big as any golfer's pet dream presented itself to American entrants. Even the finish in 304 gave naught but inspiration to those battling in the mist and rain.

There was Hagen who needed only another 76 to win the title, who needed but par for the last seven holes to win and who failed. There was Long Jim Barnes who would have tied with a 76; MacDonald Smith, who also finished three strokes behind the winners through the medium of two 6s on easy holes, and this after he had taken a 44 to the turn and the one occasion and a 42 on the other. And McDermott, the unfortunate, who needed only par on the last nine to tie at 304. And Tellier, who killed his hopes with two 6s on the first five holes coming home, blotted out international success with France as the victor.

All had finished when word was brought that Ouimet had a chance, that he was a stroke better than any of his rivals at the seventh. A thousand golfers streaked it from the shelter of the clubhouse when this news was brought. To them and the other thousand came at once dire disappointment, for the Woodland golfer messed up the next hole taking a 6 at the 380-yard eight and a 5 at the long ninth. At that he was out in 43 with a fighting chance. The tenth is 140 yards and not difficult with the tee shot from a high bank. Ouimet took a neat 5 and a dozen friends of mine strolled sadly away and back to the clubhouse broken in hopes and spirits. Who wouldn't have been?

Then began the greatest uphill fight on golf's historic pages. I hope I may live to witness such another. It was not the scores made; it was the way in which the ball was clucked down that made for excitement. The eleventh hole measures 390 yards and Ouimet's drive was only a fair, a matter of 190 yards. The lie was rotten, to use a golfer's expression. "I've got to go for the brook," said Ouimet to his little caddie. With a spoon he smashed into the turf and the ball ran to the edge of the green.

There was satisfaction indeed in his smile as he wiped the mud from the face of the wooden club. The approach putt was poor, and everyone held his breath as the next putt rolled around the edge of the cup and then dropped. But still no life to the crowd, which was figuring already on the greatness of an amateur finishing in the prize list among so many fine professionals.

GLOOM AT THE TWELFTH

If any did have hopes, they were squelched when the next hole, 415 yards, was made in a 5. The green is not far from clubhouse, and strictly speaking, there were but few left when the toilsome journey through the rain began on the way to the thirteenth hole, a matter of 320 yards. Ouimet's drive was long and straight, his approach was fifteen feet from the cup, the ball never wavered a fraction of an inch as he putted it down. He had been left with the seemingly impossible task of making the last six holes in 22, bogie for which as the card indicated was 26 in order to tie the English golfers. That 3 brought forth a round of loud hurrahs and brought scampering back the stragglers.

The fourteenth hole, 470 yards, saw a long straight drive, a hooked second, a good mashie to the green and a putt for a 4 that rimmed the lip of the cup and needed but a tap to put it in. The fifteenth hole borders on the clubhouse grounds and there came pouring forth five thousand spectators idly curious in most respects. They saw nothing to startle them, for Ouimet's drive was sliced, and his second shot was forty yards from the hole with two intervening traps.

I was immediately back of Ouimet when he made his approach shot and I consider it the second best shot in golf I have ever seen. To begin with, no ball pitched two feet over the traps could be held near the cup. The ball had to strike within six inches of the trap's edge to permit the lessening run and a windup near the cup. To make matters more difficult, Ouimet had been approaching with a mashie not laid back any too deep making the stroke ten times more severe. But he brought off the shot with a perfection to detail that has always remained in my memory. His putt of a yard he made simple.

Making a Hard One
Then at the sixteenth hole he performed again. His drive to this 123-yarder was a bit over the hole, but a 3 looked easy. The very blood in my veins chilled when I saw that from a distance of eighteen feet he was short, not one or two feet, but seven feet. I felt weak at that stage of the game, for I had been pulling for victory in spite of all the black-looking chances and wasted opportunities.

There were others in the same mood. I know, for there was little cheering when, with no hesitation, Ouimet sank the putt. He needed a 3 on the 360-yard seventeenth to tie the score at that point of Vardon and Ray. His drive was good, his approach six yards past the cup brought a smile to his mother, watching from the wall at the back of the green. Jerome Travers had a grip of my shoulder, and I knew once more where the strength came from, which had helped to win his fourth amateur championship at Garden City two weeks before.

"He's 'got' to make it and he can," said Jerry, again and again. I wondered at his excitement, having seen him as an icicle during the amateur title play.

"Ten dollars he holds it!" said Travers. There were no takers.

Of course the putt went down. That is history. In years to come, it will become more famous. Not a soul who witnessed it, including Vardon and Ray, will ever forget. The last hole, so far as the gallery goes, was played for Ouimet long before he stepped to the tee. A drive, a long approach, a run-up putt, and then, well, there were a few shivers when the young lad stepped up to a three-foot putt and without sighting from front or back, hit the ball into the cup for the very 22 for six holes needed and a tie with Vardon and Ray, a tie for America. The play next day to me seemed like an anticlimax. The game was won on the sixty-ninth and seventy-first holes.

Hypothetically Golf

A Story of Golf, Children, Love, and a Duffer

Richard Florance

NATURALLY ENOUGH YOU MIGHT EXPECT TO FIND A WOMAN VERY FOND of children, and a man enthusiastic about golf. There is no reason why a woman should not be fond of other things as well, of beer, for instance, or dancing, or Vanity Fair. By the same token, there is no reason why a man should not be enthusiastic about the modern chorus, or tennis, or sodas, or anything at all that pleases him. Only, please may I keep to golf?

Well, then, to repeat, a woman by rights ought to love children, and a man ought to like golf. But these two people didn't. The order was all tangled up, and it was Jimmy who adored children, and Margaret who played golf.

They didn't call each other Margaret and Jimmy at first. Paradoxically, they didn't meet until after they had had quite a conversation together. And although they were both staying at the same big country hotel, they hadn't even seen each other before that first conversation.

Jimmy was a healthy young chap with a tremendous lot of money and a big estate somewhere or other in the correct place for big estates to be, but he loved the hotel because there were always so many people all about. Not that he ever met them, but he liked to be near people, and to watch them. If they tried to be nice to him, at once he became shy, and as soon as their backs were turned he ran ingloriously away. The children, however, he met quite informally, and romped with them in the woods behind the hotel or took them for sudden picnics and told them wonderful stories. He was so big and good looking that the mothers gladly gave him their youngest sons and daughters, and sighed because he never asked for their older daughters. The older daughters just wrinkled up their noses, after the fashion of the unsought.

Margaret looked as though she were originally made to be the dream mother of all children, except her eyes. It was her eyes that made children intuitively suspicious of her. They were beautiful blue eyes, but they were restless, eager eyes, as are those of one who drives her own car, of one who can be sure of her dresses, her maid, her allowance, and her name, but who can never be sure of her long brassie shots. "Children?" she is quoted as saying. "Oh, yes. Wretched little things. They never keep their eyes on the ball. They just carry my clubs around and act perfectly useless."

Margaret came to the hotel for its private links. Jimmy came for the children and the theory of sociableness. So, at the end of their fourth day in the same place, neither one had as much as noticed the other one.

The fifth day they met, as might two stars rushing together meet and roar into flame. Jimmy and a horde of youngsters had invaded the golf links. That was wrong in the first place, but Jimmy knew no golf, and the links to him were not sacred, but interesting meadows wherein folk walked, hitting little balls about with long sticks. And so, when a ball bounced near him, and when one of the children, picking it up, started a game of catch, he was only mildly critical of the propriety of so doing.

Presently from a gully came striding Margaret, followed by a mite in a very, very large pair of overalls, who dragged after him her golf bag. She looked at the ground before her and frowned. Then she turned to the caddie beside her, but he stared vacantly back at her. There was evidently no ball there. She opened her mouth, and gave tongue to the accepted formula.

"You silly little idiot," she said calmly, "are you going to stand there with your mouth open?" And then, as no answer came, and as the mouth did not shut, she went on with heat, "You're a rotten caddie! Why didn't you watch it? What good are you? You little fool, I could *carry* my clubs myself! Here!" Whereupon she seized the unfortunate mite, tore from his grasp the bag of clubs, threw them on the ground, threw her own club after them, and stamped her foot. The mite smiled weakly, and burst into tears.

Jimmy's children had watched this scene in awed silence. The ball dropped from a limp hand and fell at Jimmy's feet. He picked it up and advanced sternly on the woman.

"Here," he was warmly, "is your old ball, and I'd advise you to be a little less excitable and rude."

Seemingly aware of him and his group for the first time, she took the ball from his hand and threw it down. Rage and coherence struggled in her. She bent and picked up a long wooden club; she turned on Jimmy and her eyes shot fire.

"You mind your own business, Sir!" she said. Which is quite like a famous verse, isn't it? Only, Margaret was very angry indeed. "Suppose you attend to your own business and take those dirty little creatures off the golf course. This is not a nursery!"

At first the "mind your own business" struck Jimmy as being quite undignified, and he smiled. But her final sentence, delivered icily, was crushing in the intensity of its scorn. He stared at her, and she stared back at him.

He missed a breath, and to make up for it took a deep, audible one the next time. She missed one, too, and to make up for it she missed another. He found himself wandering helplessly along the curved line of her mouth; over, around, and back; over, around, and back; he had been wandering for centuries. As for Margaret, she had slipped down into the very deepest part of his eyes and was beginning to drown. Desperately she turned her back on him and began to swing before the ball. With a start, he noticed how lithe she was. Her club swung up, hesitated the fraction of a second, and then dipped, and the ball fled away in a long arc, to land far down the course, rolling straight. Thank God! thought Margaret, and wanted terribly to look at Jimmy. How was he to know that it was the Lord and not the woman who made that shot? Again he breathed long and audibly, and without a parting glance she was gone, to lose more balls that day than ever before.

That night Jimmy forsook his usual quiet corner on the verandah, where Margaret had never come, and walked with a brave pretense of unconcern among the guests star-scattered in the card room. And Margaret, forsaking her maiden aunt in the card room where Jimmy never came, walked casually around the verandah. Therefore, that night they did not meet.

The next morning, Jimmy stealthily evaded his children, and fled into the woods. He walked in an elaborate circle, and when he at last came to a clearing, he went forward with the greatest of caution. Finally he stopped and sat down, his back against an old tree. Before him stretched the golf links and beyond them the hotel. He lit his pipe and settled himself comfortably.

Before him passed golfers in various stages of satisfaction or despair, and at last, followed by the mite, the one he waited to see. She made a short approach to the green and holed out in two careful putts. She was adorably incisive, thought Jimmy. She teed up and drove a long, low ball that sliced into the rough, whereat she stamped her foot. To her incisiveness he added a beautiful figure, and a terrible temper. Then he got up and went home, talking wisely to the birds in general, and to one old, bored-looking toad in particular.

After lunch he called to him his clan, much to the delight of the mothers and nurses, and settled himself for an afternoon of stories. Deep in the woods he sat with the clan spread before him fanwise, and he told them grizzly stories of murders and ghosts and tigers and cannibals, to their thrilled horror. There was one about a prince and a princess that was the best of all because it was so possible.

"You see," he said to the devoted circle, "the prince had never seen the princess before, so, of course, when she suddenly came over a hill, followed by a beautiful big tiger, he sat right down and stared at her. She had a little bunch of sticks with her that the tiger carried, and with these she kept hitting a tiny white dog that was all rolled up in a ball and rolled along in front of her. Now when she saw the prince, she couldn't help but sit right down and stare at him, too. So the tiger, thinking that the game was over, opened his mouth, wiggled his tail, and swallowed the little white dog right up. Then the princess got awfully angry, and stamped her foot, and said to the tiger—well, she was very angry indeed, and I mustn't tell you what she said."

At once he heard behind him a low trill of laughter, quickly smothered. He regarded a tree in front of him gravely, with an air of detachment. Then he slowly got up, and the clan chorused their regrets.

"Go on—don't stop. Please, please go on!"

He looked at the eager, upturned faces with some quiet dignity. "Let's go home," he said.

Night found Jimmy in a dark corner of the verandah where no one would object to his pipe. Margaret and her maiden aunt joined a group inside and sat down to bridge. An hour later, Margaret gave her place to an elderly lady, yawned very delicately, and said good night. On the verandah at that moment, Jimmy stuffed his pipe into his pocket, and untangled his feet from a neighboring rocking chair.

Guess I'll get a whiff of air, thought Margaret, inside.

"Hi, ho might as well turn in, murmured Jimmy, outside.

And so it came to pass that as Margaret stepped out through the doorway and stopped a moment to consider, Jimmy swung in from the night and passed her. For the briefest of seconds they looked into each other's eyes.

The man had rather imagined that when they met he would smile slightly in a superior way, and look tremendous. The woman had fancied her face assuming the most innocent look, a trifle interrogatory, perhaps, with a hint of suppressed laughter.

The very suddenness found them off their guards. Red flamed into their faces and in their startled eyes was confusion akin to terror. Jimmy felt as though he had suddenly, in the dark, run full tilt upon a wall.

Then it was over, and she was running swiftly down a cool, dim path, her hands to her face, while he fled miserably to his room.

Quote a robin to a worm early next morning, before the orthodox world had eaten its breakfast, "Just look at that man. Hoho!" The unfortunate worm twisted about to get a better view and beheld a man who whacked madly at a little white ball, but seemingly in vain, for the ball did not move. "Why, it's Jimmy!" cried the worm, and at once the robin ate him. Part of the orthodox world had breakfasted.

Jimmy was a wrathful, despairing Jimmy. Secretly he had tiptoed out into the early morning with a borrowed bag of clubs; golf he would learn, and soon. He had started well. He had addressed the ball according to the best pictures, and his first shot, a nonchalant expression of confidence, had been in the nature of a success. Then he had flubbed mildly, sending the ball rolling a few yards ahead of him. Warned by that of carelessness, he had set himself to the task, nerves and muscles tensed, with the result that he had missed the ball twice, and had plowed a deep furrow into the ground. That was an hour and four holes ago. He shook his head and ran his hand through his stubbly hair. He changed his club and bent over the ball again. Far behind him he heard a faint "Fore!" Like the shyest of birds when alarmed, he fled.

Later, from the screen of the woods, he decided that golf was a snare and a delusion. Nay, more: it was a proven impossibility to hit a ball of that size so far. Those eerie creatures who did it were a sort of goblins, possessed of inherited and unnatural powers. For him to try was mere foolishness.

So it was with mild surprise, coupled with vexation, that he found himself that afternoon approaching the bunker at number three hole with sudden, wandering little strokes. He had been careful to let no one see him play, and when a foursome moved onto a green near where his ball was lying on its way to another hole, rather than play himself he watched their putting with elaborate interest. When they quoted their best score for the hole as five, he smiled. It was manifestly impossible to do that hole in five. He himself had just taken twenty-seven strokes on the same hole; that is, not counting the five misses, and a long time spent in a gully. Wherefore, when they said that their best score was five he smiled. These polite conversations on the golf links were quite pleasant affairs. Not to be outdone, he explained to them easily how he had just made the hole in four. Then he politely waited for them to drive through him, for, as he remarked, a foursome is always more important than a single player. As his ball lay some two hundred yards from the tee, which he casually remarked to be his drive, although it was a consummation of seven strokes and a miss, the party went through him with great respect for his prowess and his old-fashioned politeness.

Later, when he finally sputtered into the bottom of a very sandy bunker, he was careful to peep over the top of it before he started thrashing at the sand. It was well that he did, for on the other slide was that which caused him to hold tightly to the tufts of grass along the slope of the bunker and flatten himself out. Below him sat Margaret, deep in conversation with the youngest, the dirtiest, and the most terrible of the clan.

Jimmy regarded her with delight. Plainly out of her element, she was struggling bravely to win the youngster's interest. It was clear that she was having a most unenjoyable time, and it was equally clear that her small companion was bored. She was asking him questions about his home life.

"And of course, you love your dear old grandmother very much," announced Margaret with the least upward inflection of her voice. The child frowned and hit his shoe with his hand.

"Why don't you play with me instead of askin' me silly old questions?" he grumbled. Soon he would scramble to his feet and run away. Margaret considered desperately.

Jimmy grinned. Then, as his roving eye caught sight of the green some hundred yards below, his grin widened. He slid back into the sand of the bunker and picked up his ball. He stood so that he could just see the top of the flag at the hole. Then he growled loudly in a deep voice. "Well, well, here I am right at the edge!"

There was an exclamation from the other side of the bunker, and the sound of a child scampering away. Loudly he cried, "Fore!" and with that threw the ball high in the air toward the flag.

A moment later when he came from around the end of the bunker, whistling blithely, his ball lay on the green miraculously near the cup, and Margaret, sitting alone, was regarding him with wide, awed eyes.

Always after supper the children marched through the halls in the wake of their respective nurses, bound for bed, a rebellious, captive procession. So there is nothing out of the ordinary in Margaret's happening to meet that night the particular child of the afternoon, nor in her stopping for a moment to say goodnight to him. Perhaps there is a bit more coincidence in the opportune arrival of Jimmy from around a corner, and in the fact that he, too, had to stop and bid the child goodnight.

"This," said the small but correct mutual friend, "is the golf lady. And this is my story, Papa."

Gravely the two nodded, smiled, and then laughed. An omniscient nurse dragged the protesting introducer off to bed, and Jimmy and Margaret were left alone with one another. Apparently they had never seen each other before.

"He's the dearest mite," said Margaret.

"Appreciative little begger," said Jimmy, and then, suddenly bethinking himself of the view from the top of the bunker, and Margaret struggling to make conversation with that same appreciative creature, laughed gleefully. Margaret laughed, too, but uneasily. She had thought of the bunker herself.

They wandered out onto the verandah and sat down in low rocking chairs. They had progressed from the particular to the general, subject: children.

"Do you know," said Margaret, "I've never been at a hotel where there were so many children. They bob up all over wherever you least expect them. You bump into them in the halls, on the lake, you fall into them on the stairs, the walks, the golf links . . ."

She was silent. He echoed her weakly, "Ah, yes—the golf links." And he was silent. Again they were thinking of the same incident. And then together they remarked:

"I love them, though."

"Rather a nuisance on the links."

Lo, it was Jimmy who said that they were a nuisance on the links. They heard each other and at once reversed their periods. Again they spoke together.

Said Margaret, "Yes, a bit of a nuisance."

Said Jimmy, "Jolly little beggars!"

Then, feeling hopelessly entangled, they lapsed into gloomy silence. When the measured creak of the rocking chairs threatened to unseat her reason, Margaret spoke again, and with a brilliant stroke carried the attack into her opponent's territory.

"I understand," she said, "that you play a very fine game of golf."

Jimmy moved in his seat. "Yes?" he murmured, correctly. She went on.

"You know, I play at it myself. Of course, I'm not in your class, but I'd love to play with you sometime—if you wouldn't mind playing with a mere amateur."

"Love to," murmured Jimmy, and moved again in his seat.

The lady pouted. He hardly need be so proud of his game and so standoffish. Jimmy sensed a dangerous gap somewhere, and sent reinforcements.

"Love to," he murmured again, weakly.

It was decidedly cool of him, but then Margaret supposed that a really fine golfer couldn't be expected to go into ecstasies at the idea of playing with an amateur lady. She had seen that one approach of his from the bunker.

"How would you like to play tomorrow morning?" she said, a bit timidly.

Jimmy stopped rocking. "Tomorrow," he said. "Tomorrow morning. Oh yes. Um. I'll tell you—I'd like to tremendously, but you see—you see, I've got to go on a picnic with the children." He smiled at himself in a pleased way. Picnics were easy affairs to arrange. He blessed the children.

To every man there must come at least once in this life some moment of brilliant strategic inspiration. Such a moment was Jimmy's, and he swept the enemy off the earth.

"Why," said he enthusiastically, "don't you come along?"

Margaret gasped. Again she saw herself, a bunker, and one child. Then she thought dimly of herself as Raphael Madonna, surrounded by cherubs, and then Raphael changed to Rose O'Neil and the cherubs changed to kewpies and made faces at her. She shuddered.

"I'm awfully sorry," she explained, "I'd adore to, of course, but you see—you see, I've promised to meet Dick on the links at ten, and so—of course—you see . . ."

The retreat, although conducted in poor order, was effective. Jimmy wondered who Dick was and frowned.

Dick was Margaret's unfortunate, small thin caddie. But how should Jimmy know that?

The next day Jimmy discovered the gentleman. Strange, how content and at peace he felt when he gazed for the first time at Dick's diminutive form and very, very large overalls.

Foreseeing difficulties, Jimmy wisely gave a hypothetical bag of clubs to the golf master and asked him quite hypothetically to reshaft his driver and his mashie. For this he paid him a real price and had thereby a two days' excuse from golf. Then he took Dick aside, and to that minute creature he tendered a large bribe. Bigger men than Dick have fallen before smaller bribes; he will be judged in heaven. Thereafter Miss Margaret's drives, Miss Margaret's putts, Miss Margaret's scores were as nothing compared to Mr. Jimmy's, and compared they were at every opportunity. When, upon an occasion, she drove the longest ball of her career, Dick even went as far as to point out the exact spot where Mr. Jimmy's drive had lain only a short week ago—some ten yards farther on.

It is not to be supposed that Margaret enjoyed this. Indeed, more than once she stamped her foot at Dick and bade him be still. Once she boxed his ears. But he hated her cordially and continued to expatiate on Jimmy's superior game. Nor would she change her caddie. Somehow there was an element of sweetness in her cup of bitterness, a sweetness, however, that she never would have admitted.

Jimmy noticed a growing coldness in Margaret, but he accepted it bravely, so bravely as to almost lead one to suspect that he rather liked it. Certainly it was not the coldness of boredom that the lady felt for him. He had daily reports from his small henchman, and he came from such councils in a highly amiable frame of mind. He managed to break his brassie early one morning before anyone else was up, and that kept him out of the game for another day, particularly as he could never play with any clubs but his own, and his brassie was his favorite shot. Margaret, seeing again that long mashie approach over the bunker, thrilled with despair.

For all of what must pass for her coldness, they were often together. For who shall delve into the heart of a golfer, and that one a woman? We can but watch the elaborately innocent ways in which they used to meet each other, the long walks they used to take together, the unaccountable silences they both loved and feared, and finally the great hatred that flamed through the woman every time Dick assured her that her drive was a little bit shorter—just a little bit shorter. Is it not consistent?

They met each other with smiles and used to hide together from the pursuing children. Sometimes they raced around hand in hand, or walked together down the dark walks and paths at night. He used to take her arm and whip her face with soft sprays of flowers. It almost seemed as though she had forgotten those long brassie shots of his, sometimes, and when one night she took his arm in such a sweet, womanly way, and walked with him for a long while in the most blissful of silences, he was so moved that later, when he went to bed, he sat for half an hour with his foot in his hand, before he could properly concentrate on the way to take off a shoe.

Therefore the blow was all the more shattering and unexpected when it fell. The next morning, when he had carefully timed his entry into the dining room so he could pass her table and smile a good morning at her, his smile stiffened and froze, and his heart fluttered and dropped through seventy miles of vacuum. For there, at Margaret's table, sat a strange, attractive man, who bore no more resemblance to the lady than does, for instance, a golf ball in a daisy field resemble a golf ball.

After the most miserable of breakfasts, Jimmy went out onto the verandah and sat stiffly in the most uncomfortable-looking chair he could find. Two children passed him, talking in the loud whisper of their kind. "Poor story Papa," said one, "his girl got another feller." Through the trees that screened the links from the hotel, Jimmy caught a glimpse of two figures swinging along the fair toward the first hole, and one of them was surely Margaret. Jimmy cursed the children.

Nor did he see much more of Margaret in the days following. She seemed to spend most of her time with the new chap. For the most part they were on the golf links together, but there Jimmy never saw them, for he buried himself in the woods, and even forgot that hypothetical bag of clubs still being repaired.

Therein Jimmy was human, but unwise. For if he had been inhuman and had peeked from out of the woods at the two golfers, he could have seen a strange thing. Between them there was only one gab, and the stranger was making frantic swats at the ball and hitting it not at all. And beside him stood Margaret, adjuring, coaxing, commanding, blasting with scorn and wheedling with praise. In this, Jimmy would have been vastly delighted, but considerably puzzled. Unless he had thought perhaps: She must love him a lot to do all that for him. Then he would have packed up and gone home. So maybe it's just as well that Jimmy stayed human and sulked in the woods.

Of course he met the stranger, and was miserably aware that he couldn't help liking him. He liked everything about him—his bigness, his blondness, his awkwardness. But he refused to go picnicking with them, refused to go walking or swimming or paddling with them, and, indeed, refused to do anything with them. Again, being human, he never saw the triumph in Margaret's eyes, nor the frank amusement in the man's. If he had, he wouldn't have understood it, anyhow. He moped miserably by himself.

It was a while he was so moping that Margaret and her friend held a little conversation that was to plunge poor Jimmy into the deepest depths that ever a man had plumbed. The two were coming in from golf, and the path was deserted. He bent toward her, and spoke in a low, doubtful voice.

"Dear," he said, "how do you know that he'll accept?"

"Don't worry, Hugh, he'll accept. He can't just refuse. It was different with me, you know—I couldn't really ask him." She broke into a low laugh. "He'll be so upset! I wonder if he has a sense of humor."

The big man laughed, but a bit doubtfully. She slipped her hand into his, and they walked silently to the hotel. Jimmy, on the verandah, saw them, and bit his lip.

Therefore he was in no mood to answer Dennison when the latter came up to him later. It seemed to make no difference to the elect of Margaret, however, for he sat down next to him and lit a cigar. There was a silence. Dennison puffed away at his cigar and then plunged in.

"I say, old man—I've been hearing interesting things about you."

"Yes?"

"I wonder if you would do me the honor of playing with me sometime."

Trapped! Jimmy crossed and uncrossed his legs, and squirmed.

"Why . . . I . . . well, now, you see . . ."

But Dennison couldn't see. Jimmy had no real reason for refusing him, and at the end of a desperate but futile ten minutes Jimmy, for all his wriggles and his squirms, was firmly impaled on the spike of his own misdeeds, to be offered up next morning as a sacrifice to the mob. No one knew what a Roman Holiday was preparing except Jimmy, but the exclusiveness of the knowledge was no balm.

Margaret went to bed that night dreaming of the morrow, seeing in her mind the proud Jimmy fuming along with her duffer Dennison, held up for hours at every hole, forced into so ridiculous a match that his vanity would suffer until the end of time. And then—but whisper it not in Gath—duffers have been known to beat veterans—sometimes—maybe.

Jimmy did not sleep. His reign was over. Tomorrow he was to be held up to scorn by Margaret's lover. Even his children would laugh at him. And Margaret . . . he turned his face miserably to the wall. One more day he would stay at that wretched hotel, and then he'd leave. And when he left, he'd leave womankind behind him, too.

Toward morning he grew defiant and swore that after all he'd put up a game fight. With that he fell asleep, and when he woke up it was late, and he wasted precious minutes trying to realize that this sunny day was the morning of his tragedy. When he came downstairs, appropriately tragic, it was too late for breakfast.

Rumors of the match had gone the rounds of the hotel, and there was a big crowd at the first tee when Jimmy got to the golf house. He went quietly into the house and cornered the golf master. From him he borrowed a bag of clubs. The golf master was all grin. Cheshire cat! thought Jimmy, and walked out to the tee.

Dennison was there, swinging professionally at the ground. Near him stood Margaret, smiling encouragement. When Jimmy came out, she started toward him, but he turned away with bowed head.

The crowed fell back, for all the world, he thought, as though to give them air. He looked at Dennison and essayed a meager smile. It seemed to him just like one of the old street fights of his infancy, when he used to circle about within a narrow wall of faces, with clenched fists and snarling face. The same curious crowd, the same ferocious will to see something beaten, the same seemingness of unreality, and the same sinking feeling in the pit of his stomach. He swung his driver nervously and waited for something to happen.

Dennison drove off first. He popped a little fly off to the right, and the crowd breathed. Dennison laughed, but Margaret frowned and shook her head at him. Jimmy compressed his lips and walked onto the tee. There was a dead silence. He stooped and arranged a tidy pile of sand for himself. Gingerly he placed the ball on this pile and stepped back. He swung his club above the ball for a moment, and then drew it up over his shoulder. He closed his eyes, took a deep breath, and swooped upon it. There was a sharp crack and a gasp from the crowed. He opened his eyes. His ball was just dipping to earth far down the course, a beautiful long drive. Dennison whistled cheerfully, but Jimmy, when he started after his ball, could hardly walk for the trembling of his legs.

Dennison continued to pop little flies until he was opposite Jimmy. Then he managed to clear the intervening bunker and landed on the green. Jimmy, closing his eyes again, flubbed into the sand and hacked furiously to get out. At the end of ten strokes, he landed exhausted on the green, and lost the hole in five wild putts. The crowd was puzzled, but Margaret's eyes were wide and amazed. She had been watching Jimmie's face that second shot.

The second hole Dennison drove a short ball, but fairly straight. The crowd smiled at Dennison—they understood him now, and pitied him, and watched for Jimmie's long drive. Jimmy, with set jaw swooping upon the ball, missed it altogether. He opened his eyes and swung again. This time he hit the earth an inch in front of the ball. The crowd tittered. Margaret was biting her lip to keep from shrieking, but Jimmy didn't care. He saw red; with all his might he came down on the ball, and the ball, plus a great deal of earth, flew off some five yards and stopped. Wild with rage, he followed it, dealing it mortal blows.

Dennison, immersed in the perilous intricacies of his own game, had no time to notice his rival. He only knew that as each hole reached up and drew down his ball, he had somehow miraculously won it from the champion. But Margaret understood, and she could have cried. If ever a woman was really sorry for something, that woman was Margaret. Only it was too late for remorse. The crowd had never enjoyed itself so hugely. The people followed the game as the bucolic nymphs might have followed Bacchus. They clutched each other in their transports of mirth, they fell over on their sides, drunk with laughter. The older daughters had the best time. . . . The sun beat down on Jimmy, the mockery and the laughter swept around him, and before him the terrible white ball kept creeping and flying and whirling in every direction. Into every bunker he slid, into every grass tuft he flubbed and he threshed and flailed and cursed in his heart.

Finally at the fifth hole human nature would stand no more. When for the fifth consecutive time he had missed the ball entirely, it was too much. Behind him howled the mob, and somewhere there was Margaret, but it all was nothing. He seized his clubs from the convulsed caddie, and threw them on the ground, he threw his hat on top of them, and with both feet he jumped upon hat and clubs. And then, with long strides, he fled away into the woods.

There his children found him calmly chewing a straw. Rage had given way to shame. He felt no anger at Margaret, nor at Dennison. He blamed himself, and mortification overwhelmed him. He thought that he would never be able to go back to the hotel again, and yet he knew that ultimately he would have to. He welcomed the children with open arms, they were his friends. They, in turn, felt sorry for him, and nestled up to him while he stroked their hair and told them stories. There was one story about a princess and a prince who wasn't a prince at all, but who masqueraded as one because he loved the princess so much.

"And so," he wound up, "the poor little chap was sent to prison to be whipped because he had dared to love the princess and to masquerade as a prince. And for some reason or other, everybody was pleased."

"I think," cried one of the clan, "that was mean of everybody!"

"And so do I!" cried a clear voice from the woods, and Margaret was with them. "Children," she said, "your mothers are looking for you." Jimmy had an overpowering desire to kiss the hem of her skirt. Finding it a considerable business to breathe noiselessly, he kicked his foot vigorously in the moss.

When the children were gone, she sat down beside him. He could say nothing, and she watched him, a little smile on her face. At last she broke the silence.

"Jimmy," she said, "Why did you?"

Then he told her. All the floodgates of the days were swept away, and he told her that he loved her—told her that he couldn't help it if she were married a thousand times—that he loved her—that he loved her. It was a tremendously dramatic moment, but there was a smile in her eyes. It worried him, for by rights it should not have been there.

"Jimmy—goose!" She laid a slim cool hand on his arm. "Jimmy—you goose . . . you dear, dear goose!" And there was a little sob in her voice, although her eyes were smiling.

Whereupon the angels descended upon Jimmy in a torrent of pink fire and brass bands and glorious little fat cherubim.

Then she explained. Dennison was her cousin, and her accomplice. How he would love that man!

"Dearest," cried Jimmy, inspired, thinking of his old estate with its many acres of stubble, "You are going to have a golf links all your own. And I'm going to learn to play. A golf links? A thousand golf links!"

"Oh!" said Margaret to the woods. From far off came to them the pealing laughter of the clan. And then her arms stole up around Jimmy's neck, and her face grew pink and white, and she whispered to him what *he* would have.

"Gee!" said Jimmy to the angels.

Playing Alone

Marrion Wilcox

"HAD NOT EXERCISE BEEN ABSOLUTELY NECESSARY FOR OUR WELL-BE-ing," said my opponent, "nature would not have made the body so proper for it by giving such an activity to the limbs, and such a pliancy to every part, as necessarily produce those compressions, extensions, contortions, dilations, and all other kinds of motions that are necessary for the preservation of such a system of tubes and glands as the physiologists describe. And that we might not want inducements to engage us in such an exercise of the body as is proper for its welfare, it is so ordered that nothing valuable can be procured without it. Not to mention riches and honor, even food and raiment are not to be come at without the toil of the hands and sweat of the brows. As for those who are not obliged to labor, by the condition in which they are born, they are more miserable than the rest of mankind, unless they indulge themselves in that voluntary labor which goes by the name of exercise."

That had a pleasant sound, I thought, and a familiar, too; like a quotation one can't quite place, or a person one must have seen before, somewhere. I looked at him more closely as he spoke—a man with shoulders like a ledge or rocks, and the palms of his hands flat and firm as a plank; such a pippin-cheeked, gray-eyed fellow as Devon especially had the habit of turning out. And to me he was still an unplaced quotation—precisely this, as I shall now explain.

After a late breakfast, I had set out from my lodgings in Abbey Crescent to spend a few hours on the Torquay links, which stretch back from cliffs overlooking the English Channel. The first hole lay beyond a long hill—so long that my drive had carried the ball little more than halfway to the top. As I expected, not a soul was in sight, for I had a mind to play through the lunching-hour—perhaps only to prove once more what I already knew well enough, that the competition of an opponent was required to put me on my mettle or keep me up to the mark. But how many of us, in golf and life, will cheerfully fall below our standard once in a while.

Nestled up against a wiry tuft of grass, the ball presented a problem that one of the sturdy irons should have solved; on the other hand, there was the tempting chance to clear the crest of the hill in two, and so make the hole in four. I accepted the risk with a brassie; the ball flew off into the bushes and ditch away to the right, and after it went the head of the broken club. The first hole cost six strokes, one new ball, and one favorite brassie.

My opponent put in an appearance as I was about to drive off from the second teeing ground. "Here is the lost ball," he began. "And, unless you prefer to go around alone, I'll play your own against you. It cleared the ditch and fell at my feet." He took acquaintanceship and consent for granted, and so did I, quite easily, for he evidently belonged in the scene, and was perhaps a "familiar spirit," so to speak, while I was comparatively a stranger.

We played along, stroke for stroke, evenly as possible, until I began to fancy that, whereas he might have done what he liked with the ball, he merely cared to keep up in order to have someone with whom to speak. When we came to the fourth putting green it was precisely twelve o'clock, and here he confided to me, with the manner of one who will not over-emphasize the value of his disclosure in making it to a friend, that high noon was really they mysterious hour—not midnight, as the vulgar suppose.

"All living things upon the earth respond to this most direct appeal from the source of life," he said, "and naturally there are some things— and some poor creatures—that are granted a short period of active life *only* at that hour, or for a little while immediately before and after the sun's supreme moment. The idea that things so lacking in vigor that they are called 'shades,' 'ghosts,' 'wraiths,' or whatnot, acquire strength to appear at midnight and must vanish at cock crow is preposterous. Is the beggar better provided for in a season of want that impoverishes even the rich? At high noon, if you will look with a seeing eye at trees and streams and hills you may become conscious of those creatures expressing their life that the Greeks knew; you may speak with dryads and nymphs and oreads if you do not prefer the rustic divinities of your own more silent six. In the hour of the fullness of life, all spirits are abroad and 'ghosts do walk': by the same token the shades of the departed eagerly drank the blood of victims and sacrificed to them in the old days."

As the exhilaration of the game and the brilliant sunshine gained upon us, the stream of his suggestions was as much livelier, and shallower, as we rather expect a stream to be when it gives over the quiet business of reflection in favor of a merry dash downhill. Unfortunately, I cannot recall many of his sayings, but a few I noted on my scorecard. Characterizing an eminent and vastly rich philanthropist who was spending the season at Torquay, he said, "He stole a pig, and gave the poor the trotters in God's name"—a homely version of a Spanish proverb, if I mistake not. A cheerful habitué of the links who had enjoyed his ups and downs my opponent described as follows: "Mr. J—is an immortal spirit who has just played at living in human form for fifty-odd years; and the wider the range of it (or, let us say, of *his*) experiences, the more fun there has been in the game. He has not desired *for* himself uninterrupted prosperity, unfailing good health, an unbroken succession of successors, in his course through life; that would have seemed to him like desiring to run a partition wall through the universe, and to live only on one side of it." Not quoted or adapted, that bit of fresh-air philosophy, I should say; and perhaps I should add one or two other suggestions from the card of my memory if I did not suspect that the reader has already noticed that, in lieu of the give and take of conversation, he is asked to be attentive to a mere monologue.

Sure enough, on the seventeenth green he read the question in my face, "Who am I? Will I finish? That's what you want to know, isn't it? I shall tell you the one thing and show you the other," he said, and began to declaim, with an effort, as I fancied:

"Out-of-Doors is the best fellow,
The very best fellow I know.
Blow soft, blow keen,
So the leaves be green,
Or blue the sky that I see between
The red leaves and the yellow.
From north, from south, the wind may blow:
Still Out-of-Doors is the best fellow,
The very best fellow I know!"
"So, then," I said, aloud, "you are only a personification—of the noon, of exercise—of out-of-doors, in a word?"
"If you like, yes."
"One thing more," said I, "who wrote that poem about you?"

"That," he said, deliberately, "belongs to me; and so," he added, "does this." Tossing my lost ball (still white and smooth) into the air, he caught it so fairly as it fell with the driver head that it flew toward the west like a martin, skimming the surface of the ground yet never touching it—away, away, to the very distant clump of bushes and the ditch in which I had vainly searched for it. And after it ran my opponent himself, to catch it up again, perhaps, or, maybe, to overtake the noon.

When You Play on Public Links

Walt Lantz

PUBLIC GOLF LINKS TO A CITY IS AS NECESSARY AS CAMOUFLAGE TO Limburger cheese. No city is complete without a playground for duffers. It wouldn't be so bad if said course was built near the town pump so you could get to it in five minutes or so, but as a rule, you have to motor—pardon me, I mean trolley—through six suburbs or so, change for a coupla more trolleys, and then walk for a mile or two before reaching the links.

The season opens as soon as the mud gets thick enough and the greens are taken out of storage and dry cleaned and pressed.

The Bureau of Parks issues brass checks, giving you the exclusive use of the link—that is with about 25,000 others. For said check, you pay five berries, which includes all privileges, such as, waiting, cheating, swearing, losing balls, etc. This isn't bad at all, considering you don't have to be ashamed to carry your own bag as you would be on a private course, thus saving caddie expense.

A golfer using a new ball is conserved a pro and should have a caddie. Here's a convenience of the municipal links. You find an auction sale of golf balls at nearly every hole, none usually less than five cents. They have been over the course a few times and the wounds have been sewed up and painted, but what would you expect to get for a dime? The duffer says, "You lose the new ones as easily as the old ones."

A tax-paying golfer must be fleet of foot. When he hits a ball for a long drive, he must be under it before it falls. Lots of the patrons have hollow heels.

A CUSTOMER GETS A HUNCH

Most of the golfers have their names stamped on the balls; a very good idea but not always beneficial, as few of them are ever retrieved. One golfer, after losing a hundred balls with his name on them and not getting one back, had the next lot stamped thusly: "A. COHN, 412 MAIN ST. Sale: 50% off on all suits." Would you believe it? He sold forty suits in one week.

Public links would be great if all the taxpayers didn't decide to play at the same time. For instance, did you ever try to get in a round before dinner on Sunday? Sure you tried, that was all. No matter how early you get up, there are a thousand others who have the same idea. The only way to go is to register before breakfast. Your number will be called after supper, and you can get in a hole or two before dark, or register on Thursday for Sunday's game.

When you do get started on an eighteen-hole excursion, golfers are thicker than the fleas on Fido's tail. There are foursomes in front of you, foursomes in back of you, and sextets in between. It's a good thing they don't all have caddies, then there would be twice as many. Stop to look for a ball a minute and they go through like a cavalry charge.

Tees on the municipal links are wonderful for niblick practice. You lose your ball and the tee if you don't remember where you put it. Glue or chewing gum should be used instead of sand so the ball wouldn't roll off.

The only way to stay on the fairway is to shoot the pill around like a billiard ball. Any time you hit the ball, you don't know whether it is going down the fairway or into somebody's back yard.

The trouble with the bunkers and traps is that they're never planted right. The proper place for them is along the edge of the fairway so the balls can't roll into the rough.

Did you ever see a lake with a rowboat in it so you could get your ball when it went in? And why do they always put a lake between the hole and the tee, when the proper place for it is in some park, where it will be appreciated. We golfers don't object to lakes, but why must there be water in them? There is a greater thrill in getting your ball out of an empty lake than losing it in a full one.

I can't understand why the moles pick on the greens, when there is so much room for their apartments out in the rough. When on the green, you usually need two niblick shots, four mashies, and six putts to sink the pill.

The holes must be cut on a bias, for the ball always misses it by a hair and when it does fall in, it bounces right out again. Never could figure why they were called greens, when it is only the rough continued, and a flag stuck in the middle of it as a decoy.

But why razz the municipal links? They are built for the benefit of those tax-paying citizens who can't find a way to amuse themselves for the taxes they pay, so they take it out on golf.

1. A few advantages the municipal golfer has over the private links are:

2. Knickers are not compulsory.

3. Initiation fees and annual dues are all included in the $5 brass check.

4. Your tailor and other enemies cannot recognize you by name, as you are called in numbers, like guests of Sing-Sing.

5. It is not considered impolite if you look for a ball for more than three hours.

6. You're just as unwelcomed whether you come in a limousine or on roller skates.

7. Instead of taking your wife to the club and buying her a $12 plate dinner you escort her to a curbstone and buy her a hot dog right off the wagon for a nickel.

The Golden Rules of Golf

O. B. Keeler

FOR THE GOVERNMENT OF ACTUAL GOLFING OPERATIONS ON THE FIELD of battle, there is a set of rules in comparison with which the much-discussed covenant of the late League of Nations resembles an extract from a primer of conduct. There are lots of contingencies in golf, and there are rules for every contingency. For example, suppose you were playing a shot with a bank right in front of you, and the ball hit the bank and hopped back and lodged in the cuff of your pants and stayed there. What would you do?

That happened to John Anderson once. What did John do? I've forgot now. But there's a rule about it somewhere. There's a rule about everything, in golf. I don't know them all. I don't know a very high percentage of them probably, except in a general sort of way. Lots of regular golfers don't know all the rules.

In the Southern Amateur Championship of 1919, played at the New Orleans Country Club, Bob Jones's tee-shot on No. 1—a one-shot hole—landed in a wheelbarrow, and not only that but went into a large shoe that was in the wheelbarrow, the footgear of some laborer, left at the edge of the course.

Bob and his partner in the qualifying round were not certain what to do about it, so to save time, Bob got up in the wheelbarrow and played the shoe out on the green with a niblick, and the ball conveniently emerged and he almost got a par 3 after all.

Did Bob do right? I know, but I ain't going to tell you. Go on and read the rules yourself. It will do you good.

However, there are rules, connected with the ancient game that are not concerned directly with the playing thereof, though they may be found under the heading of Golf Etiquette. And they are important, too, in some such fashion as the old Golden Rule is important to the welfare and happiness of a human race in the game of life. Although a good many people appear to get along in the game without observing the Golden Rule, and still remain out of jail and even seem to prosper.

This is the time of year when the clubs, most of which are becoming crowded with the influx of new members taking up golf, are getting out circular letters to the membership, urging the observance of certain regulations of the course; the not playing of gangsomes; the playing of nothing less than a foursome on Saturday afternoon; the replacing of divots; that sort of thing. Probably you have got such a letter and filed it in the wastebasket.

And yet these very matters, which harried golf and greens committees are struggling with and writing letters about, are the Golden Rules of Golf; and if you break them, through ignorance or intent, you are a good deal more unpopular a golfing citizen than if you inadvertently sole your club in a sand trap or step on the line of your opponent's putt.

The replacing of divots ought to come natural to any man with a front yard. If he hasn't got a front yard, he may have a living room in his house; and if he went into it and tipped over a chair the chances are he would upend it at once, possibly with a few remarks—but he would upend it.

Then why do not his native instincts impel him to put back the golf course when he has knocked it out of shape?

I do not know. And if you will listen to his comments when he finds his ball nestling snugly in the hole left by some unreplaced divot—possibly one of his own on a previous round—you will wonder still more how he or anybody else in the world could be so utterly and abysmally selfish and inconsiderate of the rights of other people—not to mention the golf course.

I heard a story a long time ago—it must have happened a long time ago; certainly before Mr. Volstead became a byword—about a man who was playing a hard match on a dry course and found his ball in the place where a divot ought to have been replaced; and it was a practically unplayable lie; and he stood to lose the match right here, it seemed; and he had a little something on the hip—in case he should do a hole in 1, possibly—and he got out the little flask and poured the contents heroically over the ball and lifted it out of casual licker without penalty. This seems incredible, these days.

Large, uncouth footprints in the sand traps also are left staring at the heavens by many a golfer who abandons himself to the most unguarded utterances when the ball he is playing happens to lodge in one of those tracks—as a ball has the most uncanny faculty for doing. A good golfer is not often in a trap. When he is, he smooths the sand over all depressions made by him in playing out.

Spectators as well as players require some education in this direction. In any big tournament you may see flocks of gallery racing pell-mell through beautifully smooth sand traps, all raked for the round; and the only thing Mr. and Mrs. Joi Polloi think about is that the sand certainly is inconvenient to walk through and does get in their shoes.

I got a jolt at the Engineers' Club last September during the National Amateur Championship that knocked me off the limb as a volunteer steward. The gallery was massing itself around the fourth green, and one woman in her effort to gain a point of vantage was trotting about in a big trap, making a regular pattern of tracks in the white sand.

"You're not supposed to walk in the traps," I made bold to tell her.

She looked at me with an expression in which, pity struggled bravely with scorn.

"Why not?" she returned. "I've got on golf shoes."

If you don't like people to kick wads out of your front yard—if you don't like to find your ball in a divot hole or in a heelprint in a trap, the answer is clear: Put back divots and smooth over your own footprints; these are not the sands of time you are walking in.

At that, I am persuaded that more balmy afternoons are spoiled, to say nothing of scores, by the Funeral Foursome and its variations than by empty divots and heelprints in bankers. And it is not only a matter of the Golden Rule that should regulate such affairs.

The Funeral Foursome is not innovation nor new discovery. It probably is as old as golf, which would run it back before Columbus came to America, and if he had gotten behind a Funeral Foursome, he never would have made it.

The Funeral Foursome needs no explanation to any golfer. Everybody knows what it is. But why? Why is a Funeral Foursome?

Sometimes I think it arises out of the same idea, or lack of idea, that causes a person to try desperately to get into an elevator when several people are obviously coming out. Only the person going in seems to be in a hurry, and you never could accuse a Funeral Foursome of that.

Primarily, the operations of a Funeral Foursome are based on a disregard for the feelings and rights of other golfers. They are out there to play their game, so-called. If they have four-bits a corner on the match, and have to hole out every putt, and take from there to 6 putts apiece on each green, why, that's their game. They are satisfied with it, and it's nobody else's business.

Oh, but gentlemen—gentlemen! What about the Golden Rule? Suppose (if possible) that there should be a Funeral Foursome even slower than yours in front of you. Suppose this foursome stopped to talk over each shot after it was made, instead of waiting as you do until you get on the green and are through with the 12 to 25 putts before beginning to count up and argue about the score.

Suppose, with a terrific effort, that you actually were being held up by a slower match than yours, and that it was your only afternoon that week, on the links, and that you simply had to get home by a certain time because your wife did her own cooking and you had to ride the street car while those fussy old gentlemen in front had their limousines. Now, wouldn't the funeral rites look a bit different?

Also, there is a regulation that when a match loses distance until the match head of it is a full hole beyond, that match automatically loses its place and should permit the following match to play through, as if a ball had been lost.

How many matches—Funeral Foursomes and others—observe that little variation of the Golden Rule? Some clubs are making it a regular rule this year, by the way, and imposing fines for non-observances.

In this matter of slow golf, permit the writer to say that in more than a score of years of observing golf, he could count on the thumbs of one hand the number of first-class golfers who were really slow players. I know several—though not of the top class—who spend a good deal of time studying shots and putts, but they all walk briskly between shots—and that is something anybody can do, except seemingly, the Funeral Foursome, which does nothing briskly.

And nearly all really good players are fast players. The fastest player in the world today, George Duncan, is Open Champion of Great Britain. I watched last year a foursome composed of Jock Hutchinson, Freddie McLeod, Laurie Ayton, and Bob McDonald—all Scots, and playing for "silver," so they weren't throwing anything away—and just out of curiosity I timed them for a few holes. The played four holes in exactly twenty minutes—five minutes to the hole, fifteen minutes to the side; an hour and a half to the round, granting they weren't held up.

That's a foursome, gentlemen, of regular players. Of course, if you take eight or ten shots to the hole instead of four or five, it requires longer, but the chances are that the longer you hang over the shots the more of them you take.

Anyway, there are other people on the course, and they have at least as much right to play their fast game as you have your slow game.

Golf is getting immensely more popular and golf courses are getting immensely more populous; and the clubs are finding it a problem to handle the increased number of players, practically all the newcomers being unschooled in golf, its rules, its traditions, and its etiquette. This is only natural. But it seems that something should be done with the influx to give it a right steer at the beginning—the old hands at the game have some rights, too, welcome as are the new ones.

If I were a golf committee of a club, I would not let any member go on the course until he had studied the rules of golf and its etiquette sufficiently to stand a fair examination on them.

That would help out the old Golden Rule notably, I believe.

Foursomes

John M. Ward

DEAR SIR: COMPLYING WITH YOUR REQUEST FOR A LETTER "ON THE subject of foursomes, pointing out the fine points of the game and all the arguments you can muster in its support," requires, first, a word of explanation in order to clear the way.

This question, as to the relative merits of the foursome as compared with the four-ball match, has arisen in connection with the playing of the matches between New York, Philadelphia, and Boston for the Lesley Cup; and I assume that it is in that same connection you wish me to discuss it.

Last year for the first time, when the matches were played in Boston, the foursome was substituted for the four-ball match and it was continued this year at Garden City.

None of us, who attended the banquet after the matches at the Brookline Club last year will ever forget the great forensic twosome that took place, after the dinner, between Mr. W. J. Travis, advocating the four-ball match, and Mr. Findlay Douglas, championing the foursome. Mr. Douglas, on that memorable occasion, developed a power of lung and rhetoric theretofore little suspected in him; and his eloquence and enthusiasm rose to such height that it will be recalled. The floor, his chair, and finally the festal board itself served for a rostrum. And yet, from the bristling attitude of Mr. Travis and one or two others, at the recent dinner at Garden City, it is apparent that the advocates of the four-ball match have not yet been entirely converted. Nevertheless, the foursome has made some friends, and there are now other members of the New York

95

team who are willing not only to admit that it possesses merit for the purpose of the Lesley Cup competition, but even has inherent attractions of its own.

Much has been said, and can be said, for and against the foursome. It has been sarcastically referred to as "an old man's game," presumably because the players, playing alternate strokes on the same ball, play but one half of the time. For the same reason it has been referred to as only "a half a game of golf," etc.; all of which is entirely beside the question.

The foursome has age, custom, and authority on its side. It is the original game of golf, as played by four players, and there are records to show that it is almost as old as the twosome itself. Indeed, under the Rules of Golf, it is said, "The game of golf is played by two sides, each playing its own *ball*. A side consists either of one or of two players. . . . "The four-ball match is a comparatively recent modification of the game, designed to meet the nervous requirements of the modern player; and it has attained its greatest vogue in this country, where the chief aim of most of us is to play as many holes or rounds as possible every day out. If the two players on each side are fairly well matched, the game may be quite interesting; but where they are not evenly matched, or where one of the players on one side happens to be off his game, the result is anything but a pleasure to the weaker player. He flounders along as best he can, unconsciously ignored or politely tolerated by his partner. His sense of weakness and consequent humiliation become so oppressive that he fails to render any help even when the opportunity is offered. Such good strokes as he may make are completely overshadowed by his partner's superior play and he concludes the unhappy round knowing he has figured not at all in the result. It is all well enough for players of the first class, self-reliant and accustomed to "the center of the stage," to play the four-ball match; but for *nous autres*, the players of lesser skill, the foursome offers at least some chance to appear as factors in the result.

Moreover, the foursome has always seemed to me to offer many more opportunities for the friendly interchange of advice, encouragement, and sympathy between the partners, which goes so far to make up that sociable feature that should be a part of every game of golf. In the four-ball match one is of necessity almost entirely engrossed with his own game.

Golf is so constituted that the player, playing one ball himself, must concentrate his entire attention upon that ball; and, if he happens to be paired with a weaker player, he soon unconsciously but surely loses interest in his partner's game. His ball may be on one side of the course while his partner's is on the other, and they each go about their own play with little opportunity for the interchange of any advice or encouragement. If only his own play be correct, it matters little in the final result to one partner what the other may do.

On the other hand, in the foursome, each partner is, necessarily, vitally interested in every stroke of the other. They are following the same ball and their course through the green lies along the same path. They are constantly together, advising, encouraging, and consoling each other, and thus are united by the strongest bonds of interest and sympathy. Every good play your partner makes calls for a word of heartfelt praise; and what a joy it is, when misfortune overtakes him, if you can show your appreciation and save the play by a sterling recovery! There is nothing so admirable in the field of athletics as red blood; and when you have gone through a hard match, under the conditions offered by a foursome, with a partner whose heartbeats were right, win or lose, you have added something to your love of mankind.

Getting still nearer to the point of view indicated at the outset, the foursome seems to me, in these Lesley matches, to be the fairer test. This annual competition is a departure from the original game of golf in which the unit is the individual player. Ten men are selected from each Association and play together to determine, not who are the strongest individual players, but which is the strongest team. The unit, therefore, is no longer the individual but the team. Now it is perfectly possible in a four-ball match for the losing side to have played the better golf. If one of the partners plays par golf, it matters little what the other does, even though both opponents play par golf or nearly so; and yet the combined play of the opponents is better and should entitle them to win.

Then, too, it may even happen that two partners, *both* playing good golf, are beaten by their opponents with a much inferior score. This was illustrated, in a remarkable way, in a recent four-ball match at Garden City in which Messrs. Travers and Travis were opposed by Messrs.

Stevenson and Claflin. In the morning Mr. Travis scored 75 and Mr. Travers 78, while Messrs. Stevenson and Claflin scored 85 and 82 respectively; and yet Messrs. Travers and Travis were but one up on the morning round. And in the afternoon they were actually beaten 3 and 2, though the medal scores showed much the same disparity in play. Such a result cannot possibly occur in a foursome. It is true that even in a twosome the lower medal score does not always win the hole-play, but it certainly would win where there was such a difference as occurred in the instance just mentioned. In other words, in foursome play every stroke of each partner necessarily counts in the result, which is not, and never can be, true of a four-ball match. So that as a means of determining the relative skill of two teams, the foursome registers all the faults as well as the merits of *every* player and is therefore the fairer test.

There is a practical consideration, likewise, in favor of the foursome. It moves along much more rapidly than a four-ball match and, in the fall of the year, when this contest takes place, this becomes important on account of the early coming of twilight.

These are not "all the arguments" I could muster in support of the foursome, but they have been enough to persuade me in its favor.

Golf at the White House

Heywood Broun

WARREN G. HARDING IS A RADICAL IN GOLF. THE ORTHODOXY OF THE
Republican leader ends at the first tee, for there is neither safety nor sanity in his game. All the traditions are violated in his first swing. At the top of his swing, although it is much more nearly a swipe, there comes a terrific hitch, somewhat after the manner of Ted Ray, and then Mr. Harding's club and his body come down at the ball together. The race has been going on for years, but it is always the body that wins. At the end of the drive, as one of Mr. Harding's golfing associates has described it, the President follows through with his stomach.

For all the shortness of the swing, there is a good deal of power in the driving force Mr. Harding aims at the ball. He has been known to reach 250 yards at such times as he makes a fair and square hit, but the element of chance enters over largely into the prodigious effort. Swaying, plunging, falling, Mr. Harding seems a little more like a man intent upon flying tackle than a golfer aiming at a ball. It is the hit-or-miss style of a man who is willing to go no more than ten feet every now and then, if once in a while he may reach 250 yards. "The best minds" have never been consulted about Mr. Harding's golf. It is distinctly individual, daring, and dangerous. It is golf of the extreme left wing. Indeed, the President boasts openly that he has a contempt for good form. He does not even seem to worry whether or not he stays on course. Distance is his goal, and direction is only secondary.

Very possibly no professional in the country could do much for Harding's game. It is a job for old Doctor Freud, or some member of his school; for the explanation of Harding's peculiar style and philosophy of golf must lie in the subconscious mind. Here is a man who throughout his political career has kept to the middle of the road. He has shunned excesses and experiments of all kinds. "Normalcy" has been his constant ideal. In the last campaign he never made a speech without submitting his manuscripts to a selected group of experts for revision and advice. Before taking a definite stand on anything, he invariably counted to 150 and then, on second thought, decided that perhaps it would be just as well to leave the theme until a later time and stand by his original contention that honesty and patriotism are among the virtues.

MR. HARDING'S GOLF AS AN "ESCAPE"

Golf for Mr. Harding is what the analysts term an "escape." If the sandpit that yawns in front of him were the electoral vote of the state of Ohio, Mr. Harding would undoubtedly play safe and try to make it in two conservative shots. Instead, he slugs at his ball, perfectly willing to accept the chance of glory or the bunkers. Tormented and obsessed for years with the determination never to lose a vote, if it could possibly be avoided, there is in Harding a fine carelessness about wasting a few strokes. He takes no shame to be seen in a sandpit banging away with a niblick, for few caddies will be old enough to come to the polls even in 1924.

But, for all the intense joy Mr. Harding takes in golf, it would be unfair to suggest that he is indifferent when he plays poorly enough to be worse than usual. His joy, like the joy of all true golfers, is one often closely kin to pain. He is willing to risk the hazards, but he suffers in them, for all that. At any rate, it is said that when hidden in deep gullies alone with a golf ball and niblick, far from the eyes and ears of the electorate, he swears very well. He lacks, however, something of the lines of feeling one associates with the true converts to golf. In his senatorial days, his two boon companions on the links were Senators Hale and Felinghuysen, while the fourth was generally drawn from a group consisting of Speaker Gillet of the House and Senators Frank B. Kellogg, Davis Elkins, and Gilbert H. Hitchcock.

Senator Hitchcock, to be sure, is a democrat and presumably a free trader, who would deprive the worker of the boon of a protective tariff and fill the land with soup kitchens. However, it seems to have been possible to keep such subjects in the background for eighteen holes or so, and Hitchcock never dampened the spirits of the party by remarking: "Speaking of aluminum putters, it seems to me that you gentlemen are not quite fair to Woodrow Wilson," or anything like that.

No, they seem to have been genial and rowdy parties, too genial, in fact, to be quite consistent with the reverence the true believer brings to golf. Etiquette was largely dispensed with. One of the favorite stunts consisted in attempting to make Harding foozle by suddenly shouting at him just as he was about to hit the ball. In this respect, Mr. Harding seems to have had nerves of steel. These sudden shouts never made him play a bit worse than usual, and he was always ready with some bright rejoinder. Just what terrifying taunts were used has not been disclosed, but it may be that nobody ever tried anything so disturbing as a sudden scream of, "You're going to lose Ohio," just as Harding got set for a ten-foot putt. His putting is distinctly the best part of his game, although here, too, his form is atrocious, since he uses a distinct and marked body swing.

MR. WILSON'S GOLF AND THE WAR

In one respect alone, Woodrow Wilson came closer to golfing ideals than Harding. He did bring a certain staid and reverent demeanor to the game, but in many other ways he offended golfing traditions. First of all, he very frankly used the game for finite and definite purposes, entirely foreign to the sport itself. He would, for instance, go golfing while awaiting the German reply to one of his notes. To be sure, by the faithful adherence to this practice he got in a great deal of golf for the better part of a year, but it never seemed quite fair to the game. Obviously he could not put his best efforts or attention upon it. Probably the fine turf of Chevy Chase still bears scars, because of the fact that, in the middle of an approach shot, Woodrow Wilson suddenly thought of "peace without victory." It is even said that the slice that broke the window of the clubhouse may be traced to the fact that he remembered that "we have no quarrel with the German people" at the top of a swing.

It was not a very extensive swing, for Wilson uses a shorter stroke than Harding. It is not unlike the swish of a mallet when a player is driving a croquet ball away in anger. Mr. Wilson taps at the ball and does not follow through. He gets little distance, but his game is eminently safe, for he is never off the line, except, of course, at the time of the incident we have recorded.

It isn't the golf that attracts Wilson so much as the walk. He goes through the motions in a more or less perfunctory way, not unlike that of a man touching his toes one hundred times before breakfast. He golfs for exercise. Mrs. Wilson was generally his partner, although occasionally Rear Admiral Grayson took a hand. Often there was much jesting that a rough old seadog like Grayson should have fallen under the spell of golf.

The rather tepid quality of golf under a democratic administration may be judged from the fact that generally Mr. Wilson played eleven holes. No true golfer could possibly content himself with any such fantastic number of holes. A man may play nine, or eighteen, or thirty-six or even twenty-seven holes, under extenuating circumstances, but eleven introduces a factor that does not enter into the calculations of golfers. Like Harding, Wilson excelled in putting. On the greens, his interest in the game heightened and it has been reported that upon one occasion when the ball trickled around the edge of the cup and failed to go down, he explained: "Tut! Tut!"

It is a well-established Washington tradition that presidential golf is never reported in the daily newspapers, but this incident did get into print and it proved rather deadly ammunition against the democrats. Kansas Methodists felt it was undignified for a President of the United States to give way to such emotion and violent expression over a frivolous game like golf, while hundreds of thousands of players throughout the country thought that a vigorous Mexican policy could never be expected from a man who would be content with "tuts" when a short putt lipped the cup.

THE SUPREMACY OF MR. TAFT

William Howard Taft failed disastrously of reelection. The voters of his day felt he had bungled the tariff problem. Many did not sympathize with his course of action in the Ballinger case, but when everything has been said, he remains the finest golfer who has ever held the presidency of the United States. It is just as well to establish what this means at the outset.

The best round Taft ever had was played at the difficult Myopia links one day when he seemed actually inspired and went around in 97. At his best, he could concede thirty strokes to Harding and forty or fifty to Wilson. His devotion to the game transcended that of either of the men who followed him in the White House, and before his time there was a barren century and more when not a single golfer attained the presidency. For a time, it was thought that golf was one of those things, like being born in Canada, that disqualified a man from presidency. Taft surmounted this obstacle. He was the first golfer to reach the White House.

Roosevelt was a great athlete, but he was no golfer. The only set game in which he seems to have participated actively was tennis, and in this he was far from expert. Before the days of Roosevelt, it is probably necessary to go all the way back to Washington to find a man interested in any organized form of athletic endeavor. George Washington is said to have been one of the finest quoits players of his day.

Taft was a true golfer, animated by a fine mixture of eagerness and reverence for the game. One cannot imagine his participating in a match in which the players shouted at each other to spoil the shots, and it is still more inconceivable that he should ever have stopped at the eleventh hole. Taft would have reversed the Wilsonian system. He would have played golf first and declared war afterward. Golf always came first with him. Perhaps his solution of the tariff problem might have been more effective and more popular if the question had not come up for decision during the summer in which he was experimenting with that new mashie niblick. He never took a trip without carrying his clubs with him and no sort of bad weather could discourage him. Once, in 1912, at Poland Springs, he donned hip boots and went around the course in a driving rainstorm. The afternoon was so bad that even presidential prestige was not sufficient to lure anybody out on the course except Taft and the professional who had to play when the command came.

Like Wilson and Harding, Taft uses a short swing, but he puts lots of weight into it and drives a pretty good ball.

The defeat of Mr. Taft in 1912 was most unfortunate, for at that time he was at the top of his game and constantly improving. Unfortunately, it seemed impossible to hold the campaign to this issue and Woodrow Wilson was elected. The voters had never seen him drive.

Justice Harlan and the Game of Golf

Richard D. Harlan

IT WAS THE SUMMER OF 1897, SHORTLY AFTER HE HAD PASSED HIS SIX-ty-fourth birthday, that Justice Harlan took up the royal and ancient game of golf, and of which he soon became a devotee.

From early manhood walking had been his only outdoor recreation. It had been his daily habit to walk from his residence to the court, a distance of two miles or more, and usually he would return on foot after the adjournment in the afternoon. He was fond of occasional tramps, and on holidays and not infrequently on Sunday afternoons, he was to be seen with a friend or some of his children making his way through the fields and woods of the countryside around Washington. But he had taken no other form of physical exercise and had never indulged in any sort of game, except chess and an occasional rubber of old-fashioned whist.

While he took a keen interest in current events both at home and abroad, and in a general way followed the world's progress, his chief mental diversion had been found in books of history and biography. He was a diligent reader of the lives of the great English statesmen and judges and of the great men of his own country. It is true also, as has many times been said of him, that it was his nightly habit, after retiring, to light the candles near the head of his bed, and then to read his Bible until he was ready to fall asleep. He was a constant reader of the Scriptures, and he particularly enjoyed the Psalms.

Perhaps the greatest relief to him from the tedium and pressure of his judicial labors was to meet his law students at George Washington University, where, for more than twenty years, and to very large classes, he lectured twice a week (often without notes) on the Constitution and constitutional law. For an even longer period, he conducted a men's Bible class at the New York Avenue Presbyterian Church in Washington, of which he was one of the ruling elders. This contact with young men was a source of great satisfaction and pleasure to him.

In the fulfillment of his judicial duties, he was a hard taskmaster for himself. During the long years of his service in the Supreme Court of the United States he had usually been at his desk until midnight and frequently until one or two o'clock in the morning. At times he would reverse his schedule and, retiring at about eleven o'clock, would get up before daylight to continue the study of his cases or work at his opinions until starting for the Capitol just in time for the opening of the court at the noon hour.

In the summer of 1897 he had sent his family to Murray Bay, the Canadian resort on the lower Saint Lawrence, eighty miles below Quebec, which from that time on and until his death was his summer residence, while he himself, for the month of June, went down to the summer law school of the University of Virginia to deliver a course of lectures on the Constitution. For the rest of that summer he had laid out his usual vacation tasks, having sent on to Murray Bay the records and briefs in a number of cases, in order, as was his custom, to work at them during the summer and to have his opinions ready when the court resumed its sessions in October.

In spite of the rigor of his court work, his physical strength had shown no signs of abatement; but at that time his family had reasonable grounds for fearing that the continuation of his intense labors in these different ways might within the next few years somewhat impair his vigor unless he could be persuaded to give himself more diversion, and particularly in the open air. Very fortunately, one of his sons, early that first summer at Murray Bay, had just taken up golf—the sport was then comparatively new in this country. At once he saw that it was the very game for his father. He therefore wrote several letters to him, at the University of Virginia, in which he dwelt upon the importance of an outdoor diversion for a man of his years, his sedentary habits and exacting labors. He described "this new game of golf"; he expressed the opinion that it would afford him a much-needed recreation as old age was drawing on, besides being a form of exercise in which he would find no small pleasure and interest; and he urged him to buy a set of clubs and suitable clothes and bring them up with him to Murray Bay.

Those members of his family who specially wished him to take up golf were confident that he would become a good player. He had what sportsmen call "a good eye." For example, he had always been able to defeat his boys at such a game as quoits. He was a good shot with the rifle. Often, in the shooting gallery improvised at the annual outing given by the lawyers of the District of Columbia, at Marshall Hall on the Potomac, he had been known to hit the bull's-eye nine times out of ten.

But apparently his son's enthusiasm for golf had as yet made no impression on him, for when he wrote from the University of Virginia in reply to his son's letters, he did not even refer to what had been their chief theme.

When he arrived at Murray Bay in July he found the place had gone golf-mad and that the entire summer colony was absorbed in it, either in actually playing it or in forming a gallery to watch the game of the more expert of the Canadian and American players. His own sons were among the most enthusiastic of the beginners at "this new game of golf." The result was that his summer home was somewhat deserted during the day, and during the evening there was much golf talk among his family and the friends who dropped in. All of this left him somewhat out of the running, so to speak, and this was unusual, for he had always been the center of the family interests.

The concerted efforts in the family to interest him in the game made little or no progress for a week or two. To all of the arguments in favor of a form of exercise so suitable for elderly men, and to the assurances we gave him that he would not fail to find it an interesting and beneficial diversion, his invariable reply was:

"It would never do for a judge to be seen playing a game of that kind."

That dictum represented the attitude toward sport that was then generally taken by men of his own and the other learned professions. But it had nothing in it of the austere, Puritan objection to sports as such. It was what might be called the American view, which, up to that time, had characterized our strenuous national life.

For example, up to twenty-five years ago no prominent senator or representative would have dared, in the course of a great debate in Congress, to snatch an afternoon off in order to take part in a golf match, or would even have dreamed of doing so—although that was the very thing such a leader of the British Parliament as Mr. Balfour often did at that time, without impairing in the least his prestige or reputation as a serious-minded politician.

When his oft-repeated objection as to the propriety of "a judge playing a game of this kind" showed that the justice was apparently adamant in his feeling that it would be beneath the dignity of a professional man to be "wasting his time" by indulging in any outdoor sport, one of his sons, with a carefully feigned nonchalance, casually remarked one day that he had been "teaching Chief Judge Andrews of the New York Court of Appeals to play golf," and that he had developed "quite a good game."

That far-from-innocent passing remark evidently arrested the justice's attention, for, after a few moments of eloquent silence (during which, as will appear later on in this story, he began to be attracted by the idea of beating his fellow jurist at "this new game"), he said that if he played at all he would "only play very early in the morning—long before anyone else was on the links." His son replied that it made no difference at what hour he played, and that after a few days he intended to give him his first lesson. The justice did not "know about that," and would "make no promises." There the matter was allowed to rest, and we all waited for the fruitful seed of rivalry to germinate.

A day or two thereafter his curiosity as to "this new game" tempted him to walk around the links and watch his sons play. He was probably struck by the absurd disparity between the tiny ball and the six-foot-four enthusiast who was trying so hard and ineffectually to make a good shot. At all events, after observing several very poor drives, the justice remarked rather severely that the game did not "seem to be worthy of the attention of a grown-up, serious-minded man."

The criticism must have somewhat nettled his son, for he turned on his father rather savagely and said that it was very unfair and even unjudicial to condemn a game so sweepingly without first trying it himself; and at the next tee we forced a club into his hands and insisted upon his making "one drive, anyway."

The principle embodied in the ancient legal maxim, "*Audi alleram partem,*" must have appealed to his judicial conscience, for he consented to "try one shot." He missed the ball entirely! Whereupon, with a gesture of mingled disgust and anger, he threw the club on the ground, exclaiming that the game was "even sillier" than he had "supposed." And at that moment it looked as if his objections to taking it up might prove to be insurmountable.

Nevertheless, a day or two afterward he was seen in an out-of-the-way field secretly trying a few shots in the company of a sympathetic and close-mouthed clergyman of his acquaintance. And finally he consented to allow the writer to give him his first regular lesson; and an arrangement was made with a small French-Canadian caddie to meet them on the links at six o'clock the next morning.

The night before that first lesson, in a conversation with Senator Newlands of Neveda, the justice was overheard saying, rather solemnly: "I observe that my parson son, Richard, is playing this new game of golf. I suppose it's all right, here in Murray Bay, during his vacation; but I hope he will not keep it up after returning to Rochester. I fear that his congregation would not like to see their minister playing a game of that kind." The old American idea as to the propriety of a professional man indulging in a sport was dying very hard in his mind.

Six o'clock the next morning saw the justice and his son and his caddie on the links, and he felt that for two hours he could make a thorough trial of this newfangled sport without risk of discovery.

After being given a few instructions as to his stance and the method of holding his club and approaching the ball, he took his position for the drive. He looked rather scornfully at the tiny white object perched so invitingly on the top of the high tee that had been arranged for him. Then, quickly drawing back his powerful arms, he swung the club through with a mighty effort, fully expecting, as he afterward confessed, to "knock the ball, to thunder." To his amazement, he missed it altogether!

Again, the golfer's everlasting chant, "Keep your eye on the ball," was repeated to him. He was, first, to look at the place where the ball had been, and then he could look up to see where it had gone to. But his second effort was almost as complete a failure as his first; for the breath of his powerful swing only caused the ball to slip off the tee for a foot or two.

In his angry surprise and chagrin, his great dome of a forehead turned to a bright scarlet, and he sternly commanded his amateur teacher to "put the ball up again." Once more the golfer's orthodox "Don'ts" were repeated to him. He was not to try to knock the cover off the ball," as he had been doing, but was simply to bring his arms through and let their weight "do the rest." His third attempt was a complete success. The ball went like a rifleshot, at an angle of about twenty-five degrees, to a distance of perhaps 150 yards—a pretty fair drive for ordinary players. Turning round, with a delightfully boyish look of glee upon his face, he exclaimed: "Oh, Richard, this is a great game!"

At that thrilling moment the old American idea as to the propriety of sport in the life of a professional man had received its deathblow in his mind, and from that delightful hour to the end of his life he was a confirmed golfer.

For a week or two he continued his secret, early morning lessons. He improved so rapidly and became so enthusiastic that a foursome match was suggested, consisting of himself and Judge William Howard Taft, as representing Uncle Sam, against Chief Judge Andrews and the writer, as representing the Empire State. By that time the golfing fever had so taken hold of him, and his former ideas as to the propriety of "a judge playing a game of that kind" had been so completely thrown to the winds, that he readily agreed to play the foursome during the regular hours.

The rumor of the great match having spread through the colony of summer visitors, quite a large gallery followed the contestants around the links. "Charley" Taft, now a redoubtable member of the Yale football eleven, acted as caddie for his distinguished and genial father. At the start the little lad was quite confident that Uncle Sam would win; but toward the end he followed the match with almost tearful anxiety, for the Empire State won by two or three holes.

On the way back to our cottage, the justice was very silent. Evidently he was playing the match over in his mind and was wondering just how it happened that he and the Judge Taft had lost it. Meaning to have a little quiet fun out of the situation, the writer determined to make no comments on the match, but to wait and see what his father would say and do next; and, hurrying into the cottage in advance, he enlisted the other members of the household in a conspiracy of silence. Accordingly, no questions were asked as to the result of the great match. We might have been returning from the most commonplace tramp across the Murray Bay hills.

During supper that evening no one even mentioned golf, and the justice did not open his mouth upon any topic—which was unusual, for he was fond of table talk. After supper he sat in his favorite corner near the blazing log fire, silent and very thoughtful. At about half-past eight he rose from his chimney corner and said, "I think I will go to bed," and, bidding us all "good night," he slowly climbed the stairs to his bedroom.

The next morning we were taking an early breakfast alone. Neither of us had even so much as mentioned golf since leaving the clubhouse the day before, and I was waiting to hear what he would say. Finally, he broke his long silence on the subject, and, just as if only one topic had been in our minds ever since the close of the match and he were only continuing a discussion that had been going on all night, he casually remarked that he "didn't think much of Taft's game!"

In after years the justice was in the habit of saying that "Golf is not a game, but a disease"; and from that somewhat disparaging remark about the other fellow's game, it was then evident that his own had already become a chronic case.

Hiding a smile with some difficulty, the writer admitted that Judge Taft had certainly been "clean off his game" the day before, and that he had never seen him play so badly—for the ex-President, even then as a beginner, was a very dangerous antagonist; possibly "Charley's" ill-concealed filial anxiety had affected him. To that explanation, slowing nodding his head up and down, with an air of having reached a final and thoroughly judicial conclusion, the justice replied: "Well, I think I can learn this game; but Andrews never will!"

From that time on, my father's interest in the game increased apace. Especially during that first summer, he practiced his strokes at all hours and in all places, whether suitable or not. For him, the sitting room rug was a good imitation of the putting green and a salt cellar an excellent counterfeit of the inviting but elusive hole. But woe betide the chandelier, or the passerby in the rear, when at night he practiced some new idea as to stance or swing he had gotten from Harry Vardon or Travers, and the numerous other books by famous golfers he read with great avidity at that period.

A week or two after he had thus tasted blood in his first real match game, he saw one of his daughters-in-law knitting a fancy red-and-black waistcoat, and he asked her what it was. Being told it was a golf waistcoat for her husband, he asked her to let him try it on—which he immediately proceeded to do. It was never seen again except upon his portly form! Not only did he thus commandeer another man's waistcoat, but he also bought a red coat to match it. He balked, however, at the knickerbockers then in vogue even for elderly men; but he compromised by putting on leggings, which gave him a very trim, sportsmanlike appearance.

Another anecdote is perhaps worth repeating, as additional evidence that a large amount of a very lovable kind of "human nature" went into the makeup of his character.

At the close of his first season at Murray Bay, he played a match with a distinguished French-Canadian judge, and somewhat to his surprise he was badly beaten. Some friend of the Quebec jurist had evidently seen the match and been interested in its spicy international aspect, for several days afterward there appeared in one of the Montreal papers a full and rather amusing account of it, in which special emphasis was laid on the fact that the Canadian jurist had worsted "the United States Supreme Court at the ancient and royal game of golf," and the justice had to stand quite a bit of good-humored chaffing on the subject at the hands of his boys and his Canadian and American friends at Murray Bay. Of course he took it most good-naturedly, but it was evident to his family that his growing pride as a golfer and his pride as an American had both received a rude shock, and we boys had premonitions then of a challenge from him for a return match at the very opening of the next summer.

Thanks to the opportunities for practice snatched at intervals during the open Washington winters at the Chevy Chase Country Club (which he joined immediately upon his return that autumn), his game had greatly improved by the following summer, and as soon as the Quebec jurist arrived at Murray Bay he was served with a good-humored, formal challenge to a return match in the "Canadian-American Champion Series." On that occasion the justice, to his great delight, was decidedly victorious.

For several days afterward it was observed that he carefully examined the sporting columns of that same Montreal paper—the part of a newspaper he had never been known so much as to glance at. Finally, pointing accusingly at the paper in his hands, he said to the writer, somewhat quizzically (his very words are quoted substantially as he uttered them): "Last year, when Judge B., who had played golf all his life, beat me, that Montreal paper took nearly a half-column to tell its readers how the French-Canadian jurist had downed the Supreme Court of the United States; but I wish simply to call your attention to the fact that, this year, when the American judge was even more victorious than his opponent had been last year, this same enterprising Canadian newspaper doesn't even give a line to the return match."

It was a touch of "human nature" in a golfer that bridged all the years between father and son.

By the end of his second or third year on the links his descent of the golfer's Avernus had become so complete that, quite as a matter of course, he accepted an election for one or two years to the presidency of the Murray Bay Golf Club, and for twelve or more years, during the happy summers spent in the bracing air of the lower Saint Lawrence region, he rarely missed a day on the links. In the first two or three summers he often played twice a day, making his thirty-six holes. To him an ordinary rain was no obstacle at all; he would say that it was "only a Scotch mist," and that it could easily be negotiated with the help of an umbrella and, blissfully oblivious of even a sharp shower, he would follow up his ball with a stately and springy step, full of high hopes for his next stroke. And when he returned to the cottage, he would tell us how he had made one hole in four strokes and a certain very difficult hole in five, and another, a short and very "sporty" hole, in three; and what hard luck he had on another, "perfectly simple hole," and so on.

Eventually he developed a very accurate and effective game. Many a better golfer was quite often beaten by him because of his steady playing through the fair green—his safer though shorter shots more than making up for the longer but erratic shots of his more brilliant opponent. And on the putting green he won many a hole with his deadly eight- and ten-foot putts, which, standing erect like a flagstaff, he generally made with one hand.

He became such a familiar and welcome figure on the Murray Bay links, and was so closely associated with the development of the club, that when, in later years, the course was rearranged and names given to the holes, one of his favorites was named "The justice," in his honor, another hole being called "The President," in honor of his partner in that first foursome match of "Uncle Sam vs. the Empire State."

So contagious was his pleasure in the game and such was his genial camaraderie that he became a much sought-after companion on the links, both at Murray Bay and at Chevy Chase. Younger men were especially keen to try conclusions with "the Justice."

The writer remembers one instance where the much younger golfer (a certain Mr. S.) came home from the links "a sadder and a wiser man." This gentleman was the writer's guest at Murray Bay about the summer of 1900, by which time the justice was among the best of the group listed in golf clubs as "Class C."

Mr. S. was inclined to take his own game rather seriously. Though at the time he was on the shady side of fifty-five and was at least ten years younger than the justice, he never admitted his age, preferring to be classed with the "boys" in the forties. He confessed to the writer that he would like to see what he could do against the justice. Slyly encouraged thereto by the writer, he sent him a respectful challenge, which was gleefully accepted. Upon his return from the links, when asked by the writer how the match had turned out, Mr. S. exclaimed: "He's a wonder! Why, he beat me seven up, with six to play. I felt like that Texan whose house and barns and chickens and wife had been swept away by a tornado; it was 'so d—d complete' that I had to laugh."

The next morning Mr. S. had a caller in the person of Jackson, the messenger assigned to the justice by the marshal of the court. Jackson had become so much attached to the family, and they to him, and had so identified himself with the justice and all that concerned him, that, in speaking to or of the justice, he never used the pronouns of the second or third persons, but always said "we and "our." The following dialogue then ensued:

"How are you feeling this morning, Mr. S.?"

"Oh, I'm feeling very well, Jackson. Why?"

"Well, Mr. S., we were just wondering how you felt this morning, after the game; for we have made up our minds that, after this season, we are only going to play with the young men, with the men of our class."

And this double shot came from the faithful henchman of a man of sixty-seven, who was also a novice! Mr. S., however, was a good enough "sport" to tell this good story himself all over Rochester. He is probably still telling it.

The writer can vouch for the truth of a certain other story about the justice that even now, every once in a while, some paragrapher sends on its fresh rounds through the newspapers.

Among his favorite companions on the Chevy Chase links was a prominent Episcopalian clergyman in Washington. The reverend doctor had just missed his drive completely. Though greatly surprised and disgusted, not a word escaped his lips. Whereupon the justice (quoting unconsciously from one John Kendrick Bang's delightful golf talks, which he had recently read) remarked: "Doctor Sterrett, the things you didn't say were something awful. That was the most profane silence I ever heard!"

Often, during the mild Washington winters, when he was troubled by a knotty point in some case before the court, he would go out very early in the morning to Chevy Chase, for a short singleton on the links, his caddie being his only companion; and then returning home, with a freshened mind, he would successfully attack the legal problem that had perplexed him. And as the spring approached, he would begin to look forward to the good times he meant to have, during the next summer, on the wind-swept links at Murray Bay, drinking in the glorious views of the majestic Saint Lawrence between strokes, and accumulating new strength of body and clearness of mind for his arduous work on the bench.

There can be on doubt that "this game of golf," at which he shied so decidedly when first he was urged and tempted to try it, added not a few years to his life. It certainly kept him physically and mentally vigorous to the very end of his days.

A telegram of congratulations that was sent to him by a fellow golfer on his seventieth birthday will make an appropriate finish to this story:

"Many happy returns of the day.

Seventy years up, and many more to play."

And he did "play" eight years more—keenly enjoying his game up to almost the very last, when the curtain dropped upon his earthly life.

Cowboy Golf

Zane Grey

IN THE WHIRL OF THE SUCCEEDING DAYS, IT WAS A MOOTED QUESTION whether Madeline's guests or her cowboys or herself got the keenest enjoyment out of the flying time. Considering the sameness of the cowboys' ordinary life, she was inclined to think they made the most of the present. Stillwell and Stewart, however, had found the situation trying. The work of the ranch had to go on, and some of it got sadly neglected. Stillwell could not resist the ladies any more than he could resist the fun in the extraordinary goings-on of the cowboys. Stewart alone kept the business of cattle-raising from a serious setback. Early and late he was in the saddle, driving the Mexicans he had hired to relieve the cowboys.

One morning in June, Madeline was sitting on the porch with her merry friends when Stillwell appeared on the corral path. He had not come to consult Madeline for several days—an omission so unusual as to be remarked.

"Here comes Bill—in trouble," laughed Florence.

Indeed, he bore some faint resemblance to a thundercloud as he approached the porch; but the greetings he got from Madeline's party, especially from Helen and Dorothy, chased away the blackness from his face and brought the wonderful wrinkling smile.

"Miss Majesty, sure I'm a sad demoralized old cattleman," he said, presently. "An' I'm in need of a heap of help."

"What's wrong now?" asked Madeline, with her encouraging smile.

"Wal, it's so amazin' strange what cowboys will do. I jest am about to give up. Why, you might say my cowboys were all on strike for vacations.

What do you think of that? We've changed the shifts, shortened hours, let one an' another off duty, hired Greasers, an',' in fact, done everythin' that could be thought of. But this vacation idee growed worse. When Stewart set his foot down, then the boys begin to get sick. Never in my born days as a cattleman have I heerd of so many diseases. An' you ought to see how lame an' crippled an' weak many of the boys have got all of a sudden. The idee of a cowboy comin' to me with a sore finger an' askin' to be let off for a day! There's Booly. Now I've knowed a hoss to fall all over him, an' onct he rolled down a canyon. Never bothered him at all. He's got a blister on his heel, a ridin' blister, an' he says it's goin' to blood-poisonin' if he doesn't rest. There's Jim Bell. He's developed what he says is spinal mengalootis, or some such like. There's Frankie Slade. He swore he had scarlet fever because his face burnt so red, I guess, an' when I hollered that scarlet fever was contagious an' he must be put away somewhere, he up an' says he guessed it wasn't that. But he was sure awful sick an' needed to loaf around an' be amused. Why, even Nels doesn't want to work these days. If it wasn't for Stewart, who's had Greasers with the cattle, I don't know what I'd do."

"Why all this sudden illness and idleness?" asked Madeline.

"Wal, you see, the truth is every blamed cowboy on the range except Stewart thinks it's his bounden duty to entertain the ladies."

"I think that is just fine!" exclaimed Dorothy Coombs; and she joined in the general laugh.

"Stewart, then, doesn't care to help entertain us?" inquired Helen, in curious interest. "Wal, Miss Helen, Stewart is sure different from the other cowboys," replied Stillwell. "Yet he used to be like them. There never was a cowboy fuller of the devil than Gene. But he's changed. He's foreman here, an' that must be it. All the responsibility rests on him. He sure has no time for amusin' the ladies."

"I imagine that is our loss," said Edith Wayne, in her earnest way. "I admire him."

"Stillwell, you need not be so distressed with what is only gallantry in the boys, even if it does make a temporary confusion in the work," said Madeline.

"Miss Majesty, all I said is not the half, nor the quarter, nor nuthin' of what's troublin' me," answered he, sadly.

"Very well; unburden yourself."

"Wal, the cowboys, exceptin' Gene, have gone plumb batty, jest plain crazy over this heah game of gol-lof."

A merry peal of mirth greeted Stillwell's solemn assertion.

"Oh, Stillwell, you are in fun," replied Madeline.

"I hope to die if I'm not in daid earnest," declared the cattleman. "It's an amazin' strange fact. Ask Flo. She'll tell you. She knows cowboys, an' how if they ever start on somethin' they ride it as they ride a hoss."

Florence being appealed to, and evidently feeling all eyes upon her, modestly replied that Stillwell had scarcely misstated the situation.

"Cowboys play like they work or fight," she added. "They give their whole souls to it. They are great big simple boys."

"Indeed they are," said Madeline. "Oh, I'm glad if they like the game of golf. They have so little play."

"Wal, somethin's got to be did if we're to go on raisin' cattle at Her Majesty's Rancho," replied Stillwell. He appeared both deliberate and resigned.

Madeline remembered that despite Stillwell's simplicity he was as deep as any of his cowboys, and there was absolutely no gaging him where possibilities of fun were concerned. Madeline fancied that his exaggerated talk about the cowboys' sudden craze for golf was in line with certain other remarkable tales that had lately emanated from him. Some very strange things had occurred of late, and it was impossible to tell whether or not they were accidents, mere coincidents, or deep-laid, skillfully worked-out designs of the fun-loving cowboys. Certainly there had been great fun, and at the expense of her guests, particularly Castleton. So Madeline was at a loss to know what to think about Stillwell's latest elaboration. From mere force of habit she sympathized with him and found difficulty in doubting his apparent sincerity.

"To go back a ways," went on Stillwell, as Madeline looked up expectantly, "you recollect what pride the boys took in fixin' up that gol-lof course out on the mesa? Wal, they worked on that job, an' though I never seen any other course, I'll gamble yours can't be beat. The boys was sure curious about that game. You recollect also how they all wanted to see you an' your brother play, an' be caddies for you? Wal, whenever you'd quit they'd go to work tryin' to play the game. Monty Price, he was the leadin' spirit. Old as I am, Miss Majesty, an' used as I am to cowboy excentrikities, I nearly dropped daid when I heered that little hobble-footed, burned-up Montana cowpuncher say there wasn't any game too swell for him, an' gol-lof was just his speed. Serious as a preacher, mind you, he was. An' he was always practicin.' When Stewart gave him charge of the course an' the clubhouse an' all them funny sticks, why, Monty was tickled to death. You see, Monty is sensitive that he ain't much good anymore for cowboy work. He was glad to have a job that he didn't feel he was hangin' to by kindness. Wal, he practiced the game, an' he read the books in the clubhouse, an' he got the boys to doin' the same. That wasn't very hard, I reckon. They played early an' late an' in the moonlight. For a while Monty was coach, an' the boys stood it. But pretty soon Frankie Slade got puffed on his game, an' he had to have it out with Monty. Wal, Monty beat him bad. Then one after another the other boys tackled Monty. He beat them all. After that they split up an' begin to play matches, two on a side. For a spell this worked fine. But cowboys can't never be satisfied long onless they win all the time. Monty an' Link Stevens, both cripples, you might say, joined forces an' elected to beat all comers. Wal, they did, an' that's the trouble. Long an' patient the other cowboys tried to beat them two game legs, an' hevn't done it. Mebbe if Monty an' Link was perfectly sound in their legs like the other cowboys there wouldn't hev been such a holler. But no sound cowboys'll ever stand for a disgrace like that. Why, down at the bunks in the evenin's it's some mortifyin' the way Monty an' Link crow over the rest of the outfit. They've taken on superior airs. You couldn't reach up to Monty with a trimmed spruce pole. An' Link—wal, he's just amazin' scornful.

"'It's a swell game, ain't it?' says Link, powerful sarcastic. 'Wal, what's hurtin' you low-down common cowmen? You keep harpin' on Monty's game leg an' on my game leg. If we hed good legs we'd beat you all the wuss. It's brains that wins in gol-lof. Brains an' airstoocratik blood, which of the same you fellers sure hev little.'

"An' then Monty he blows smoke powerful careless an' superior, an' he says:

"'Sure it's a swell game. You cow-headed gents think beef an' brawn ought to hev the call over skill an' gray matter. You'll all hev to back up an' get down. Go out an' learn the game. You don't know a baffy from a sandwich. All you can do is waggle with a club an' fozzle the ball.'

"Whenever Monty gets to usin' them strange names, the boys go round kind of dotty. Monty an' Link hev got the books an' directions of the game, an' they won't let the other boys see them. They show the rules, but that's all. An,' of course, every game ends in a row almost before it's started. The boys are all turrible in earnest about this gol-lof. An' I want to say, for the good of ranchin,' not to mention a possible fight, that Monty an' Link hev got to be beat. There'll be no peace round this ranch till that's done."

Madeline's guests were much amused. As for herself, in spite of her scarcely considered doubt, Stillwell's tale of woe occasioned her anxiety. However, she could hardly control her mirth.

"What in the world can I do?"

"Wal, I reckon I couldn't say. I only come to you for advice. It seems that a strange kind of game has locoed my cowboys, an' for the time bein' ranchin' is at a standstill. Sounds ridiculous, I know, but cowboys are as strange as wild cattle. All I'm sure of is that the conceit has got to be taken out of Monty an' Link. Onct, just onct, will square it, an' then we can resoome our work."

"Stillwell, listen," said Madeline, brightly. "We'll arrange a match game, a foursome, between Monty and Link and your best picked team. Castleton, who is an expert golfer, will umpire. My sister, and friends, and I will take turns as caddies for your team. That will be fair, considering yours is the weaker. Caddies may coach, and perhaps expert advice is all that is necessary for your team to defeat Monty's."

"A grand idee," declared Stillwell, with instant decision. "When can we have this match game?"

"Why, to-day—this afternoon. We'll all ride out to the links."

"Wal, I reckon I'll be some indebted to you, Miss Majesty, an' all your guests," replied Stillwell, warmly. He rose with sombrero in hand, and a twinkle in his eye that again prompted Madeline to wonder. "An' now I'll be goin' to fix up for the game of cowboy gol-lof. Adios."

The idea was as enthusiastically received by Madeline's guests as it had been by Stillwell. They were highly amused and speculative to the point of taking sides and making wagers on their choice. Moreover, this situation so frankly revealed by Stillwell had completed their deep mystification. They were now absolutely nonplussed by the singular character of American cowboys. Madeline was pleased to note how seriously they had taken the old cattleman's story. She had a little throb of wild expectancy that made her both fear and delight in the afternoon's prospect.

The June days had set in warm; in fact, hot during the noon hours: and this had inculcated in her insatiable visitors a tendency to profit by the experience of those used to the Southwest. They indulged in the restful siesta during the heated term of the day.

Madeline was awakened by Majesty's well-known whistle and pounding on the gravel. Then she heard the other horses. When she went out, she found her party assembled in gala golf attire, and with spirits to match their costumes. Castleton, especially, appeared resplendent in a golf coat that beggared description. Madeline had faint misgivings when she reflected on what Monty and Nels and Nick might do under the influence of that blazing garment.

"Oh. Majesty," cried Helen, as Madeline went up to her horse, "don't make him kneel! Try that flying mount. We all want to see it. It's so stunning."

"But that way, too, I must have him kneel," said Madeline, "or I can't reach the stirrup. He's so tremendously high."

Madeline had to yield to the laughing insistence of her friends, and after all of them except Florence were up, she made Majesty go down on one knee. Then she stood on his left side, facing back, and took a good firm grip on the bridle and pommel and his mane. After she had slipped the toe of her boot firmly into the stirrup, she called to Majesty. He jumped and swung her up into the saddle.

"Now just to see how it ought to be done watch Florence," said Madeline.

The Western girl was at her best in riding-habit and with her horse. It was beautiful to see the ease and grace with which she accomplished the cowboys' flying mount. Then she led the party down the slope and across the flat to climb the mesa.

Madeline never saw a group of her cowboys without looking them over, almost unconsciously, for her foreman, Gene Stewart. This afternoon, as usual, he was not present. However, she now had a sense—of which she was wholly conscious—that she was both disappointed and irritated. He had really not been attentive to her guests, and he, of all her cowboys, was the one of whom they wanted most to see something. Helen, particularly, had asked to have him attend the match. But Stewart was with the cattle. Madeline thought of his faithfulness, and was ashamed of her momentary lapse into that old imperious habit of desiring things irrespective of reason.

Stewart, however, immediately slipped out of her mind as she surveyed the group of cowboys on the links. By actual count there were sixteen, not including Stillwell. And the same number of splendid horses, all shiny and clean, grazed on the rim in the care of ranch hands. The cowboys were on dress-parade, looking very different in Madeline's eyes, at least, from the way cowboys usually appeared. But they were real and natural to her guests; and they were so picturesque that they might have been stage cowboys instead of real ones. Sombreros with silver buckles and horsehair bands were in evidence; and bright silk scarfs, embroidered vests, fringed and ornamented chaps, huge swinging guns, and clinking silver spurs lent a festive appearance.

Madeline and her party were at once eagerly surrounded by the cowboys, and she found it difficult to repress a smile. If these cowboys were still remarkable to her, what must they be to her guests?

"Wal, you all raced over, I seen," said Stillwell, taking Madeline's bridle. "Get down—get down. We're sure amazin' glad an' proud. An,' Miss Majesty, I'm offerin' to beg pawdin for the way the boys are packin' guns. Mebbe it ain't polite. But it's Stewart's orders."

"Stewart's orders!" echoed Madeline. Her friends were suddenly silent.

"I reckon he won't take no chances on the boys bein' surprised sudden by raiders. An' there's raiders operatin' in from the Guadalupes. That's all. Nothin' to worry over. I was just explainin.'"

Madeline, with several of her party, expressed relief, but Helen showed excitement and then disappointment.

"Oh, I want something to happen!" she cried.

Sixteen pairs of keen cowboy eyes fastened intently upon her pretty, petulant face; and Madeline divined, if Helen did not, that the desired consummation was not far off.

"So do I," said Dot Coombs. "It would be perfectly lovely to have a real adventure."

The gaze of the sixteen cowboys shifted and sought the demure face of this other discontented girl. Madeline laughed, and Stillwell wore his strange, moving smile.

"Wal, I reckon you ladies sure won't have to go home unhappy," he said. "Why, as boss of this heah outfit I'd feel myself disgraced forever if you didn't have your wish. Just wait. An' now, ladies, the matter on hand may not be amusin' or excitin' to you; but to this heah cowboy outfit it's powerful important. An' all the help you can give us will sure be thankfully received. Take a look across the links. Do you all see them two apologies for human bein's prancin' like a couple of hobbled broncs? Wal, you're gazin' at Monty Price an' Link Stevens, who have of a sudden got too swell to associate with their old bunkies. They're practicin' for the toornament. They don't want my boys to see how they handle them crooked clubs."

"Have you picked your team?" inquired Madeline.

Stillwell mopped his red face with an immense bandana and showed something of confusion and perplexity.

"I've sixteen boys, an' they all want to play," he replied. "Pickin' the team ain't goin' to be an easy job. Mebbe it won't be healthy, either. There's Nels and Nick. They just stated cheerful-like that if they didn't play we won't have any game at all. Nick never tried before, an' Nels, all he wants is to get a crack at Monty with one of them crooked clubs."

"I suggest you let all your boys drive from the tee and choose the two who drive the farthest," said Madeline.

Stillwell's perplexed face lit up.

"Wal, that's a plumb good idee. The boys'll stand for that."

Wherewith he broke up the admiring circle of cowboys round the ladies.

"Grap a rope—I mean a club—all you cowpunchers, an' march over hyar an' take a swipe at this little white bean."

The cowboys obeyed with alacrity. There was considerable difficulty over the choice of clubs and who should try first. The latter question had to be adjusted by lot. However, after Frankie Slade made several ineffectual attempts to hit the ball from the teeing ground, at last to send it only a few yards, the other players were not so eager to follow. Stillwell had to push Booly forward, and Booly executed a most miserable shot and retired to the laughing comments of his comrades. The efforts of several succeeding cowboys attested to the extreme difficulty of making a good drive.

"Wal, Nick, it's your turn," said Stillwell.

"Bill, I ain't so all-fired particular about playin'," replied Nick.

"Why? You was roarin' about it a little while ago. Afraid to show how bad you'll play?"

"Nope, jest plain consideration for my feller cowpunchers," answered Nick, with spirit. "I'm appreciatin' how bad they play, an' I'm not mean enough to show them up."

"Wal, you've got to show me," said Stillwell. "I know you never seen a gol-lof stick in your life. What's more, I'll bet you can't hit that little ball square—not in a dozen cracks at it."

"Bill, I'm also too much of a gent to take your money. But you know I'm from Missouri. Gimme a club."

Nick's angry confidence seemed to evaporate as one after another he took up and handled the clubs. It was plain he had never before wielded one. But, also, it was plain he was not the kind of a man to give in. Finally he selected a driver, looked doubtfully at the small knob, and then stepped into position on the teeing ground.

Nick Steele stood six feet four inches in height. He had the rider's wiry slenderness, yet he was broad of shoulder. His arms were long. Manifestly, he was an exceedingly powerful man. He swung the driver aloft and whirled it down with a tremendous swing. Crack! The white ball disappeared, and from where it had been rose a tiny cloud of dust.

Madeline's quick sight caught the ball as it lined somewhat to the right. It was shooting low and level with the speed of a bullet. It went up and up in swift, beautiful flight, then lost its speed and began to sail, to curve, to drop; and it fell out of sight beyond the rim of the mesa. Madeline had never seen a drive that approached this one. It was magnificent, beyond belief except for actual evidence of her own eyes.

The yelling of the cowboys probably brought Nick Steele out of the astounding spell with which he beheld his shot. Then Nick, suddenly alive to the situation, recovered from his trance and, resting nonchalantly upon his club, he surveyed Stillwell and the boys. After their first surprised outburst, they were dumb.

"You all seen thet?" Nick grandly waved his hand. "Thaught I was joshin,' didn't you? Why, I used to go to Saint Louis an' Kansas City to play this here game. There was some talk of the golf clubs takin' me down East to play the champions. But I never cared fer the game. Too easy fer me! Them fellers back in Missouri were a lot of cheap dubs, anyhow, always kickin' because whenever I hit a ball hard, I always lost it. Why, I hed to hit sort of left-handed to let 'em stay in my class. Now you all can go ahead an' play Monty an' Link. I could beat 'em both, playin' with one hand, if I wanted to. But I ain't interested. I jest hit thet ball off the mesa to show you. I sure wouldn't be seen playin' on your team."

With that Nick sauntered away toward the horses. Stillwell appeared crushed. And not a scornful word was hurled after Nick, which fact proved the nature of his victory. Then Nels strode into the limelight. As far as it was possible for this iron-faced cowboy to be so, he was bland and suave. He remarked to Stillwell and the other cowboys that sometimes it was painful for them to judge of the gifts of superior cowboys such as belonged to Nick and himself. He picked up the club Nick had used and called for a new ball. Stillwell carefully built up a little mound of sand and, placing the ball upon it, squared away to watch. He looked grim and expectant.

Nels was not so large a man as Nick, and did not look so formidable as he waved his club at the gaping cowboys. Still he was lithe, tough, strong. Briskly, with a debonair manner, he stepped up and then delivered a mighty swing at the ball. He missed. The power and momentum of his swing flung him off his feet, and he actually turned upside down and spun round on his head. The cowboys howled. Stillwell's stentorian laugh rolled across the mesa. Madeline and her guests found it impossible to restrain their mirth. And when Nels got up, he cast a reproachful glance at Madeline. His feelings were hurt.

His second attempt, not by any means so violent, resulted in as clean a miss as the first, and brought jeers from the cowboys. Nels's red face flamed redder. Angrily he swung again. The mound of sand spread over the teeing ground and the exasperating little ball rolled a few inches. This time he had to build up the sand mound and replace the ball himself. Stillwell stood scornfully by, and the boys addressed remarks to Nels.

"Take off them blinders," said one.

"Nels, your eyes are shore bad," said another.

"You don't hit where you look."

"Nels, your left eye has sprung a limp."

"Why, you dog-goned old fule, you cain't hit thet bawl."

Nels essayed again, only to meet ignominious failure. Then carefully he gathered himself together, gaged distance, balanced the club, swung cautiously. And the head of the club made a beautiful curve round the ball.

"Shore it's jest thet crooked club," he declared.

He changed clubs and made another signal failure. Rage suddenly possessing him, he began to swing wildly. Always, it appeared, the illusive little ball was not where he aimed. Stillwell hunched his huge bulk, leaned hands on knees, and roared his riotous mirth. The cowboys leaped up and down in glee.

"You cain't hit thet bawl," sang out one of the noisiest. A few more whirling, desperate lunges on the part of Nels, all as futile as if the ball had been thin air, finally brought to the dogged cowboy a realization that golf was beyond him.

Stillwell bawled: "Oh, haw, haw, haw! Nels, you're—too old—eyes no good!"

Nels slammed down the club, and when he straightened up with the red leaving his face, then the real pride and fire of the man showed. Deliberately he stepped off ten paces and turned toward the little mound upon which rested the ball. His arm shot down, elbow crooked, hand like a claw.

"Aw, Nels, this is fun!" yelled Stillwell.

But swift as a gleam of light Nels flashed his gun, and the report came with the action. Chips flew from the golf ball as it tumbled from the mound. Nels had hit it without raising the dust. Then he dropped the gun back in its sheath and faced the cowboys.

"Mebbe my eyes ain't so orful bad," he said, coolly, and started to walk off.

"But look ah-heah, Nels," yelled Stillwell, "we come out to play gol-lof! We can't let you knock the ball around with your gun. What'd you want to get mad for? It's only fun. Now you an' Nick hang round heah an' be sociable. We ain't depreciatin' your company none, nor your usefulness on occasions. An' if you just hain't got inborn politeness sufficient to do the gallant before the ladies, why, remember Stewart's orders."

"Stewart's orders?" queried Nels, coming to a sudden halt.

"That's what I said," replied Stillwell, with asperity. "His orders. Are you forgettin' orders? Wal, you're a fine cowboy. You an' Nick an' Monty, 'specially, are to obey orders."

Nels took off his sombrero and scratched his head. "Bill, I reckon I'm some forgetful. But I was mad. I'd 'a' remembered pretty soon, an' mebbe my manners."

"Sure you would," replied Stillwell. "Wal, now, we don't seem to be proceedin' much with my gol-lof team. Next ambitious player step up."

In Ambrose, who showed some skill in driving, Stillwell found one of his team. The succeeding players, however, were so poor and so evenly matched that the earnest Stillwell was in despair. He lost his temper just as speedily as Nels had. Finally Ed Linton's wife appeared riding up with Ambrose's wife, and perhaps this helped, for Ed suddenly disclosed ability that made Stillwell single him out.

"Let me coach you a little," said Bill.

"Sure, if you like," replied Ed. "But I know more about this game than you do."

"Wal, then, let's see you hit a ball straight. Seems to me you got good all-fired quick. It's amazin' strange." Here Bill looked around to discover the two young wives modestly casting eyes of admiration upon their husbands. "Haw, haw! It ain't so darned strange. Mebbe that'll help some. Now, Ed, stand up and don't sling your club as if you was ropin' a steer. Come round easy-like an' hit straight."

Ed made several attempts which, although better than those of his predecessors, were rather discouraging to the exacting coach. Presently, after a particularly atrocious shot, Stillwell strode in distress here and there, and finally stopped a dozen paces or more in front of the teeing ground. Ed, who for a cowboy was somewhat phlegmatic, calmly made ready for another attempt.

"Fore!" he called.

Stillwell stared.

"Fore!" yelled Ed.

"Why're you hollerin' that way at me?" demanded Bill.

"I mean for you to lope off the horizon. Get back from in front."

"Oh, that was one of them durned crazy words Monty is always hollerin.' Wal, I reckon I'm safe enough hyar. You couldn't hit me in a million years."

"Bill, ooze away," urged Ed.

"Didn't I say you couldn't hit me? What am I coachin' you for? It's because you hit crooked, ain't it? Wal, go ahaid an' break your back."

Ed Linton was a short, heavy man, and his stocky build gave evidence of considerable strength. His former strokes had not been made at the expense of exertion, but now he got ready for a supreme effort. A sudden silence clamped down upon the exuberant cowboys. It was one of those fateful moments when the air was charged with disaster. As Ed swung the club, it fairly whistled.

Crack! Instantly came a thump. But no one saw the ball until it dropped from Stillwell's shrinking body. His big hands went spasmodically to the place that hurt, and a terrible groan rumbled from him.

Then the cowboys broke into a frenzy of mirth that seemed to find adequate expression only in dancing and rolling accompaniment to their howls. Stillwell recovered his dignity as soon as he caught his breath, and he advanced with a rueful face.

"Wal, boys, it's on Bill," he said. "I'm a livin' proof of the pig-headedness of mankind. Ed, you win. You're captain of the team. You hit straight, an' if I hadn't been obstructin' the general atmosphere that ball would sure have gone clear to the Chiricahuas."

Then making a megaphone of his huge hands, he yelled a loud blast of defiance at Monty and Link.

"Hey, you swell gol-lofers! We're waitin.' Come on if you ain't scared."

Instantly Monty and Link quit practicing, and like two emperors came stalking across the links.

"Guess my bluff didn't work much," said Stillwell. Then he turned to Madeline and her friends. "Sure I hope, Miss Majesty, that you all won't weaken an' go over to the enemy. Monty is some eloquent, an,' besides, he has a way of gettin' people to agree with him. He'll be plumb wild when he heahs what he an' Link are up against. But it's a square deal, because he wouldn't help us or lend the book that shows how to play. An,' besides, it's policy for us to beat him. Now, if you'll elect who's to be caddies an' umpire I'll be powerful obliged."

Madeline's friends were hugely amused over the prospective match; but, except for Dorothy and Castleton, they disclaimed any ambition for active participation. Accordingly, Madeline appointed Castleton to judge the play, Dorothy to act as caddie for Ed Linton, and she herself to be caddie for Ambrose. While Stillwell beamingly announced this momentous news to his team and supporters, Monty and Link were striding up.

Both were diminutive in size, bowlegged, lame in one foot, and altogether unprepossessing. Link was young, and Monty's years, more than twice Link's, had left their mark. But it would have been impossible to tell Monty's age. As Stillwell said, Monty was burned to the color and hardness of a cinder. He never minded the heat, and always wore heavy sheepskin chaps with the wool outside. This made him look broader than he was long. Link, partial to leather, had, since he became Madeline's chauffeur, taken to leather altogether. He carried no weapon, but Monty wore a huge gun sheath and gun. Link smoked a cigarette and looked coolly impudent. Monty was dark-faced, swaggering, for all the world like a barbarian chief.

"That Monty makes my flesh creep," said Helen, low-voiced. "Really, Mr. Stillwell, is he so bad—desperate—as I've heard? Did he ever kill anybody?"

"Sure. 'Most as many as Nels," replied Stillwell, cheerfully.

"Oh! And is that nice Mr. Nels a desperado, too? I wouldn't have thought so. He's so kind and old-fashioned and soft-voiced."

"Nels is sure an example of the dooplicity of men, Miss Helen. Don't you listen to his soft voice. He's really as bad as a sidewinder rattlesnake."

At this juncture Monty and Link reached the teeing ground, and Stillwell went out to meet them. The other cowboys pressed forward to surround the trio. Madeline heard Stillwell's voice, and evidently he was explaining that his team was to have skilled advice during the play. Suddenly there came from the center of the group a loud, angry roar that broke off as suddenly. Then followed excited voices all mingled together. Presently Monty appeared, breaking away from restraining hands, and he strode toward Madeline.

Monty Price was a type of cowboy who had never been known to speak to a woman unless he was first addressed, and then he answered in blunt, awkward shyness. Upon this great occasion, however, it appeared that he meant to protest or plead with Madeline, for he showed stress of emotion. Madeline had never gotten acquainted with Monty. She was a little in awe, if not in fear, of him, and now she found it imperative for her to keep in mind that more than any other of the wild fellows on her ranch this one should be dealt with as if he were a big boy.

Monty removed his sombrero—something he had never done before—and the single instant when it was off was long enough to show his head entirely bald. This was one of the hallmarks of that terrible Montana prairie fire through which he had fought to save the life of a child. Madeline did not forget it, and all at once she wanted to take Monty's side. Remembering Stillwell's wisdom, however, she forebore yielding to sentiment, and called upon her wits.

"Miss—Miss Hammond," began Monty, stammering, "I'm extendin' admirin' greetin's to you an' your friends. Link an' me are right down proud to play the match game with you watchin.' But Bill says you're goin' to caddie for his team an' coach 'em on the fine points. An' I want to ask, all respectful, if thet's fair an' square?"

"Monty, that is for you to say," replied Madeline. "It was my suggestion. But if you object in the least, of course we shall withdraw. It seems fair to me, because you have learned the game; you are expert, and I understand the other boys have no chance with you. Then you have coached Link. I think it would be sportsmanlike of you to accept the handicap."

"Aw, a handicap! Thet was what Bill was drivin' at. Why didn't he say so? Every time Bill comes to a word thet's pie to us old golfers he jest stumbles. Miss Majesty, you've made it all clear as print. An' I may say with becomin' modesty thet you wasn't mistaken none about me bein' sportsmanlike. Me an' Link was born thet way. An' we accept the handicap. Lackin' thet handicap, I reckon. Link an' me would have no ambish to play our most be-ootiful game. An' thankin' you, Miss Majesty, an' all your friends, I want to add thet if Bill's outfit couldn't beat us before, they've got a swell chanct now, with you ladies a-watchin' me an' Link."

Monty had seemed to expand with pride as he delivered this speech, and at the end he bowed low and turned away. He joined the group round Stillwell. Once more there was animated discussion and argument and expostulation. One of the cowboys came for Castleton and led him away to exploit upon ground rules.

It seemed to Madeline that the game never would begin. She strolled on the rim of the mesa, arm in arm with Edith Wayne, and while Edith talked she looked out over the gray valley leading to the rugged black mountains and the vast red wastes. In the foreground on the gray slope, she saw cattle in movement and cowboys riding to and fro. She thought of Stewart. Then Boyd Harvey came for them, saying all details had been arranged. Stillwell met them halfway, and this cool, dry, old cattleman, whose face and manner scarcely changed at the announcement of a cattle raid, now showed extreme agitation.

"Wal, Miss Majesty, we've gone an' made a foozle right at the start," he said, dejectedly.

"A foozle? But the game has not yet begun," replied Madeline.

"A bad start, I mean. It's amazin' bad, an' we're licked already."

"What in the world is wrong?"

She wanted to laugh, but Stillwell's distress restrained her.

"Wal, it's this way. That darn Monty is as cute an' slick as a fox. After he got done declaimin' about the handicap he an' Link was so happy to take, he got Castleton over hyar an' drove us all dotty with his crazy gol-lof names. Then he borrowed Castleton's gol-lof coat. I reckon borrowed is some kind word. He just about took that blazin' coat off the Englishman. Though I ain't sayin' but that Casleton was agreeable when he tumbled to Monty's meanin.' Which was nothin' more 'n to break Ambrose's heart. That coat dazzles Ambrose. You know how vain Ambrose is. Why, he'd die to get to wear that Englishman's gol-lof coat. An' Monty forestalled him. It's plumb pitiful to see the look in Ambrose's eyes. He won't be able to play much. Then what do you think? Monty fixed Ed Linton, all right. Usually Ed is easy-goin' an' cool. But now he's on the rampage. Wal, mebbe it's news to you to learn that Ed's wife is powerful, turrible jealous of him. Ed was somethin' of a devil with the wimmen. Monty goes over an' tells Beulah—that's Ed's wife—that Ed is goin' to have for caddie the lovely Miss Dorothy with the goo-goo eyes. I reckon this was some disrespectful, but with all doo respect to Miss Dorothy she has got a pair of unbridled eyes. Mebbe it's just natural for her to look at a feller like that. Oh, it's all right; I'm not sayin' any-thin'! I know it's all proper an' regular for girls back East to use their eyes. But out hyar it's bound to result disastrous. All the boys talk about among themselves is Miss Dot's eyes, an' all they brag about is which feller is the luckiest. Anyway, sure Ed's wife knows it. An' Monty up an' told her that it was fine for her to come out an' see how swell Ed was prancin' round under the light of Miss Dot's brown eyes. Beulah calls over Ed, figgertively speakin,' ropes him for a minnit. Ed comes back huggin' a grouch as big as a hill. Oh, it was funny! He was goin' to punch Monty's haid off. An' Monty stands there an' laughs. Says Monty, sarcastic as alkali water: 'Ed, we all knowed you was a heap married man, but you're some locoed to give yourself away.'

That settled Ed. He's some touchy about the way Beulah henpecks him. He lost his spirit. An' now he couldn't play marbles, let alone gol-lof. Nope, Monty was too smart. An' I reckon he was right about brains bein' what wins."

The game began. At first Madeline and Dorothy essayed to direct the endeavors of their respective players. But all they said and did only made their team play the worse. At the third hole they were far behind and hopelessly bewildered. What with Monty's borrowed coat, with its dazzling effect upon Ambrose, and Link's oft-repeated allusion to Ed's matrimonial state, and Stillwell's vociferated disgust, and the clamoring good intention and pursuit of the cowboy supporters, and the embarrassing presence of the ladies, Ambrose and Ed wore through all manner of strange play until it became ridiculous.

"Hey, Link," came Monty's voice booming over the links, "our esteemed rivals are playin' shinny."

Madeline and Dorothy gave up, presently, when the game became a rout, and they sat down with their followers to watch the fun. Whether by hook or crook, Ed and Ambrose forged ahead to come close upon Monty and Link. Castleton disappeared in a mass of gesticulating, shouting cowboys. When that compact mass disintegrated, Castleton came forth rather hurriedly, it appeared, to stalk back toward his hostess and friends.

"Look!" exclaimed Helen, in delight. "Castleton is actually excited. Whatever did they do to him? Oh, this is immense!"

Castleton was excited, indeed, and also somewhat disheveled.

"By Jove! that was a rum go," he said, as he came up. "Never saw such blooming golf! I resigned my office as umpire."

Only upon considerable pressure did he reveal the reason. "It was like this, don't you know. They were all together over there, watching each other. Monty Price's ball dropped into a hazard, and he moved it to improve the lie. By Jove! they've all been doing that. But over there the game was waxing hot. Stillwell and his cowboys saw Monty move the ball, and there was a row. They appealed to me. I corrected the play, showed the rules. Monty agreed he was in the wrong. However, when it came to moving his ball back to its former lie in the hazard there was more blooming trouble. Monty placed the ball to suit him, and then he transfixed me with an evil eye.

"'Dook,' he said. I wish the bloody cowboy would not call me that. 'Dook, mebbe this game ain't as important as international politics or some other things relatin,' but there's some health an' peace dependin' on it. Savvy? For some space our opponents have been dead to honor an' sportsmanlike conduct. I calculate the game depends on my next drive. I'm placin' my ball as near to where it was as human eyesight could. You seen where it was same as I seen it. You're the umpire, an,' Dook, I take you as an honorable man. Moreover, never in my born days has my word been doubted without sorrow. So I'm askin' you, wasn't my ball layin' just about here?'

"The bloody little desperado smiled cheerfully, and he dropped his right hand down to the butt of his gun. By Jove, he did! Then I had to tell a blooming lie!"

Castleton even caught the tone of Monty's voice, but it was plain that he had not the least conception that Monty had been fooling. Madeline and her friends divined it, however; and, there being no need of reserve, they let loose the fountains of mirth.

Shush!!!

Ring Lardner

To the Editor: I want to call your tension to something about golf that has been ranking in my bosom for a long wile and I would have said something about it yrs. ago only I thought a man of your brains and intelligents would take steps, but I suppose you are afraid of the Old Guard amist your readers and scared of offending them, but where they's a principal involved I never fail to speak out my mind and my friends say I have done it so often that it is what you might call spoken out.

Well, it looks to me like they was room for improvement in the game and when I say the game I don't mean my game but the game itself as gotten up by Saint Andrew and Simon Peter his brother and the next time the rules committee gets together I wished they would make a change in the code witch looks to me to be a whole lot more important than taking the endearing terms out of tennis or making a pitcher keep his finger nails pared so as he can't scratch baseball or self.

According to what I have read golf is suppose to be the most sociable game in the world and in my $1.50 dictionary one of the definitions of sociable is "suited for, or characterized by, much conversation." Well, then, why and the he-ll don't they mend the golf rules so as a man can talk wile they're playing? Instead of witch, if you say a word to a regular golfer wile he is making a shot, why the first thing he will do is suffer a nervous break down and then he will give you a dirty look and likely as not he will pick up his toys and walk off the links, as I have nicknamed them. And when you ask somebody what was the idear they will tell you that your ethics is rancid and you must be scum, because how can a man concentrate on their shot when somebody is makeing remarks at them. And if you was in the gallery at the national amateur and even wispered wile Bobby Ouimet was trying to run down a millimeter put, why the head linesman would reach in his hip pocket for a sawed off niblick and knock you for a safety.

Well, gents, I have seen a good many different kinds of athaletics and took a small part in a few of them and I ask you as man to man what other event is they where comments is barred?

"Yes," you will say, "but they's no other sport where a man has got to concentrate on what they are doing. If your mind is distracted wile you are playing golf you're gone."

How true.

And now leave us suppose that Ty Cobb is up in the ninth inning of a ball game with 2 out and the score 7 to 4 vs. Detroit like it usually is and Young and Bush on base. Well, the bench warmers on the other club is yelling "Pop up, Ty! You been a good old wagon but you done broke down." And the catcher is wispering "What shall I have him throw up here, Ty? Do you want a slow ball?" And the boys in the stands is hollering "Strike the big cheese out, Lefty. He's through."

But all this don't worry Ty because he is thinking to himself, "I mustn't forget to send my laundry out when I get back to the hotel." His mind ain't on the game at all and when Lefty throws one up there, why it's just from force of habit that he swings and next thing you know Felsch is beating it back to the left center field fence and Jackson is getting set to make the relay. But suppose Ty had been thinking about that next pitch instead of his shirts, why the uproar would of give him neurasthenia and they'd of had to send the trainer up to hit for him.

Or suppose for inst. they's a horse race and they are comeing down the stretch and Vagabond the favorite is out in front and the second horse is Willie the Wisp that's 20 to 1 and a lot of waiters has a bet down on him and they all begin screaming "Come on Willie" so loud that Vagabond can't help from hearing them, but he don't even look up as he is thinking about a couple of libr To the Editor: I want to call your tension to something about golf that has been ranking in my bosom for a long wile and I would have said something about it yrs. ago ary books that he promised to bring home to his mare.

Or you take what happened down to Toledo last 4 of July. Dempsey lept up and crowned Jessica in the left eye and Jessica suddenly set down but he got up again and 60 thousand and no hundreds larnyxs was shreeking "Kill the big dog, Jack!" and as I recall it, instead of the remarks bothering Dempsey, why he hit Jessica again with the same Gen. results and I would of swore he was concentrateing, but I found out afterwards that he was trying to figure out weather he would have veal chops or a steak for supper. Otherwise he would of raised his hand unlocked and told the referee that he wouldn't go on unlest the fans shut up their d-m noise.

Or leave us consider that extra inning game that wound up in Europe a couple yrs. ago and they was a guy name Frank Foch or something that was suppose to be figureing out how to put on the finishing touchs to it and he was setting down with a map in front of him, but the Germans kept on shooting Big Bertha and Little Eva with the loud pedal on, so finely a orderly come in and asked Mr. Foch if the noise bothered him. And Mr. Foch says "Oh no. It might if I was rapped up in what I am doing. But I was just wondering if I would look better with my mustache off or on, so let them keep on shooting." So it looks like if Mr. Foch had of been really forced to think about the job they had wished on him the Germans would probably be in Harrisburg by this time, changeing engines.

And then they's examples in the more intimate sports like shooting craps or driveing a car. For inst. you have made four passes and you've left it all ride and you come out with a deuce and a four and all the boys that's fadeing you begins yelping "Billy Hicks can't six" and "How many wonders in the world?" and etc. and you might get rattled and seven only that you ain't concentrated on the crap game a-tall, but you're thinking what a good time you might of had in Yellowstone Park last summer if you hadn't went to the 1000 Islands. Or let's say you're driveing up Fifth Ave. at 4 P.M. and your wife keeps pinching one of your arms and the gals in the back seat screek every little wile and say "Look out be careful!"

why you might bump somebody if your mind was on the traffic instead of Dr. C. Roach Straton's latest sermon.

Now in regards to golf itself, leave me give you a couple of incidence that happened to me personly witch will show that the boys who crabs against a little sociability is making a mountain climber out of a mole trap. Well, once I was playing out to Riverside near Chi with Albert Seckel and he was giveing me seven and no hundreds strokes per hole and when we came to the last tee we was even up. Well, the last hole was about 260 yds. but you had to drive over the Blue Ridge Mts. of Virginia and you couldn't see the green from the tee and if you didn't get your drive over the Mts. you was utterly lost. Well, for some reason another Seck had the honor and just as he was going to drive, I says "I hope you don't miss the ball entirely" so he drove onto the green and went down in two.

And down to Toledo last July, a few days before Willard became an acrobat, I and Rube Goldberg met in a match game out to Inverness and we was playing for a buck a hole and my caddie was Harry Witwer and he had broughten along a alarm clock and when we would get on the green, witch was seldom, why just as Rube was going to put, Harry would set off the alarm, and Rube got so nervous that on the 15th. hole Harry throwed my towel into the ring and I was seven down.

So all and all, Mr. Editor, I say pass a rule makeing it legal to open your clam when you feel like it and leave us forget this old obsleet law of silent golf witch was gotten up in Scotland where they wouldn't no more talk for nothing than Harry Lauder would sing for the same price. But weather the rule is past or no, when I am playing at golf I am going to say what I want to when I want to and if my oppts. don't like my ethics, why they's showers in the locker room.

Yours Truely,

Do We Play Golf for Pleasure?

R. L. Goldberg

As THIS IS MY FIRST ESSAY ON THE SUBJECT OF GOLF, I DO NOT CARE TO be a piker. I shall begin with a very sweeping statement.

I honestly believe we owe our success in the late world war to that hectic and goat-procuring pastime wherein the noble niblick plays a tragic part.

A greater part of our three million or so boys in the American army had dabbled more or less before the war in the game of keeping the head down and following through. A man fights his darndest when he is fighting mad. He's got to be sore to register the K. O. Luckily, most of us took up golf before the war startled. That's what made us sore.

Here is the subject of the thesis I have to lay before the dean of the College of Relaxation: "Is golf a pleasure or an incurable rash?

I shall cite my own case, for instance, as I am a great believer in the theory that we have no one to blame for misfortunes but ourselves. Several years ago, I did not know a mashie from a banana sundae. I had never set foot upon the fair green, and I was utterly free from caddie trouble. I was as innocent and happy as a newborn giraffe. Nothing irritated me. I could ride in the New York subway from the Battery to Bronx Park with thirty-seven elbows pressing against my ribs, and fifty-five bags of herring caressing my nose, and smile.

Today the light of happiness is nowhere to be seen in the contour of my deep-lined features. The baby prattle of my two young sons does not arouse in me the sense of living in a world of beauty and glory. Why?

I took up golf.

Never mind who talked me into it. He's more miserable than I am. He knows more about the game. The amount of unhappiness you get out of golf is in direct proportion to the knowledge you have of the game. The more you know, the worse you feel. I am still a dub, so at least remember that there is such a thing as a sun and that Charley Chaplin still makes big money making people laugh.

The first intimation that all is not going to be as snappy and delightful as you expected comes when you put on your first pair of the short golf trousers and stand in front of the mirror. Luckily you kid yourself into blaming it upon your imagination. You are sure your legs were never that shape. You had recently seen Charley Bone, the living skeleton in the circus and you had him on the brain. Of course you don't look like that!

The next blow comes when you steal a look around the locker room and see the oddest looking things running back and forth from the shower-bath without a stitch of clothing on. You thought golf was played by the better class of people. Could these animated cartoons belong to the American aristocracy of sport? Had the House of Kuppenheimer been hiding such terrible things all these years? But no! You were nervous on account of the newness of the surroundings and it was your imagination again.

As you walk toward the first tee, you spot old Joe Marmelade standing on the left side waiting his turn to drive. You recall the old saying that good fellowship is the essence of sport. Everything will be great from now on. You are among friends. You rush up, slap Marmelade in the back of his twenty-two-dollar sweater coat and yell at the top of your voice, "Hello, Joe. How's the boy!" Before the echo of the last word has had a chance to hit the side of the clubhouse fifteen feet away, you know you have committed treason, grand larceny, mayhem, sorcery, arson, and murder in the first degree. A man with whiskers, who is standing on the tee ready to drive, gives you a look that shrivels you up to the size of a German mark. Anything but a nasty look for a guy with whiskers! Even your pal, Marmelade, the man whose father picked prunes with your father out in California back in the early fifties, turns away in disgust. You look out of the corner of your eye and see your caddie whispering with another freckled hyena. You are the prize boob!

You can't turn back now. On the veranda overlooking the tee, your wife is telling another lady how easily you pick up new games. Besides, don't doctors and nurses say one gets hardened to scenes of suffering. You are the principal character in the scene, and you may as well let the hardening process start immediately.

Ah, it is your turn to drive. Suddenly you realize there is someone watching you. In fact, there is quite a crowd watching you. They must have sent out invitations for the affair. The whole membership of the club seems to be standing there. No one bats an eyelash. No one moves. No one smiles. "Who died?" you ask yourself.

But why should you worry? Haven't you memorized all the rules of the game and mastered the theory of golf? Let 'er go! There's nothing to it after all: hold the head down, follow through, don't drop the right shoulder, change the weight of the body from one foot to the other, don't press, keep your eye on the ball, and all the rest. It's a cinch.

Zam! Hurray, you did it. As luck would have it, you hit the ball right square on the nose. You could tell by the click it was a wonderful shot. You did not forget a single thing the instructor told you the day before.

But where is the caddie walking? Sure enough, the funeral directors were right. You were the corpse and didn't know it. The caddie stops right in the middle of the Argonne Forest twenty-seven feet and six inches away from the tee and points. Sure enough, it's your ball. There are your initials in the northeast corner.

Well, anyway you are away from that crowd of petrified undertakers, and you can go to your grave privately. It takes you four shots to get out of the jungle and you land right in the center of a sandpit behind what looks like Mount Vesuvius. It is in full eruption, too. There is another duffer in a sandpit on the other side of the mountain throwing sand, and rocks, and lava, and mud, and tin cans all over you in an attempt to get out into the open himself.

You come out into the open to enjoy the big, open expanse of Nature's hospitality, and you spend half the day down in a hole originating a sandstorm effect for the Hippodrome. You wish to inhale the fresh, pure exhilarating ozone, and discover yourself carrying home half the Sahara Desert inside your chest!

Finally, you reach the green with the help of the Lord and the demon of necessity, take four putts, put your ball in the hole, and try to crawl in after it.

Your opponent is standing there holding the score card nonchalantly and he asks, "How many did you get, Stupid?"

"Fourteen," you answer, under your breath, feeling that you have no right to live.

Suddenly you are overcome by a strange desire to know just how many strokes it took your opponent to reach the hole.

"How many did you make?" you summon up the courage to ask, with a note of apology verging on a sob. You haven't seen each other since you left the tee together, so he ought to tell you just as a matter of pure charity.

He puts the pencil thoughtfully in his mouth, looks back over the ground you have just covered and says, "Let me see, I didn't keep track of my shots. My drive took me just to that big tree. My next shot was past the bunker, my third was over there just short of the green, and two putts, making five in all."

You know he is lying, but you have no right to tell him so. Why didn't he keep track of the shots as he made them? Has he such a good memory that he doesn't have to count as he goes along? If he has such a retentive brain, why doesn't he pay you back the five he borrowed two years before?

And so on down through the eighteen holes—misery, pain, anguish, dishonesty, and darkness! So this is golf? No more for you. Pinochle is the thing.

But what happens the following week, and the week after that, and the week after that?

There you are cursing and fuming and slicing all over the place. And if you miss a Sunday, you are more miserable off the links than on the links.

All of which may prove that golf is an incurable rash. It itches forever!

Gentlemen, You Can't Go Through!

Charles E. Van Loan

I

There has been considerable argument about it—even a mention of ethics—though where ethics figures in this case is more than I know. I'd like to take a flat-footed stance as claiming that the end justified the means. Saint George killed the Dragon, and Hercules mopped up the Augean stables, but little Wally Wallace—142 pounds in his summer underwear—did a bigger job and a better job when the betting was odds-on-and-write-your-own-ticket that it couldn't be done. I wouldn't mind heading a subscription to present him with a gold medal about the size of a soup plate, inscribed as follows, to wit and viz.: W. W. Wallace—He Put the Fore in Foursome.

Every golfer who ever conceded himself a two-foot putt because he was afraid he might miss it has sweated and suffered and blasphemed in the wake of a slow foursome. All the clubs I have ever seen—and I've traveled a bit—are cursed with at least one of these Creeping Pestilences that you observe mostly from the rear.

You're a golfer, of course, and you know the makeup of a slow foursome as well as I do: Four nice old gentlemen, prominent in business circles, church members who remember it even when they top a tee shot, pillars of society, rich enough to be carried over the course in palanquins, but too proud to ride, too dignified to hurry, too meek to argue except among themselves, and too infernally selfish to stand aside and let the younger men go through. They take nine practice swings before hitting a shot, and then flub it disgracefully; they hold a prayer meeting on every putting green and a post-mortem on every tee, and a rheumatic snail could give them a flying start and beat them out in a fifty-yard dash. Know 'em? What golfer doesn't?

But nobody knows why it is that the four slowest players in every club always manage to hook up in a sort of permanent alliance. Nobody knows why they never stage their creeping contests on the off days when the course is clear. Nobody knows why they always pick the sunniest afternoons, when the locker room is full of young men dressing in a hurry. Nobody knows why they bolt their luncheons and scuttle out to the first tee, nor where that speed goes as soon as they drive and start down the course. Nobody knows why they refuse to walk any faster than a bogged mooley cow. Nobody knows why they never look behind them. Nobody knows why they never hear any one yell, "Fore!" Nobody knows why they are so dead set against letting anyone through.

Everybody knows the fatal effect of standing too long over the ball, all dressed up with nowhere to go. Everybody knows of the tee shots that are slopped and sliced and hooked; of the indecision caused by the long wait before playing the second; of the change of clubs when the first choice was the correct one; of the inevitable penalty exacted by loss of temper and mental poise. Everybody knows that a slow foursome gives the Recording Angel a busy afternoon and leaves a sulphurous haze over an entire course. But the aged reprobates who are responsible for all this trouble—do they care how much grief and rage and bitterness simmers in their wake? You think they do? Think again. Golf and Business are the only games they have ever had time to learn, and one set of rules does for both. The rest of the world may go hang! Golf is a serious matter with these hoary offenders, and they manage to make it serious for everybody behind them—the fast-walking, quick-swinging fellows who are out for a sweat and a good time and lose both because the slow foursome blocks the way.

Yes, you recognize the thumbnail sketch—it is the slow foursome that infests your course; the one you find in front of you when you go visiting. You think four men who are inconsiderate enough to ruin your day's sport and ruffle your temper ought to be disciplined, called up on the carpet, taken in hand by the Greens Committee. You think they are the worst ever—but wait! You are about to hear of the golfing renegades known as the Big Four, who used to sew us up twice a week as regularly as the days came round; you are about to hear of Elsberry J. Watlington, and Colonel Jim Peck, and Samuel Alexander Peebles, and W. Cotton Hamilton—world's champions in the Snail Stakes, undisputed holders of the Challenge Belt for Practice Swinging, and undefeated catch-as-catch-can loiterers on the Putting Green.

Six months ago, we would have backed Watlington, Peck, Peebles, and Hamilton against the wide world, bet dollars against your dimes and allowed you to select your own stakeholders, timekeepers, and judges. That's how much confidence we had in the Big Four. They were without doubt and beyond argument the slowest and most exasperating quartette of obstructionists that ever laid their middle-aged stomachs behind the line of a putt.

Do I hear a faint murmur of dissent? Going a little strong, am I? All right, glad you mentioned it, because we may as well settle this question of supremacy here and now.

To save time, I will admit that your foursome is slower than Congress and more irritating than the Senate. Permit me to ask you one question: Going back over the years, can you recall a single instance when your slow foursome allowed you to play through? . . . A lost ball, was it? . . . Well, anyway, you got through them. . . . Thank you, and your answer puts you against the ropes. I will now knock you clear out of the ring with one well-directed statement of fact. Tie on your bonnet good and tight and listen to this: The Big Four held up our course for seven long and painful years, and during that period of time they never allowed anyone to pass them, lost ball or no lost ball.

That stops you, eh? I rather thought it would. It stopped us twice a week.

II

Visitors used to play our course on Wednesdays and Saturdays—our big days—and then sit in the lounging room and try hard to remember that they were our guests. There were two questions they never failed to ask:

"Don't they ever let anybody through?"

And then, "How long has this been going on?"

When we answered them truthfully, they shook their heads, looked out the windows, and told us how much better their clubs were handled. Our course was all right—they had to say that much in fairness. It was well trapped and bunkered, and laid out with an eye to the average player; the fair greens were the best in the state; the putting greens were like velvet; the holes were sporty enough to suit anybody; but—and then they looked out of the window again.

You see, the trouble was that the Big Four practically ran the club as they liked. They had financed it in its early days, and as a reward had been elected to almost everything in sight. We used to say they shook dice to see who should be president and so forth, and probably they did. They might as well have settled it that way as any other, for the annual election and open meeting was a joke.

It usually took place in the lounging room on a wet Saturday afternoon. Somebody would get up and begin to drone through a report of the year's activities. Then somebody else would make a motion and everybody would say, "Ay!" After that the result of the annual election of officers would be announced. The voting members always handed in the printed slips they found on the tables, and the ticket was never scratched—it would be Watlington, Peck, Peebles, and Hamilton all the way. The only real question would be whether or not the incoming president of the club would buy a drink for all hands. If it was Peck's turn the motion was lost.

As a natural result of this sort of thing, the Big Four never left the saddle for an instant. Talk about perpetuation in office—they had it down to a fine point. They were always on the Board of Directors; they saw to it that control of the Greens Committee never slipped out of their hands; they had two of the three votes on the House Committee, and no outsider was even considered for treasurer. They were dictators with a large D, and nobody could do a thing about it.

If a mild kick was ever made or new blood suggested, the kicker was made to feel like an ingrate. Who started the club anyway? Who dug up the money? Who swung the deal that put the property in our hands? Why, Watlington, Peck, Peebles, and Hamilton, to be sure! Could anyone blame them for wanting to keep an eye on the organization? Cer-tain-ly not. The Big Four had us bluffed, bulldozed, buffaloed, licked to a whisper.

Peck, Peebles, and Hamilton were the active heads of the Midland Manufacturing Company, and it was pretty well known that the bulk of Watlington's fortune was invested in the same enterprise. Those who knew said they were just as ruthless in business as they were in golf— quite a strong statement.

They seemed to regard the Sundown Golf and Country Club as their private property, and we were welcome to pay dues and amuse ourselves five days a week, but on Wednesdays and Saturdays we were not to infringe on the sovereign rights of the Big Four.

They never entered any of the club tournaments, for that would have necessitated breaking up their foursome. They always turned up in a body, on the tick of noon, and there was an immediate scramble to beat them to Number One tee. Those who lost out stampeded over to Number Ten and played the second nine first. Nobody wanted to follow them; but a blind man, playing without a caddie, couldn't have helped but catch up with them somewhere on the course.

If you wonder why the club held together, you have only to recall the story of the cowpuncher whose friend beckoned him away from the faro layout to inform him that the game was crooked.

"Hell!" said the cowpuncher. "I know that; but—it's the only game in town, ain't it?"

The S. G. & C. C. was the only golf club within fifty miles.

III

When Wally Wallace came home from college he blossomed out as a regular member of the club. He had been a junior member before, one of the tennis squad.

Wally is the son of old Hardpan Wallace, of the Trans-Pacific outfit—you may have heard of him—and the sole heir to more millions than he will ever be able to spend; but we didn't hold this against the boy. He isn't the sort that money can spoil, with nothing about him to remind you of old Hardpan, unless it might be a little more chin than he really needs.

Wally's first act as a full-fledged member of the club was to qualify for the James Peck Annual Trophy—a pretty fair sort of cup, considering the donor.

He turned in a nice snappy 81, which showed us that a college education had not been wasted on him, and also caused several of the Class-A men to sit up a bit and take notice.

He came booming through to the semifinals with his head up and his tail over the dashboard. It was there that he ran into me. Now I am no Jerry Travers, but there are times when I play to my handicap, which is 10, and I had been going fairly well. I had won four matches—one of them by default. Wally had also won four matches, but the best showing made against him was 5 down and 4 to go. His handicap was 6, so he would have to start me 2 up; but I had seen enough of his game to know I was up against the real thing and would need a lot of luck to give the boy anything like a close battle. He was a strong, heady match player, and if he had a weakness the men whom he had defeated hadn't been able to spot it. Altogether it wasn't a very brilliant outlook for me; but, as a matter of fact, I suppose no 10-handicap man ever ought to have a brilliant outlook. It isn't coming to him. If he has one it is because the handicapper has been careless.

Under our rules a competitor in a club tournament has a week in which to play his man, and it so happened that we agreed on Wednesday for our meeting. Wally called for me in his new runabout, and we had lunch together—I shook him and stuck him for it, and he grinned and remarked that a man couldn't be lucky at everything. While we were dressing, he chattered like a magpie, talking about everything in the world but golf, which was a sign he wasn't worrying much. He expected easy picking, and under normal conditions he would have had it.

We left the first tee promptly at one-forty-five p. m., our caddies carrying the little red flags that demand the right of way over everything. I might have suggested starting at Number Ten if I had thought of it, but to tell the truth I was a wee mite nervous and was wondering whether I had my drive with me or not. You know how the confounded thing comes and goes. So we started at Number One, and my troubles began. Wally opened up on me with a 4–4–3, making the third hole in a stroke under par, and when we reached the fourth tee we were all square and my handicap was gone.

It was on the fourth tee that we first began to notice signs of congestion ahead of us. One foursome had just driven off and beckoned us to come through, another was waiting to go, and the fair green on the way to the fifth looked like the advance of the Mexican standing army.

"Somebody has lost the transmission out of his wheelchair," said Wally. "Well, we shouldn't worry—we've got the red flags and the right of way. Fore!" And he proceeded to smack a perfect screamer down the middle of the course—250 yards if it was an inch. I staggered into one and laid my ball some distance behind his, but on the direct line to the pin. Then we had to wait a bit while another foursome putted out.

"There oughtn't to be any congestion on a day like this," said Wally. "Must be a bunch of old men ahead."

"It's the Big Four," said I. "Watlington, Peck, Peebles, and Hamilton. They always take their time."

From where we were we could see the seventh and eighth fair greens. There wasn't a player in sight on either one.

"Good Lord!" said Wally. "They've got the whole United States wide open ahead of 'em. They're not holding their place on the course."

"They never do," said I, and just then the foursome moved off the putting green.

"Give her a ride, old top!" said Wally.

I claim that my second shot wasn't half bad—for a 10-handicap man. I used a brassie and reached the green about thirty feet from the pin, but the demon Wally pulled a mid-iron out of his bag, waggled it once or twice, and then made my brassie look sick. When we reached the top of the hill, there was his ball ten feet from the cup. I ran up, playing it safe for a par 4, but Wally studied the roll of the green for about ten seconds—and dropped a very fat three. He was decent enough to apologize.

"I'm playing over my head," said he.

I couldn't dispute it—two 3s on par 4s might well be over anybody's head. One down and fourteen to go; it had all the earmarks of a massacre.

We had quite an audience at the fifth tee—two foursomes were piled up there, cursing.

"What's the matter, gentlemen?" asked Wally. "Can't you get through?"

"Nobody can get through," said Billy Williams. "It's the Big Four."

"But they'll respect the red flags, won't they?"

It was a perfectly natural question for a stranger to ask—and Wally was practically a stranger, though most of the men knew who he was. It brought all sorts of answers.

"You think they will? I'll bet you a little two to one, no limit, that they're all color-blind!"

"Oh, yes, they'll let you through!"

"They'll ask you to come through—won't they, Billy? They'll insist on it, what?"

"They're full of such tricks!"

Wally was puzzled. He didn't quite know what to make of it. "But a red flag," said he, "gives you the right of way."

"Everywhere but here," said Billy Williams.

"But in this case, it's a rule!" argued Wally.

"Those fellows in front make their own rules."

"But the Greens Committee . . ."

And this was where everybody laughed.

Wally stooped and teed his ball.

"Look here," said he, "I'll bet you anything you like that they let us through. Why, they can't help themselves!"

"You bet that they'll let you through of their own accord?" asked Ben Ashley, who never has been known to pass up a plain cinch.

"On our request to be allowed to pass," said Wally.

"If you drive into 'em without their permission, you lose," stipulated Ben.

"Right!" said Wally.

"Got you for a dozen balls!" said Ben.

"Anybody else want some of it?" asked Wally.

Before he got off the tee, he stood to lose six dozen balls; but his nerve was unshaken and he slammed out another tremendous drive. I sliced into a ditch and away we went, leaving a great deal of promiscuous kidding behind us. It took me two shots to get out at all, and Wally picked up another hole on me.

Two down—murder!

On the sixth tee we ran into another mass meeting of malcontents. Old Man Martin, our prize grouch, grumbled a bit when we called attention to our red flags.

"What's the use?" said he. "You're on your way, but you ain't going anywhere. Might just as well sit down and take it easy. Watlington has got a lost ball, and the others have gone on to the green so's nobody can get through. Won't do you a bit of good to drive, Wally. There's two foursomes hung up over the hill now, and they'll be right there till Watlington finds that ball. Sit down and be sociable."

"What'll you bet that we don't get through?" demanded Wally, who was beginning to show signs of irritation.

"Whatever you got the most of, Sonny—provided you make the bet this way: They got to let you through. Of course you might drive into 'em or walk through 'em, but that ain't being done—much."

"Right! The bet is that they let us through. One hundred fish."

Old Martin cackled and turned his cigar round and round in the corner of his mouth—a wolf when it comes to a cinch bet.

"Gosh! Listen to our banty rooster crow! Want another hundred, Sonny?"

"Yes—Grandpa!" said Wally, and sent another perfect drive soaring up over the hill.

Number Six is a long hole, and the ordinary player never attempts to carry the cross-bunker on his second. I followed with a middling-to-good shot, and we bade the congregation farewell.

"It's ridiculous!" said Wally as we climbed the hill. "I never saw a foursome yet that wouldn't yield to a red flag, or one that wouldn't let a twosome through—if properly approached. And we have the right of way over everything on the course. The Greens Committee . . ."

"Is composed," said I, "of Watlington, Peck, and Peebles—three members of the Big Four. They built the club, they run the club, and they have never been known to let anybody through. I'm sorry, Wally, but I'm afraid you're up against it."

The boy stopped and looked at me.

"Then those fellows behind us," said he, "were betting on a cinch, eh?"

"It was your proposition," I reminded him.

"So it was," and he grinned like the good game kid he is. "The Greens Committee, eh? 'Hast thou appealed unto Caesar? unto Caesar shalt thou go.' I'm a firm believer in the right method of approach. They wouldn't have the nerve . . ."

"They have nerve enough for anything," said I, and dropped the subject. I didn't want him to get the idea that I was trying to argue with him and upset his game. One foursome was lying down just over the hill; the other was piled up short of the bunker. Watlington had finally found his ball and played onto the green. The others, of course, had been standing around the pin and holding things up for him.

I took an iron on my second and played short, intending to pitch over the bunker on my third. Wally used a spoon and got tremendous height and distance. His ball carried the bunker, kicked to the right, and stopped behind a sand trap. It was a phenomenal shot, and with luck on the kick would have gone straight to the pin.

I thought the Big Four would surely be off the green by the time I got up to my ball, but no, Peck was preparing to hole a three-foot putt. Any ordinary dub would have walked up to that pill and tapped it in, but that wasn't Peck's style. He got down on all fours and sighted along the line to the hole. Then he rose, took out his handkerchief, wiped his hands carefully, called for his putter, and took an experimental stance, tramping about like a cat "making bread" on a woolen rug.

"Look at him!" grunted Wally. "You don't mind if I go ahead to my ball? It won't bother you?"

"Not in the least," said I.

"I want to play as soon as they get out of the way," he explained.

The Colonel's first stance did not suit him, so he had to go all through the tramping process again. When he was finally satisfied, he began swinging his putter back and forth over the ball, like the pendulum of a grandfather's clock—ten swings, neither more nor less. Could anyone blame Wally for boiling inside?

After the three-footer dropped—he didn't miss it, for a wonder—they all gathered around the hole and pulled out their cards. Knowing each other as well as they did, nobody was trusted to keep the score.

"Fore!" called Wally.

They paid not the slightest attention to him, and it was fully a half a minute before they ambled leisurely away in the direction of the seventh tee.

I played my pitch shot, with plenty of backspin on it, and stopped ten or twelve feet short of the hole. Wally played an instant later, a mashie shot intended to clear the trap, but he had been waiting too long and was burning up with impatience. He topped the ball, hit the far edge of the sand trap, and bounced back into a bad lie. Of course I knew why he had been in such a hurry—he wanted to catch the Big Four on the seventh tee. His niblick shot was too strong, but he laid his fifth dead to the hole, giving me 2 for a win. Just as a matter of record, let me state that I canned a nice rainbow putt for a 4. A 4 on Number Six is rare.

"Nice work!" said Wally. "You're only 1 down now. Come on, let's get through these miserable old men!"

Watlington was just addressing his ball, the others had already driven. He fussed and he fooled and he waggled his old dreadnaught for fifteen or twenty seconds, and then shot straight into the bunker—a wretchedly topped ball.

"Bless my heart!" said he. "Now why—why do I always miss my drive on this hole?"

Peck started to tell him, being his partner, but Wally interrupted, politely but firmly.

"Gentlemen," said he, "if you have no objection we will go through. We are playing a tournament match. Mr. Curtiss, your honor, I believe."

Well, sir, for all the notice they took of him he might have been speaking to four graven images. Not one of them so much as turned his head. Colonel Peck had the floor.

"I'll tell you, Wat," said he, "I think it's your stance. You're playing the ball too much off your right foot—coming down on it too much. Now if you want it to rise more . . ." They were moving away now, but very slowly.

"Fore!"

This time they had to notice the boy. He was mad clear through, and his voice showed it. They all turned, took one good look at him, and then toddled away, keeping well in the middle of the course. Peck was still explaining the theory of the perfect drive. Wally yelled again; this time they did not even look at him. "Well!" said he. "Of all the damned swine! I . . . I believe we should drive anyway!"

"You'll lose a lot of bets if you do." Perhaps I shouldn't have said that. Goodness knows I didn't want to see his game go to pieces behind the Big Four—I didn't want to play behind them myself. I tried to explain. The kid came over and patted me on the back.

"You're perfectly right," said he. "I forgot all about those fool bets, but I'd gladly lose all of 'em if I thought I could hit that long-nosed stiff in the back of the neck!" He meant the Colonel. "And so that's the Greens Committee, eh? Holy jumping Jemima! What a club!"

I couldn't think of much of anything to say, so we sat still and watched Watlington dig his way out of the bunker, Peck offering advice after each failure. When Watlington disagreed with Peck's point of view he took issue with him, and all hands joined in the argument. Wally was simply sizzling with pent-up emotion, and after Watlington's fifth shot he began to lift the safety valve a bit. The language he used was wonderful, and a great tribute to higher education. Old Hardpan himself couldn't have beaten it, even in his mule-skinning days.

At last the foursome was out of range and I got off a pretty fair tee shot. Wally was still telling me what he thought of the Greens Committee when he swung at the ball, and never have I seen a wider hook. It was still hooking when it disappeared in the woods, out of bounds. His next ball took a slice and rolled into long grass.

"Serves me right for losing my temper," said he with a grin. "I can play this game all right, old top, but when I'm riled it sort of unsettles me. Something tells me I'm going to be riled for the next half hour or so. Don't mind what I say. It's all meant for those hogs ahead of us."

I helped him find his ball, and even then we had to wait on Peebles and Hamilton, who were churning along down the middle of the course in easy range. I lighted a cigarette and thought about something else—my income tax, I think it was. I had found this a good system when sewed up behind the Big Four. I don't know what poor Wally was thinking about—man's inhumanity to man, I suppose—for when it came time to shoot, he failed to get down to his ball and hammered it still deeper into the grass.

"If it wasn't for the bets," said he, "I'd pick up and we'd go over to Number Eight. I'm afraid that on a strict interpretation of the terms of agreement, Martin could spear me for two hundred fish if we skipped a hole."

"He could," said I, "and what's more to the point, he would. They were to let us through—on request."

Wally sighed.

"I've tried one method of approach," said he, "and now I'll try another one. I might tell 'em that I bet two hundred dollars on the suspicion that they were gentlemen, but likely they'd want me to split the winnings. They look like that sort."

Number Seven was a gift on a golden platter. I won it with a frightful 8, getting into all sorts of grief along the way, but Wally was entirely up in the air and blew the short putt that should have given him a half.

"All square!" said he. "Fair enough! Now we shall see what we shall see!"

His chin was very much in evidence as he hiked to Number Eight tee, and he lost no time getting into action. Colonel Peck was preparing to drive as Wally hove alongside. The Colonel is very fussy about his drive. He has been known to send a caddie to the clubhouse for whispering on the bench. Wally walked up behind him.

"Stand still, young man! Can't you see I'm driving?"

It was in the nature of a royal command.

"Oh!" said Wally. "Meaning me, I presume. Do you know, it strikes me that for a golfer with absolutely no consideration for others, you're quite considerate—of yourself!"

Now I had always sized up the Colonel for a bluffer. He proved himself one by turning a rich maroon color and trying to swallow his Adam's apple. Not a word came from him.

"Quiet," murmured old Peebles, who looks exactly like a sheep. "Absolute quiet, please."

Wally rounded on him like a flash.

"Another considerate golfer, eh?" he snapped. "Now, gentlemen, under the rules governing tournament play I demand for my opponent and myself the right to go through. There are open holes ahead; you are not holding your place on the course . . ."

"Drive, Jim," interposed Watlington in that quiet way of his. "Don't pay any attention to him. Drive."

"But how can I drive while he's hopping up and down behind me? He puts me all off my swing!"

"I'm glad my protest has some effect on you," said Wally. "Now I understand that some of you are members of the Greens Committee of this club. As a member of the said club, I wish to make a formal request that we be allowed to pass."

"Denied," said Watlington. "Drive, Jim."

"Do you mean to say that you refuse us our rights—that you won't let us through?"

"Absolutely," murmured old Peebles. "Absolutely."

"But why—why? On what grounds?"

"On the grounds that you're too fresh," said Colonel Peck. "On the grounds that we don't want you to go through. Sit down and cool off."

"Drive, Jim," said Watlington. "You talk too much, young man."

"Wait a second," said Wally. "I want to get you all on record. I have made a courteous request . . ."

"And it has been refused," said old Peebles, blinking at both of us. "Gentlemen, you can't go through!"

"Is that final?"

"It is—absolutely."

And Watlington and Peck nodded.

"Drive, Jim!"

This time it was Hamilton who spoke.

"Pardon me," said Wally. He skipped out in front of the tee, lifted his cap, and made a low bow. "Members of the Greens Committee," said he, "and one other hog as yet unclassified, you are witnesses that I default my match to Mr. Curtiss. I do this rather than be forced to play behind four such pitiable dubs as you are. Golf is a gentleman's game, which doubtless accounts for your playing it so poorly. They tell me that you never let anyone through. God giving me strength, the day will come when you will not only allow people to pass you, but you will beg them to do it. Make a note of that. Come along, Curtiss. We'll play the last nine—for the fun of the thing."

"Oh, Curtiss!" It was Watlington speaking. "How many did you have him down when he quit?"

The insult would have made a saint angry, but no saint on the calendar could have summoned the vocabulary with which Wally replied. It was a wonderful exhibition of blistering invective. Watlington's thick hide stood him in good stead. He did not turn a hair or bat an eye, but waited for Wally to run out of breath. Then:

"Drive, Jim," said he.

Now I did not care to win that match by default, and I did everything in my power to arrange the matter otherwise. I offered to play the remaining holes later in the day or skip the eighth and begin all square on the ninth tee.

"Nothing doing," said Wally. "You're a good sport, but there are other men still in the tournament, and we're not allowed to concede anything. The default goes, but tell me one thing—why didn't you back me up on that kick?"

I was afraid he had noticed that I had been pretty much in the background throughout, so when he asked me, I told him the truth.

"Just a matter of bread and butter," said I. "My uncle's law firm handles all the Midland's business. I'm only the junior member, but I can't afford . . ."

"The Midland?" asked Wally.

"Yes, the Midland Manufacturing Company—Peck, Peebles, and Hamilton. Watlington's money is invested in the concern too."

"Why," said Wally, "that's the entire gang, isn't it—Greens Committee and all?"

"The Big Four," said I. "You can see how it is. They're rather important—as clients. There has been no end of litigation over the site for that new plant of theirs down on Third Avenue, and we've handled all of it."

But Wally hadn't been listening to me.

"So all the eggs are in one basket!" he exclaimed. "That simplifies matters. Now, if one of 'em had been a doctor and one of 'em a lawyer and one of 'em . . ."

"What are you talking about?" I demanded.

"Blest if I know!" said Wally.

So far as I could learn no official action was taken by the Big Four because of conduct and language unbecoming a gentleman and a golfer. Before I left the clubhouse, I had a word or two with Peebles. He was sitting at a table in the corner of the lounging room, nibbling at a piece of cheese and looking as meek as Moses.

"We—ah—considered the source," said he. "The boy is young and— rash, quite rash. His father was a mule skinner—it's in the blood—can't help it possibly. Yes, we considered the source. Absolutely!"

I didn't see very much of Wally after that, but I understood that he played the course in the mornings and gave the club a wide berth on Wednesdays and Saturdays. His default didn't help me any. I was handsomely licked in the finals—4 and 3, I believe it was. About that time something happened that knocked golf completely out of my mind.

IV

I was sitting in my office one morning when Atkinson, of the C. G. & N., called me on the phone. The railroad offices are in the same building, on the floor above ours.

"That you, Curtiss? I'll be right down. I want to see you."

Now, our firm handles the legal end for the C. G. & N., and it struck me that Atkinson's voice had a nervous worried ring to it. I was wondering what could be the matter when he came breezing in all out of breath.

"You told me," said he, "that there wouldn't be any trouble about that spur track along Third Avenue."

"For the Midland people, you mean? Oh, that's arranged for. All we have to do is appear before the City Council and make the request for a permit. Tomorrow morning it comes off. What are you so excited about?"

"This," said Atkinson. He pulled a big red handbill out of his pocket and unfolded it. "Possibly I'm no judge, Curtiss, but this seems to be enough to excite anybody."

I spread the thing out on my desk and took a look at it. Across the top was one of those headlines that hit you right between the eyes:

SHALL THE CITY COUNCIL LICENSE CHILD MURDER?

Well, that was a fair start, you'll admit, but it went on from there. I don't remember ever reading anything quite so vitriolic. It was a bitter attack on the proposed spur track along Third Avenue, which is the habitat of the downtrodden working man and the playground of his children. Judging solely by the handbill, anyone would have thought that the main idea of the C. G. & N. was to kill and maim as many toddling infants as possible. The Council was made an accessory before the fact, and the thing wound up with an appeal to class prejudice and a ringing call to arms.

"Men of Third Avenue, shall the City Council give to the bloated bondholders of an impudent monopoly the right to torture and murder your innocent babes? Shall your street be turned into a speedway for a modern car of Juggernaut? Let your answer be heard in the Council Chamber tomorrow morning—'No, a thousand times, no!'"

I read it through to the end. Then I whistled.

"This," said I, "is hot stuff—very hot stuff! Where did it come from?"

"The whole south end of town is plastered with bills like it," said Atkinson glumly. "What have we done now that they should be picking on us? When have we killed any children, I would like to know? What started this? Who started it? Why?"

"That isn't the big question," said I. "The big question is: Will the City Council stand hitched in the face of this attack?"

The door opened and the answer to that question appeared—Barney MacShane, officially of the rank and file of the City Council of our fair city, in reality the guiding spirit of that body of petty pirates. Barney was moist and nervous, and he held one of the bills in his right hand. His first words were not reassuring.

"All hell is loose—loose for fair!" said he. "Take a look at this thing."

"We have already been looking at it," said I with a laugh intended to be light and care-free. "What of it? You don't mean to tell me that you are going to let a mere scrap of paper bother you?"

Barney mopped his forehead and sat down heavily.

"You can laugh," said he, "but there is more than paper behind this. The whole west end of town is up in arms overnight, and I don't know why. Nobody ever kicked up such a rumpus about a spur track before. That's my ward, you know, and I just made my escape from a deputation of women and children. They treed me at the City Hall—before all the newspaper men—and they held their babies up in their arms and they dared me—yes, dared me—to let this thing go through. And the election coming on and all. It's hell, that's what it is!"

"But, Barney," I argued, "we are not asking for anything the city should not be glad to grant. Think what it means to your ward to have this fine big manufacturing plant in it! Think of the men who will have work . . ."

"I'm thinking of them," said Barney sorrowfully. "They're coming to the Council meeting tomorrow morning, and if this thing goes through, I may as well clean out my desk. Yes, they're coming, and so are their wives and their children, and they'll bring transparencies and banners and God knows what all . . ."

"But listen, Barney! This plant means prosperity to every one of your people . . ."

"They're saying they'll make it an issue in the next campaign," mumbled MacShane. "They say that if that spur track goes down on Third Avenue it's me out of public life—and they mean it too. God knows what's got into them all at once—they're like a nest of hornets. And the women voting now too. That makes it bad—awful bad! You know as well as I do that any agitation with children mixed up in it is the toughest thing in the world to meet." He struck at the poster with a sudden spiteful gesture. "From beginning to end," he snarled, "it's just an appeal not to let the railroad kill the kids!"

"But that's nonsense—bunk!" said Atkinson. "Every precaution will be taken to prevent accidents. You've got to think of the capital invested."

Barney rolled a troubled eye in his direction.

"You go down on Third Avenue," said he, "and begin talking to them people about capital! Try it once. What the hell do they care about capital? They was brought up to hate the sound of the word! You know and I know that capital ain't near as black as it's painted, but can you tell them that? Huh! And a railroad ain't ever got any friends in a gang standing round on the street corners!"

"But," said I, "this isn't a question of friends—it's a straight proposition of right and wrong. The Midland people have gone ahead and put up this big plant. They were given to understand there would be no opposition to the spur track going down. They've got to have it! The success of their business depends on it! Surely you don't mean to tell me that the Council will refuse this permit?"

"Well," said Barney slowly, "I've talked with the boys—Carter and Garvey and Dillon. They're all figuring on running again, and they're scared to death of it. Garvey says we'd be damned fools to go against an agitation like this—so close to election, anyhow."

I argued the matter from every angle—the good of the city, the benefit to Barney's ward—but I couldn't budge him.

"They say the voice of the people is the voice of God," said he, "but we know that most of the time it's only noise. Sometimes the noise kind of dies out, and then's the time to step in and cut the melon. But any kind of noise so close to election? Huh! Safety first!"

Before the meeting adjourned it was augmented by the appearance of the president and vice-president of the Midland Manufacturing Company, Colonel Jim Peck and old Peebles, and never had I seen those stiff-necked gentlemen so humanly agitated.

"This is terrible!" stormed the Colonel. "Terrible! This is unheard of! It is an outrage—a crime—a crying shame to the city! Think of our investment! Other manufacturing plants got their spur tracks for the asking. There was no talk of killing children. Why—why have we been singled out for attack—for—for blackmail?"

"You can cut out that kind of talk right now!" said Barney sternly. "There ain't a nickel in granting this permit, and you know it as well as I do. Nobody ain't trying to blackmail you! All the dough in town won't swing the boys into line behind this proposition while this rumpus is going on. And since you're taking that slant at it, here's the last word—sit tight and wait till after election!"

"But the pl-plant!" bleated Peebles, tearing a blotter to shreds with shaking fingers. "The plant! Think of the loss of time—and we—we expected to open up next month!"

"Go ahead and open up," said Barney. "You can truck your stuff to the depots, can't you? Yes, yes—I get you about the loss! Us boys in the Council—we got something to lose too. Now here it is, straight from the shoulder, and you can bet on it." Barney spoke slowly, wagging his forefinger at each word. "If that application comes up tomorrow morning, with the Council chamber jammed with folks from the south end of the town—good-a-by, John! Fare thee well! It ain't in human nature to commit political suicide when a second term is making eyes at you. Look at our end of it for a while. We got futures to think of, too, and Garvey—Garvey wants to run for mayor someday. You can't afford to have that application turned down, can you? Of course not. Have a little sense. Keep your shirts on. Get out and see who's behind this thing. Chances are somebody wants something. Find out what it is—rig up a compromise—get him to call off the dogs. Then talk to me again, and I'll promise you it'll go through as slick as a greased pig!"

"I believe there's something in that," said I. "We've never run into such a hornets' nest as this before. There must be a reason. Atkinson, you've got a lot of gumshoe men on your staff. Why don't you turn 'em loose to locate this opposition?"

"You're about two hours late with that suggestion," said the railroad representative. "Our sleuths are on the job now. If they find out anything I'll communicate with you P. D. Q."

"Good!" ejaculated Colonel Peck. "And if it's money . . ."

"Aw, you make me sick!" snapped Barney MacShane. "You think money can do everything, don't you? Well, it can't! For one thing, it couldn't get me to shake hands with a stiff like you!"

I was called away from the dinner table on the following Friday evening. Watlington was on the telephone.

"'That you, Curtiss? Well, we think we've got in touch with the bug under the chip. Can you arrange to meet us in Room 85 at the Hotel Brookmore at nine tonight? . . . No, I can't tell you a thing about it. We're asked to be there—you're asked to be there—and that's as far as my information goes. Don't be late."

When I entered Room 85, four men were seated at a long table. They were Elsberry J. Watlington, Colonel Jim Peck, Samuel Alexander Peebles, and W. Cotton Hamilton. They greeted me with a certain amount of nervous irritability. The Big Four had been through a cruel week and showed the marks of strain.

"Where's Atkinson?" I asked.

"It was stipulated, expressly stipulated," said old Peebles, "that only the five of us should be present. The whole thing is most mysterious. I—I don't like the looks of it."

"Probably a hold-up!" grunted Colonel Peck.

Watlington didn't say anything. He had aged ten years, his heavy smooth-shaven face was set in stern lines and his mouth looked as if it might have been made with a single slash of a razor.

Hamilton mumbled to himself and kept trying to light the end of his thumb instead of his cigar. Peck had his watch in his hand. Peebles played a tattoo on his chin with his fingers.

"Good thing we didn't make that application at the Council meeting," said Hamilton. "I never saw such a gang of thugs!"

"Male and female!" added Colonel Peck. "Well, time's up! Whoever he is, I hope he won't keep us waiting!"

"Ah!" said a cheerful voice. "You don't like to be held up on the tee, do you, Colonel?"

There in the doorway stood Wally Wallace, beaming upon the Big Four. Not even on the stage have I ever seen anything to match the expressions on the faces around that table. Old Peebles's mouth kept opening and shutting, like the mouth of a fresh caught carp. The others were frozen, petrified. Wally glanced at me as he advanced into the room, and there was a faint trembling of his left eyelid.

"Well," said Wally briskly, "shall we proceed with the business of the meeting?"

"Business!" Colonel Peck exploded like a firecracker.

"With—you?" It was all Watlington could do to tear the two words out of his throat. He croaked like a big bullfrog.

"With me," said Wally, bowing and taking his place at the head of the table. "Unless," he added, "you would prefer to discuss the situation with the rank and file of the Third Avenue Country Club."

The silence that followed that remark was impressive. I could hear somebody's heart beating. It may have been my own. As usual Colonel Peck was first to recover the power of speech, and again as usual he made poor use of it.

"You—you young whelp!" he gurgled. "So it was . . ."

"Shut up, Jim!" growled Watlington, whose eyes had never left Wally's face. Hamilton carefully placed his cigar in the ashtray and tried to put a match into his mouth. Then he turned on me, sputtering.

"Are you in on this?" he demanded.

"Be perfectly calm," said Wally. "Mr. Curtiss is not in on it, as you so elegantly express it. I am the only one who is in on it. Me, myself, W. W. Wallace, at your service. If you will favor me with your attention, I will explain . . ."

"You'd better!" ripped out the Colonel.

"Ah," said the youngster, grinning at Peck, "always a little nervous on the tee, aren't you?"

"Drive, young man!" said Watlington.

A sudden light flickered in Wally's eyes. He turned to Elsberry J. with an expression that was almost friendly.

"Do you know," said he, "I'm beginning to think there may be human qualities in you after all."

Watlington grunted and nodded his head. "Take the honor!" said he.

Wally rose and laid the tips of his fingers on the table.

"Members of the Greens Committee and one other"—and here he looked at Hamilton, whose face showed he had not forgotten the unclassified hog—"we are here this evening to arrange an exchange of courtesies. You think you represent the Midland Manufacturing Company at this meeting. You do not. You represent the Sundown Golf and Country Club. I represent the Third Avenue Country Club—an organization lately formed. You may have heard something of it, though not under that name."

He paused to let this sink in.

"Gentlemen," he continued, "you may recall that I once made a courteous request of you for something that was entirely within my rights. You made an arbitrary ruling on that request. You refused to let me through. You told me I was too fresh and advised me to sit down and cool off. I see by your faces that you recall the occasion.

"You may also recall that I promised to devote myself to the task of teaching you to be more considerate of others. Gentlemen, I am the opposition to your playing through on Third Avenue. I am the Man Behind. I am the Voice of the People. I am a singleton on the course, holding you up while I sink a putt. If you ask me why, I will give you your own words in your teeth: You can't go through because I don't want you to go through."

Here he stopped long enough to light a cigarette, and again his left eyelid flickered, though he did not look at me. I think if he had I should have erupted.

"You see," said he, flipping the match into the air, "it has been necessary to teach you a lesson—the lesson, gentlemen, of courtesy on the course, consideration for others. I realized this could never be done on a course where you have power to make the rules—or break them. So I selected another course. Members of the Greens Committee and one other, you do not make the rules on Third Avenue. You are perfectly within your rights in asking to go through; but I have blocked you. I have made you sit down on the bench and cool off. Gentlemen, how do you like being held up when you want to play through? How does it feel?"

I do not regret my inability to quote Colonel Peck's reply to this question.

"Quit it, Jim!" snapped Watlington. "Your bark was always worse than your bite, and it's not much of a bark at that—'Sound and fury, signifying nothing.' Young man, I take it you are the chairman of the Greens Committee of this Third Avenue Country Club, empowered to act. May I ask what are our chances of getting through?"

"I know I'm going to like you—in time!" exclaimed Wally. "I feel it coming on. Let's see, tomorrow is Saturday, isn't it?"

"What's that got to do with it?" mumbled Hamilton.

"Much," answered Wally. "Oh, much, I assure you! I expect to be at the Sundown Club tomorrow." His chin shot out and his voice carried the sting of a lash. "I expect to see you gentlemen there, playing your usual crawling foursome. I expect to see you allowing your fellow members to pass you on the course. You might even invite them to come through—you might insist on it, courteously, you understand, and with such grace as you may be able to muster. I want to see every member of that club play through you—every member!"

"All d-damned nonsense!" bleated Peebles, sucking his fingers.

"Shut up!" ordered Watlington savagely. "And, young man, if we do this—what then?"

"Ah, then!" said Wally. "Then the reward of merit. If you show me you can learn to be considerate of others—if you show me you can be courteous on the course where you make the rules—I feel safe in promising that you will be treated with consideration on this other course that has been mentioned. Yes, quite safe. In fact, gentlemen, you may even be asked to play through on Third Avenue!"

"But this agitation!" began Hamilton.

"Was paid for by the day," smiled the brazen rascal, with a graceful inclination of his head. "People may be hired to do anything—even to annoy prominent citizens and frighten a City Council."

Hamilton stirred uneasily, but Wally read his thought and froze him with a single keen glance. "Of course," said he, "you understand that what has been done once may be done again. Sentiment crystallizes—when helped out with a few more red handbills—a few more speeches on the street corners . . . "

"The point is well taken!" interrupted Watlington hurriedly. "Damn well taken! Young man, talk to me. I'm the head of this outfit. Pay no attention to Jim Peck. He's nothing but a bag of wind. Hamilton doesn't count. His nerves are no good. Peebles—he's an old goat. I'm the one with power to act. Talk to me. Is there anything else you want?"

"Nothing," said Wally. "I think your streak of consideration is likely to prove a lasting one. If not—well, I may have to spread this story round town a bit . . . "

"Oh, my Lord!" groaned Colonel Peck.

It was a noble and inspiring sight to see the Big Four, caps in hand, inviting the common people to play through. The entire club marched through them—too full of amazement to demand explanations. Even Purdue McCormick, trudging along with a putter in one hand and a mid-iron in the other, without a bag, without a caddie, without a vestige of right in the wide world, even Purdue was coerced into passing them. At dusk he was found wandering aimlessly about on the seventeenth fairway, babbling to himself. We fear he will never be the same again.

I have received word from Barney MacShane that the City Council will be pleased to grant a permit to lay a spur track on Third Avenue. The voice of the people, he says, has died away to a faint murmuring. Someday I think I will tell Barney the truth. He does not play golf, but he has a sense of humor.

Winning the Double Crown

Chick Evans

THERE WAS AN UNUSUAL CIRCUMSTANCE CONNECTED WITH THE National Amateur Championship of 1916, on the links of the Merion Cricket Club near Philadelphia. It was the first time since the national championships had been instituted that the holders of the two titles dwelt in the same city. Robert Gardner, the Amateur champion, and I, the Open champion, had been delayed a little in setting out for the scene of conflict; he by an infected finger, and I by business, but oddly enough we happened to pick the same train going east. The qualifying rounds of the big event were to begin on Monday, September 4, but we arrived only two days prior to the start.

Play for the American Golfer Trophy, a team event, was staged as a preliminary. In that competition Robert and I represented the Chicago Golf Club, and came in third with a 72, not a bad showing for the first time over the course. In view of the result of the 1920 championship, it may be interesting to state that we were one stroke better than Davidson Herron and Max Marston.

On account of his ailing finger, Robert only played the eighteen holes of the event, but in the afternoon Clayton Ingraham, a former Midlothain member, and I played Willie Howland and Paul Hunter of Chicago, and I see from notes made at the time that Howland played extremely well and the rest of us fairly so.

The Merion Cricket Club is fortunate in possessing two good courses, and in consequence it was able to try the experiment of having the qualifying rounds played over two courses, thus relieving the great congestion, and shortening the time.

The east links, the Merion course proper, is fine and well-trapped with large greens but not so fast, I was happy to observe, as the usual eastern greens. The west course had few artificial hazards, but many natural ones, and the greens were small and a bit tricky. It was one of those courses on which it seemed easy to make a phenomenally small score or an extraordinarily big one. I went over it on Sunday and set an amateur record of 71. The next day, in the qualifying round, I played rather badly, thus justifying my description of its qualities.

When the officials began to write the scores in the qualifying rounds on the board, a distinct shock passed over the spectators, for never have I known them so high in a national tournament, for 80s were plentiful. Those who played over the east course in the morning finished over the west course in the afternoon and, as the big figures were written down, there was much speculation over the ability of prominent players to pass.

The low medal score of 153 was made by W. C. Fownes of Oakmont. Max Marston came in second with 155, and E. M. Byers, another Pittsburgher, was third with 157. Herron failed to qualify. There were only eight scores under 160, and six played off a tie at 167 for last place. Out of the dozen or more Chicagoans who had entered, only four qualified: F. R. Blossom and I at 158, Robert Gardner, 160, and D. E. Sawyer at 162. John Anderson had a peculiar experience, making a 90 on the east course and a 70 on the west, safely qualifying and shattering my record of the day before. The two Atlanta boys, Perry Adair and Bobby Jones, the latter a youngster of fourteen years, both qualified.

When the draw was concluded I found myself paired with Nelson Whitney of New Orleans, a man whose playing, the early part of the season, had led me to consider as one of the strongest contenders for championship honors. I knew a hard day was before me, but I was glad to see that no Chicagoans would be brought together in the first round. It was the first time since I had played in the event that this had been the ease.

The first day of match-play rounds was baking hot, the course was dry, and the greens lightning fast. My match with Whitney was trying, both in and out, with never more than a hole separating us in the morning. In the afternoon, however, the game was more my way, and it was a relief when it ended on the thirty-fourth green in my favor. It was my hardest match in the whole tournament until I reached the final.

Ned Sawyer had an inch-by-inch match with John Anderson, the former losing on the thirty-seventh green when he missed a three-foot putt. Gardner did not have much trouble defeating John Ward, but a great deal of surprise was expressed when Fownes, the medalist of the event, went down before Buxton. The latter, however, had beaten the Pittsburgher before, and is really a very fine player. Henry Topping was defeated by W. P. Smith by a single putt that hit the cup, poised on its edge, and stayed there. But the wonder of the day was Bobby Jones, the fourteen-year-old boy from Atlanta. His defeat of E. M. Byers, ex-National champion, was sensational. Perry Adair, also won his match.

At the end of the day when the slain were all accounted for, we found that half of the Chicagoans had been swept away, only Robert Gardner and I remaining.

On Wednesday, Bob Gardner was expected to have a difficult match with Max Marston, and the Mrs. Gardner had come down from Maine to see it, but the game was rather disappointing, for at no time did Marston have a chance. It was pleasantly spectacular, however, for the gallery was very large, and the golf was well worth looking at.

Bobby Jones went on his victorious way, defeating Dyer, who himself is a fine player, by uncanny golf. White defeated Kirkby, Hunter lost to Anderson, and Ormiston to Guilford, and I defeated W. P. Smith rather easily. After our matches Bob Gardner and I shook hands with the hope that we might meet in the final. The day's weather was fine, gray skies, and less slippery greens.

It was blazing hot on Thursday, but in spite of it a tremendous crowd followed the Gardner-Jones match. Philadelphia had taken mightily to the little Southerner. It was hard on the more experienced player because popular sympathy usually goes out to youngsters. The Atlanta marvel came to luncheon one up, but Gardner played a strong game in the afternoon, winning by 4 and 3.

I had no trouble in my match with Anderson, my game was coming right and I defeated him 9 and 8.

The four left in the semifinals were compelled to play under sultry weather conditions. The very ball seemed sticky, and never have I found the heat more oppressive. Gardner was playing Guilford, but I did not see any of the match being busily engaged with my own. Apparently Guilford never had a chance, and I was told that Bob was steadily out-driving the long-distance player from Massachusetts.

In my match with Corkran, I lost the second hole, but after squaring that I led him all the way. He was a good little player, however, but I won on the sixteenth hole in the afternoon, which meant I was safely past the semifinal round. The afternoon had been marked by a shower, accompanied by violent thunder and lightning and fierce winds.

When Saturday came the weather and course had both been freshened by the rain of the previous day. I thought I had never seen a more beautiful morning than when Gardner and I stood at the first tee ready for the match that would decide the National Amateur Championship. Even at that early hour there was a big gallery, estimated at three thousand, and this was more than trebled before the day was over, for Philadelphia is a fine gallery town.

I began well, winning the first hole in 3, a stroke under par. It was a good start, but Robert squared the match three times in the course of the morning round. I went to luncheon, however, gaily enough, 3 up. At the clubhouse a friend from Edgewater summed up the prospect with the remark that "Bob Gardner can't give Chick Evans three on 18 holes— and win." That sounded encouraging, but very early in the afternoon it began to look as if he could.

The gallery had seemed large when we started in the morning, but the crowd at the first tee in the afternoon spread out in all directions. We made our tee shots down a long aisle lined with people. This time I began badly, and the hole I had played so beautifully under par in the morning, I messed up into a 5 in the afternoon. We both played the second hole under par, but by the firth hole Gardner had wiped away my lead of 3, and it was looking bad for Chick Evans. There may have been a little overconfidence on my part, but there was certainly good playing on his.

I won the sixth by a full midiron shot, the like of which I had practiced over and over again, dozens of times during the twelve years of climb to this opportunity. I won the seventh. Gardner took the ninth with a beautiful 2 to my 3. On the tenth I holed the longest putt—a thirty-footer—that I had ever made in a championship. It gave me a half, and I followed my advantage by holing a sloping four-footer.

The thirteenth is only 125 yards. It has a villainously undulating green with a brook on two sides and traps on the other. That day the pin was on the far edge of the fast, hard green. If I played safe it would give Gardner an easy half. I determined to play the psychological shot as close to the flag as possible, knowing that if I got a good one he would be obliged to try for a 2. Danger yawned everywhere, and my heart gave a tug as my ball stopped a foot from the back edge. Bob's went into a trap. From then on it was easy.

The crowd that had swept the course like a mighty army all the afternoon had now been increased by the people at the clubhouse and they swarmed everywhere over to the fourteenth hole, which we halved in 4.

The end came on the next hole. When Robert grasped my hand in acknowledgment of defeat, someone in the crowd shouted: "The double crown for Evans!"

As we got our medals, in a sort of daze, someone pushed my mother forward. She was looking very little in that immense crowd as we embraced. A free ride to the clubhouse half a mile away on the shoulders of Eddie Moore of Edgewater and others, with a cheering crowd following, furnished the climax.

A paper said that evening: "When a slight, elderly woman under whose glasses tears of joy glistened came through the crowd, Chick threw his arms about her and kissed her, and the crowd went wild with enthusiasm, for it was his mother and all week she had followed her son over the course."

One of the papers called it "the greatest ovation ever given to an American golfer." I am no judge of that, but I do know that a Philadelphia gallery is a delightful one.

When the wires flashed broadcast the news of my final victory, a deluge of congratulations poured in. One reason for a special interest in my success was that I had been trying for the prize a long time. Then the fact that it was the first time in this country that an open champion had ever played an amateur champion for the amateur title, made the event unique. Also Robert Gardner and I had never before played against each other in the national event. Those congratulations were as sweet as the victory.

My victory gave me the proud distinction of being the only golfer in this country who had ever held both amateur and open title at the same time. In England, John Ball had won both British amateur and open titles the year in which I was born.

Boy Golfer Falls Before Champion

Special to the *New York Times*

Philadelphia, Sept. 7—The blow has fallen. At one fell swoop, the last metropolitan players and Bobby Jones, the youthful marvel from Atlanta, were eliminated from the competition for the national amateur championship in the third round of match play over the links of the Merion Cricket Club today. It took a full-grown national champion to overcome the prodigy of the links, however, and Bobby succumbed to the prowess of Bob Gardner only after the gamest kind of struggle, leading by 1 up at the end of the morning round, to lose out in the afternoon by 4 up and 8 to play.

Though his rise to fame was meteoric, the end of the little Georgia golf marvel in the national amateur championship was long and lingering. At the start of the first round he looked like a winner, and at the end of the round, 1 up on the national champion, it seemed more and more as if the stalwart athlete, former holder of the world's pole vaulting record, famed alike for his prowess on the athletic field and the links, was to fail by the hand of the chunky, rosy-cheeked, blond little Southerner, who was driving like a wizard, playing his irons with his touch of a professional, and putting with that supreme confidence that youth alone knows.

The lad, lest but out of the thousands who watched and followed the match, Bobby Jones Jr., Atlanta, was the last person in the throng to expect his defeat. His courage was high, and his confidence was unshaken until Bob Gardner curled into the cup on the fifteenth green, the twenty-foot putt that settled the match, 4 and 3.

The boy's chubby hand shot out and grasped the less-muscular fingers of Gardner in a congratulating clasp, and then he mingled with the multi-color clad throng that followed the contest over hill and dale, under the glare of the hottest sun of the season. In his short-sleeved white shirt, soaked through with perspiration, with his dusty gray trousers and his well-worn shoes singling him out from the gayly comparisoned onlookers, he trudged his way alone to the clubhouse, with his dreams of a national championship vanished in a short half hour. Crying; not a bit of it. Whistling; whistling a comic song, twirling his golf club in his hands, and greeting sympathetic words with a smile, he strolled off the links where in the last few days he has made for himself a reputation that will long endure in the history of American golf. When such a boy takes a beating, he will come back for another, and another, until finally victory is his.

It was strange for Gardner to feel that a golf gallery was against him. The present national champion is beloved alike by players and spectators. No more popular champion has arisen in late years at any sport, yet hardly a person in the great crowd that followed the match around the links was hoping Gardner would defeat the game little Southerner, who has proved the sensation of the tournament. Mild handclapping greeted the fine shots of the national champion, but the successes of the boy were signals for outbursts of enthusiasm that fairly carried away the multitude. When Bobby holed on the ninth green in the morning match, the applause was spontaneous and prodigious.

For a national amateur champion, Gardner made a most inauspicious start in the morning round against the boy. He heeled his toe shot and it scooted off through the long grass behind two apple trees that barred a clear shot to the green. He took his brassie and endeavored to play to the green through a narrow opening in the trees, but his ball crossed a bunker to the right of the green and ran out of bounds across a road. Dropping another ball and attempting to carry out his original plan, he smote the bough of one of the apple trees a stunning blow. The apple tree was not seriously injured, but Gardner's chances of winning the hole were absolutely ruined. He played up short of the green, however, and then gave

Bobby a chance to play a second shot after his fine drive. The boy overran the green a little and came to rest in a mound of sand.

"Never give up," is Gardner's motto, so he made his fifth shot and put the ball within twelve feet of the pin, waiting to see how many shots the youngster would take to get out of trouble. Bobby walked over to the sand pile, chipped out the ball with a little motion of his wrists, and holed his putt for a 4, standing 1 up on the title holder.

The youngster drove first from the next tee and hooked his ball into a bunker. "There I knew it," chorused some of the faint hearts in the galley, "he can't stand prosperity; he'll lose this surely." Calling for his jigger, the boy picked the ball from the top of the sand and sent it 150 yards toward the green. Gardner placed his drive in some long grass near the fence, and then tumbled his second into a pit on the other side of the course. The boy was nicely on the green in 3, took two putts, won the hole, and was 2 up on the national champion with only two holes played.

This was too good to be true, so the youngster proceeded to give away the third hole when it seemed he had a fair-sized mortgage on it. Gardner was in the long grass by a fence on his tee shot, and rolled into more long grass on a mound to the left of the green on his second. With a fine drive and a clear shot to the green, the boy unaccountably sent his second shot far to the right of the green, with a dangerous pitch back across to be within hailing distance of the pin. The lad tried it—and failed, dropping short into a yawning trap and going over the green entirely on his fourth shot.

The fourth hole was in a way one of the most remarkable of the match, and well displayed the qualities that have brought this youngster to the fore, even if he did lose out and square the match. Gardner got a wonderful drive with just a short chip to the green, which is 355 yards from the tee. The Atlanta youth was in the long grass by the out-of-bounds fence on his tee shot, tried for the green on his second, but failed to get out of the grass, tried again on his third, but struck the side of the green and rolled down by Gardner's drive. Gardner then chipped up to within fifteen feet of the pin, and the boy just hopped up on the edge of the green and stayed there, some twenty-five feet from the flag. He had played 4, and the title holder lay with 2 putts for a sure 4.

The hole was lost and everyone knew it—that is everyone except the boy. Give up the hole? Never! He stepped up and banged that twenty-five-foot putt into the back of the cup for his 5. Certainly he lost, when Gardner had an easy 4, but he holed that putt and gave the crowd an inkling of the courage and skill that defeated Eben Byers, former national champion, on two successive days.

Young Jones had lost two holes, and he lost two more, four in succession, enough to worry the most hardened veteran, or to weaken the stoutest heart. The fifth hole he lost by playing to the green by way of bunkers and rough instead of the neatly clipped fair green, and the sixth was given to Gardner by the youngster when he took three putts from the edge of the green.

The short seventh hole across the gully was a terrible strain on the nerves of the youngster, but he has become hardened to such things in the last few days and survived the ordeal. Gardner drove first, or rather he attempted to drive, missing his shot so completely that it barely rolled off the front of the tee into the long grass. The boy made the long carry successfully and was on the green in 1.

The interest in the boy was certainly taking away from the credit due to Gardner, for on this shot and on that he was showing the prowess that won his title for him, and yet the crowd was plainly first and last for the youngster. Gardner put an iron shot right upon the green and holed out in two putts for his 4, and by taking three putts from his landing place the boy gained only a half, where he should have had a safe margin of victory.

The youngster was still 2 down, but he gained one hole on the eight, where the national title holder drove out of bounds, and on the ninth green, after Gardner had run up for a sure 3, the boy dropped a twenty-foot putt for a 2 that squared the match. Then the welkin rang with applause for the boy. For a fourteen-year-old lad to lose four holes in succession to take three putts on three successive greens, to stand 2 down to the national amateur champion at the sixth hole, and to square it at the ninth bespoke a stout arm and a bold heart, and the feat received the appreciation it merited.

The boy went into the lead at 1 up on the twelfth green when Gardner missed a short putt, and he would have been 2 up at the thirteenth had not the title holder made a beautiful putt to get a half. The boy's second shot laid Gardner's second a three-quarter stymie, with a fair-sized putt still to be made. The Hinsdale player had only a small portion of the cup to aim for, but he aimed truly and the ball dropped in for a half in 2.

The putt he made on this green, however, he more than missed on the next, and the boy was 2 up at the fourteenth. The youngster put his second within twelve feet of the pin for a sure 4. He just missed getting his 3, but, as Gardner barely got on the green, and took three putts, no harm was done, and he was 2 up again.

Both drove to the seventeenth green in the face of the wind, but the boy made a poor approach putt, and seemed to have lost the hole. Gardner ran his ball up for a sure 3, when, to his unbounded astonishment, the youngster took a circuitous side-hill route to the cup, and his ball disappeared for a half in 3. The boy lost the home hole by topping his drive, and was only 1 up at the end of the round.

Only 1 up! Could even that be expected of a fourteen-year-old boy in his first national championship, playing against the defending champion? But the youngster should have been at least 3 up, with any kind of luck and with any sort of putting on half a dozen greens.

All through the morning round, the rangy Gardner was looking quizzically at the short, stumpy figure of "the pride of the South," and the wondering look was still on the face of the champion when he stopped for luncheon. "It's too much for me to figure out," he confessed. "I can't see how he does it."

Gardner is one of the longest drivers in the country, yet the boy was right up with him every time. On his irons to the green, on chip shots for the pin, on putting in a pinch the boy matched him stroke for stroke and came out a little the better. And as for a fighting heart, not even Bob Gardner, who is the last word in courage, could outgame the little fellow.

The first hole in the afternoon found the match all square after the boy bounced into and out of a pit on his second. He was short of the green, and lost the hole, 4 to 5. He lost the second and was 1 down when he hooked his drive into the rough and put his second in a bunker, but he squared things on the next hole in beautiful style. Both he and Gardner were bunkered to the left of the green on their second shots. Gardner had a bad lie and was lucky to get out, but the boy was well located, and chipped up within four feet of the pin, getting a 4 that won the hole.

With an easy chip to the fourth green, the youngster made one of his few poor shots of the day, falling short into a bunker on the left. He failed to get out on his third, messed things up considerably, and surrendered to Gardner who had a sure 4. Although the sixth, seventh, and eighth were halved, these were really the holes that decided the match, for the youngster seemed to have each and every one of them at his mercy, only to have the irrepressible Mr. Gardner chip up for a half each time, taking only one putt on each green.

The ninth hole was a sad affair for the youngster, and after putting his tee shot into a bunker to the left, he shot his ball far over the green in his attempt to get out and found himself 2 down at the turn. On the tenth he allotted into a bunker and became 3 down, and on the twelfth a shot out of bounds, and another that brought up close to a concrete bridge, put him 4 down, the ultimate depths to which he sank.

The next two holes were halved, and Gardner was dormie 4 as he stood on the fifteenth tee. He put his first shot out of bounds, his second well on the fairway, and his third twenty feet from the pin. The youngster played the hole perfectly with a sure 4, but what could such a little fellow do against the big, tall national champion from Chicago, who dove out of bounds and still persisted in getting a par 4 on the hole? For the title holder sent a twenty-foot putt spinning into the cup that dashed the youngster's hopes to the ground, defeated him 4 and 3, and eliminated him from further play in the twenty-second national amateur golf championship.

So passed the boy, amid the mourning of the assembled multitude, but he left a record that will be claimed with pride in future years by his descendants to the third and fourth generation, and by their sisters and their cousins and their aunts to the tenth degree of kinship.

Homebred and Foreign Pros Compared

Walter C. Hagen

THERE HAS ALWAYS BEEN A GREAT RIVALRY IN ENGLAND BETWEEN THE English and the Scottish over their respective abilities at golf. The question of which was the better player, the English pro or the Scottish pro, came up for discussion some three hundred years ago and is still an open debate on the other side of the Atlantic.

Of recent years, a new factor has appeared in the field that has at last come to be recognized as an important institution, this the American-made professional, often referred to as the "Homebred." It took over twenty years to develop this branch of golf, but once developed it has made its presence felt in the golf world. For six years, not a foreign-born professional has been able to annex our open championship and although we are still in the minority we have been more than able to hold our own on the links in competitions.

This is no attempt to gloat over the Scottish or English pro, to whom every homebred professional owes a great debt of gratitude. We have learned our golf from the foreign-born pro. We also learned the art of club making and green keeping and if we have succeeded in becoming more or less proficient in our line, it speaks well for our teachers. Our success has not been due to the fact that there are a poorer class of foreign pros in this country. This was the argument first advanced when home talent began to win tournaments. It is, in fact, far from the truth. The old crowd that came over at first swept everything before them. If it wasn't a Scotchman winning, it was an Englishman and no thought was ever given to the American pro principally because there was no such a thing.

There must be caddies, however, and as they couldn't very well import them, this job fell to the American youth. Then as golf became popular, there were club makers and assistant to the pro and naturally the boys were keen to enter tournaments once they had something to stand on.

It has taken all of twenty-five years to bring about this change. Almost every spring the foreign professionals have been reinforced with high class material from across the big water hazard. The homebred has developed at a fast rate until at the present time we are able to make a creditable showing in point of numbers as well as good players.

I wish there was some sort of friendly rivalry between the homebred and the foreigner that would bring about an annual team match between them such as they have in Great Britain each year in the international matches between the Scotch and the English pros. The foreigners say this is one of the important events of the year in golf—or was before the war—and is cagerly looked forward to. Such a tournament would help to make better golfers our of our own players. The time to stage this event would be the day before the Professional Golfers' Championship in the fall. I believe it would attract more attention than the amateur-professional four-ball contest. This is no presumption on my part to pick a team, but I can think of a dozen or more homebreds who would fit in nicely.

The Scot gets the most enjoyment out of his golf. The English pro, too, takes the game less seriously than the American. It was a Scotchman who told me this. He said the homebred had come to the front because he was becoming a student of the game and was willing to give no end of time to practice to perfect his playing. The Scot, as a rule, is content with what he has and is perhaps less keen to practice.

The American boy is divided between baseball and golf. The lure of professional baseball attracts a lot of youths who otherwise might have taken to golf and become professionals. In England there is no game that requires as many players as baseball. Professional cricket is not a menace to golf, nor is professional soccer. It is little wonder that so many of them turn their attention to the royal and ancient pastime.

My own case was like that of thousands of American boys who play baseball. It was one time my ambition to be a great pitcher, and I was having no little success pitching for the school team. My colleagues insisted I was good enough to play on a big-league team and one day I got my chance. I received an offer from a certain famous club that would almost have turned any boy's head. About this time I heard the call of the links. It was with great difficulty that I was able to make up my mind between the baseball diamond and the golf links. I had luring offers from both fields and I realized it must be one or the other. It is hard to tell just what leads a person to make up his mind when opportunity knocks at his door with two tempting offers at the same time. It may be fate, or perhaps it is only luck which way you turn, but in this case golf appealed to me a little stronger than baseball and won my affections. I have never had any reason to regret having selected a golf career. The golf pro undoubtedly has a much longer career ahead of him than the ballplayer has, although the professional golfer is not paid in anywhere near the proportion that the ballplayer is.

However over the stretch of time, the odds must be greatly in favor of the golf pro. The latter at the age of fifty is by no means an old man or has he outlived his usefulness. Just at this time of life, by his great experience on the links, he is as much if not of more value to the club than in the heyday of his youth when he is thinking only of championship titles and trying to hold up some sort of a reputation as a tournament player.

Until the open championship at Englewood in 1909, the home-bred pro was never considered as a serious contender in any of the important open tournaments. It was therefore little wonder that Tommy McNamara's feat of finishing second to George Sargent in this even attracted a great deal of attention and led a certain amateur to predict that sooner or later the American-born professional would hold his own with the foreign pro. But hardly did this gentleman realize that this would come true so soon. On the following year, Johnnie McDermott, one of the most sensational professionals this country has ever turned out, entered the limelight for the first time and finished in a tie with Alex Smith and his brother Macdonald, at Philadelphia. Alex won in the play oft, but Johnnie got second place. This was the last time the foreign-born pro has been able to take away an open championship from the home talent.

McDermott's success encouraged a great many youngsters to take up tournament play. Heretofore the American-made professional had kept strictly in the background principally through modesty. He felt he had no chance measuring strokes with the English and the Scotch, but when on the following year, to be exact in 1911, McDermott again finished in a three-cornered tie for first place, having for one of his rivals Mike J. Brady of Boston, another homebred, the American golfing public began to realize that home talent amounted to something. McDermott won the play-off and Mike Brady finished second, both beating out G. O. Simpson, who, by the way, was the professional at Wheaton, the Chicago course, where the championship was held.

The next year at Buffalo, McDermott had things his own way, finishing in front with a lead of two strokes, but the man in second place was another homebred, Tom McNamara of Boston, who proved that his former good showing at Englewood three years before was no mere flash in the pan. In this same tournament, four out of the first seven players were American pros. The list included the three mentioned before and Jack Dawling, who joined the star performers for the first time.

Two other American boys earned recognition in 1913. This was the year that Francis Ouimet gained his sensational victory over Vardon and Ray. The situation was becoming desperate according to the English way of looking at it, as Lord Northcliffe, evidently believing it would take more than the present foreign talent in America to head off the homebred uprising, sent over Vardon and Ray, two of the very best English pros, and with them came Reid and Tellier, two other stars from the other side. How Ouimet, then comparatively unknown, first tied and then defeated Vardon and Ray in the play-off is history of the game that we are all familiar with. The other American boy to make a showing for the first time that year was myself. I landed in a tie with three others for fourth place, and as this was my first tournament I was just as much pleased at this performance as I was to win the championship the next year at Chicago. This time I was closely pressed by Chick Evans and a little lower down the list were the names of Francis Ouimet and Mike Brady. Again the home talent got in its deadly work as among the first six there were two American amateurs and two American pros.

By this time I think the English and the Scotch realized we had come to the front to stay or at least to hold our own in the campaigns to follow. The open tournament at Baltusrol, notable for the fine entry list of stars, including a number of players who had just come over from England, brought another pair of Americans to the front. This time it was Jerry Travers who won and added an open title to his list of amateur championships. For the third time, Tommy McNamara landed in second place. Then came last year's championship at Minneapolis. The foreign pros thought it about time to call a halt on the steady march of the homebreds and a group of players, headed by the irrepressible Jock Hutchinson, got most of the money. Among the leaders were Long Jim Barnes, Wilfred Reid, Gil Nicholls, and George Sargent. While heading off the local talent, they were not quite good enough, however, to stop the steady advances of Chick Evans, who got the coveted title, bringing American golf once more to the fore and making the third time that an amateur had been successful in landing this blue ribbon event.

The last two championships were played without the entry of J. J. McDermott, who through illness was forced to retire from tournament play. This recalls to mind the sensational career of little "Mac" who seven years ago at the Philadelphia Cricket Club in the open championship announced to a group of pros who were speculating on the chances of the various players, that he would have to be reckoned with. "Mac" was then almost unknown, and he, nor any other American-made golfer, was considered as a possibility. If he had failed to make good, the incident would have been quickly forgotten as only an idle boast of an over enthusiastic youth. But "Mac" did make good by tying the Smith brothers, although he lost first place in the play-off. That same year, two months later, he showed that his sudden rise to fame was well earned as he finished second at Deal in the Metropolitan open. Again, Alex Smith was his conqueror, but "Mac" won a place for himself at the top of the heap in the next two National championships.

A Rub of the Green

William Almon Wolff

IT SHOULD HAVE BEEN CLEAR ON THE DAY THAT OLD BURNETT FIRST appeared at the club with a bright new bag and a lot of bright, new, shiny sticks, and a badly worried expression that something cataclysmic had happened to him. A man born with Burnett's disposition, who had lived until his middle thirties with an unregenerate contempt of the royal and ancient game of golf, wasn't going to be converted to it overnight, so to speak, unless there was something mighty important behind the conversion. But if you have ever lived in a community that revolves about its golf club as the earth and the other planets revolve about the sun, you will understand that Burnett's leap for the mourner's bench—and that isn't a far-fetched a figure as it sounds, either—didn't cause so much as a ripple.

It didn't seem odd to anyone that the old chap should suddenly decide he wanted to play golf. The odd thing, you see, was that he hadn't done it years before. There'd been plenty of talk about his refusal to play. It wouldn't be quite accurate to say that it had been held against him; he had always been awfully well liked. But—well, there hadn't been that perfect communion between him and everyone else in the club and in Edgeburn that there would have been had he been a golfer. If one plays golf, you know, one does want to talk about it.

Naturally Burnett didn't choose a Saturday afternoon or a Sunday morning for his baptism of fire. He was shrewd enough; he was one of those lawyers who get enormous fees for handling obscure, unsensational cases. So he arranged matters for his first plunge with a view to as much seclusion as he could ever hope to achieve. Yet it is a matter of record that Mrs. Capping was on the veranda when he made his hesitating way to the first tee and that she saw through the whole mystery forthwith.

"The man's in love!" said Mrs. Chapin.

She said it aloud, although she was alone, and she spoke more distinctly than she had intended to. Burnett heard her and trembled in the wretchedly uncomfortable shoes that his look of being a novice had nerved some criminal to sell to him. The trouble was that Mrs. Chapin was so absolutely right. And Burnett, frantically trying to discover how he had betrayed himself, couldn't do it. He was ready to swear that neither in word nor deed had he given himself away. This was true. Mrs. Chapin's conviction arose simply from what you may, if you like, call feminine intuition, but what is, actually, a sublimated sort of deductive ability. Burnett supposed, naturally, in his shame and distress, that Mrs. Chapin would not only proclaim her discovery, but would publish the name of the lady in the case. But there he did her less than justice, as well as more. Mrs. Chapin was not a gossip. Moreover, she was not actually a mind reader. She had to have some foundation, however slender, upon which to rear her edifices of deduction. And Burnett was perfectly right when, in his hasty review of his checkered recent past, he failed to perceive any betraying action. Mrs. Chapin had something to think about; for the moment, that was all.

Have you ever amused yourself by looking in the catalogue of a great library at the titles listed under the heading love? There are pages and pages of entries. The subject is one, it appears, that is not without ramifications. Leaving love stories, from the "Odyssey" down to the works of Laura Jean Libbey, out of the reckoning altogether, all sorts of learned persons seem to have spent their lives writing about love. They have earned the right to put down whole sections of the alphabet after their silly names by turning out theses and treatises in explanation of love.

They wander, these portentous people, into abstruse discussions of chemical affinity, and they write whole tomes about sensations and reactions and primary, secondary, and tertiary impulses. They work out formulate and equations by the score, and they convince you, if you waste your time in reading them, of how little they must know about love by exposing, without apparent shame, their vast erudition in embryology and zoology and the higher mathematics and other irrelevant nonsense of the sort.

And when they've finished, they haven't cleared the thing up. They're really no further along than Solomon was when he gave up his search for the answer. And that isn't so surprising. Solomon had opportunities for original research, and an experience, too, that the average scientific inquirer can't duplicate. So, in the matter of love, we haven't come along very fast since Solomon's time. We may know a little more about the eagle in the air and the ship in the sea, but when it comes to the way of a man with a maid . . .

Now here was old Burnett taking up a game he had hated all his life because he had fallen in love with one of a species he had always been afraid of, a girl. Odd? Well, it was, as you'll agree when you've heard the end of it.

Burnett had never been a woman hater, or anything like that. Let a girl get married, a girl he had been avoiding ever since she put up her hair and forced her mother to let her wear long skirts, and Burnett would become devoted to her at once. Especially when she had a baby or two for him to make a fuss about and give things to. He was a sort of semiofficial uncle to half the kids in town. And that was one of the things that made people think he was older than he was. That, and a rigorous sort of look he had. Yes—that's the word, rigorous.

You've seen his sort often. There was something square about him, from head to foot. He had rather a square head, and you were especially likely to think so when he didn't wear a hat, and you could see his high forehead, with his light-ish hair brushed back rather stiffly. That impression of squareness one got was repeated half a dozen times—in his body, for instance, and in his movements. He had blue eyes that seemed to be searching out the secrets of those who faced him, while his prominent eyebrows rather accentuated their aggressive quality . . . Then he had a firm jaw—very firm that jaw was.

Why had the old duffer had to fall in love with Mary Crandall no one could guess. It was just the sort of silly performance that made Solomon throw up his hands. Not that she wasn't an awfully nice girl. She was all of that. She wouldn't have pleased people, whose standards were those of the early Victorians, perhaps, but in this day and generation she got a pretty high rating. Old Burnett saw her for the first time when she was pretty nearly at her best, too. Someone had telephoned him to come over for some bridge before dinner, on a Saturday afternoon, and he reached the club early, and went out to watch the foursome he was waiting for coming up to the last green.

Mary was just driving off. He saw a tall girl, with brown hair and blue eyes, and checks that were full of color; a girl who stood squarely on her feet, and whose arms, bare to the elbows, were round and firm and brown, like her bare throat; a girl with grace in her every movement, as she swung her driver, and swept the ball from the tee with a fine, easy stroke deceptively casual in its look, unless you knew something about the game. She turned and looked at him a moment, appraisingly, in a curiously frank fashion she had. She'd been away for a long time; school, and college, and Europe, you know. And now she had come home to live and settle down—and to get married, one supposed, and otherwise fulfill her destiny.

Burnett didn't know who she was at all; he supposed she was one of the visiting girls who were always around for weekends. But she recognized him, all right, and there was a funny little look in her eyes as she came over to him, with her hand held out to him boyishly.

"What a shame of you!" she said. "You don't remember me at all, do you, Frank? You're just the same old stick in the mud, though, aren't you? Do you mean to tell me you haven't learned to play golf since I've been away?"

He was scared to death at once. But he managed to remember her, and shook hands. "I'm glad to see you, Molly," he told her. "But—you're so much better looking than I supposed you would be!"

"Thanks," she said indifferently. She'd been abroad long enough not to be excited by compliments; the Anglo-Saxon technique, you know, is pretty poor when it comes to that sort of thing. She looked him up and down. "I can't say as much for you, Frank," she went on rather brutally. "You ought to diet—or exercise—or something! Well, see you at the dance tonight, I suppose. I'll be going on."

That was absolutely all the direct, immediate contact he had with her between her home-coming and the day he first tried to play golf, about six weeks later. She didn't see him at the dance, of course; he was afraid of dances. But he saw her. He sneaked over, with some poor pretext of being out of cigarettes, about half past ten, and stared at her from the veranda. She danced just as well as she played golf, which was very well indeed. And something about the way a dancing frock feminized her settled the old chap completely—a frilly, white thing, it was, that contrasted in the oddest and most delightful way with her sunburned arms and throat. To all practical intents and purposes, you know, he fell in love with her that day, at sight, so to speak. But he didn't know it, and, and besides he'd known her practically ever since she'd been born.

Mary Crandall upset a few precedents in the club that summer. She really was a stunning girl, and it happened that she didn't have much competition. That year's crop of girls who were coming to dances and grown-up parties for the first time wasn't quite up to standard, and Molly was older than the rest of them, too, and had had the experience they lacked. As a rule, no one girl had any monopoly of attention in the club and the Edgeburn crowd generally. Couples would pair off and play around together, and in due course there'd be an engagement and a wedding.

But from the moment of her return, you could see that Molly was going to have her choice, and that most of the other girls would have to wait until she'd made up her mind—after which the usual paring off would begin again. That first dance was just a foretaste of what was coming. Burnett, peeping in, saw what was going on. They didn't go in for cards and dance orders at the Saturday night dances at Edgeburn, and before every dance Molly was surrounded about five deep by those who wanted to dance with her, while most of the other girls had to wait until she had made her selection.

Well, that was the way it went on. Molly enjoyed it, of course. She wouldn't have been a human girl if she hadn't, but she was nice about it, too, and wasn't hated as much by the other girls as you might have supposed she would be. They would have forgiven her unconditionally if she had been willing to choose one of the moths who fluttered about her, and so had released the rest of them. But she wouldn't do that. She seemed determined to distribute her favors with a good deal of impartiality. Even after a month had gone by scarcely any of her worshippers were prepared to admit themselves out of the running to the extent of resuming their attendance at other shrines, although by that time Edgeburn was disposed to think that two of them had outdistanced the field.

It was only natural that these two, Jimmy Hunter and Steve Murray, should have gained their lead through their golfing prowess. Molly spent most of her waking hours on the links, and, leaving sentiment out of the reckoning, it was to be expected that she would make her rounds with those who could make the best showing. Here it was a toss-up between Steve and Jimmy. They were both good; criminally, uncannily good, when you come to that. Men who had played the game for years and spent small fortunes in buying clubs and taking lessons, who had abandoned their affairs in the middle of winter to go south to keep their hands and eyes in, and still felt good when they beat eighty, used to damn those two youngsters very heartily. They both seemed to play golf by instinct.

The truth was, of course, that they'd been playing ever since they could walk. Places like Edgeburn are the nurseries of champions. When a kid's father is a keen golfer and takes the boy around with him from the time he is five or six years old, that boy is bound to play good golf, if there's anything normal about him. And that was the way it had worked out with Steve and Jimmy. There wasn't much to choose between them. Each had been intercollegiate champion, and each had been the other's runner-up. Both were handicapped at scratch on the Metropolitan list; both of them felt disgraced with anything worse than a seventy-six at Edgeburn, which is not an easy course.

And yet it was Molly with whom old Burnett, after his years of immunity, had to go and fall in love! It was the sort of competition he was bound to meet in Steve and Jimmy that he deliberately courted! A fine chance he had! He admitted that to himself, you know. He wasn't like some of these shy birds, an egoist in disguise. He had no illusions. But he started to learn to play golf just the same.

Jamie Park, the Edgeburn professional, was a conscientious man and an honest one. He instructed Burnett in the swing; he marked the places for his feet. And after fifteen minutes of a dour silence, broken only by pleas, growing in fervor, to his pupil, he spoke his mind.

"I'll no do it," he said. "I'll no can do it, man! Ye're sinfu'! Go back to your books, Mr. Burnett! Ye're a grand lawyer, and a,'but a gowfer—never!"

"Can't you teach me, Jamie?" asked Burnett.

"To play gowf—? No!" said Jamie flatly. "An' I'll no can take your money under false pretense!"

"I've got to learn," said old Burnett. "You get that, Jamie! You've given me fair warning—caveat emptor! You'll go on giving me lessons, or I'll complain to the committee and have you fired! What are you here for, anyhow?"

So Jamie continued to try to do what couldn't be done. As a golfer Burnett was hopeless. He must have been born stiff, and he couldn't loosen himself. Jamie plucked up a bit, after a while. He didn't want to take Brunett's money for lessons; he wanted to use him as a horrible example instead. He said if he could assemble all his other pupils as a gallery when Burnett was playing around he could make finished golfers of them, because they would be able to see all the things they must avoid doing if they wanted to play well.

Old Burnett was sensitive; he always had been. He'd been afraid of ridicule all his life. Really, that had been at the bottom of his odd refusal to play golf, and, of course, it had accounted for his avoidance of girls of the marriageable age. Yet, now that he had gone and fallen in love, the one thing he was possessed to do was the one thing that was sure, above all others, to make him ridiculous in the eyes of all who beheld him. Because that was what his golfing did, of course. He was probably the worst golfer in the civilized world. He never kept a score, but if he had, it would have been about two hundred strokes for the Edgeburn course—actual strokes, that is, and not counting penalties, which he didn't understand very well.

His game didn't have a single redeeming quality. He simply couldn't keep his eye on the ball. There was no coordination at all between his muscles; his swing was a ghastly, jerky thing that brought tears to the eyes of Jamie Park whenever he witnessed it.

"It's no fair," said Jamie bitterly. "It's not, indeed. They'll see you, and they'll say I taught it! Hard, it is, cruel hard!"

Probably no more than the average amount of masculine brutality was latent in the membership at Edgeburn. But there was something in Burnett's golf that brought out all that was worst and most base in his friends. It wasn't that they jeered, exactly. It was worse than that. Men used to invite their friends to watch him. When he really hit a ball there would be an outburst of cheering, so that people on the veranda or in the locker room in the basement would look at one another and grin. Billy Doone, who had a friend in the movie-picture business, begged Burnett tearfully to allow a series of one-reel comedies to be built about him. He said the films would drive Charley Chaplin into the discard, and that he, Burnett, and everyone concerned in the pictures would make a fortune and be able to retire.

But the old chap went on serenely, playing by himself. He must have hated it. If his whole past life was anything to go by, he must have nerved himself, every time he appeared on the course, to a degree of fortitude approaching that of an early Christian martyr. But he went on and he pretended he enjoyed it, and didn't mind the ribald comments he provoked.

"Greatest game in the world," he used to say with enthusiasm. "By Jove, you chaps were right all the time, and I wouldn't listen to you! I've taken off ten pounds and I feel great! But it isn't only the exercise. It's a fascinating game! I love the uncertainty of it!"

He always got a laugh with that line, but he always stuck to it too. As Edgeburn saw it, there was nothing uncertain about his game.

And all the time Mrs. Chapin, who had stuck to her first impulsivity formed opinion as to the origin of Burnett's interest in the game, tried to fathom his idea. She couldn't do it. He certainly paid no attention to Mary Crandall. He was just a little less shy when it came to girls, but he didn't single her out at all. He didn't invite her to share his lonely rounds. He took no such chances of being made ridiculous with Mary as he had in the ease of golf. Yet Mrs. Chapin persisted in the belief that it was because he had fallen in love with some girl that he had begun to play. She thought of Mary, because she tried to connect him with every eligible skirted creature in the club, but only to dismiss the thought at once. It was a little too far-fetched, even for Mrs. Chapin!

Actually, however, Burnett saw a good deal of Mary in a furtive, sneaking fashion. He stalked her. He discovered that she wouldn't let the weather keep her from playing, and after that he used to drop his work whenever it grew stormy and rush for a train and the club. He could always manage his own round in such a way as to bring him up to the eighteenth green just in time to carry her bag up to the club, and then he would shyly suggest that, since they were the only ones around, they might as well have tea together.

He couldn't have enjoyed their tête-à-têtes very much, though, because golf was Mary's principal topic of table talk, and when it came to golf, they lived in different worlds. She used to set forth the merits of the games of Jimmy Hunter and Steve Murray. According to her, both were assured of a brilliant future.

"I don't know which of them will do it first," she would say pensively. "But each of them ought to win the amateur championship. Jimmy's a little steadier than Steve when it comes to match play. Steve's nerves get frayed a little after a week's golf, so I'd rather back Jimmy in the finals. But Steve's much better at medal play. If he works hard on his short approaches, he'll have a chance in the open next year."

"I suppose they'll have to settle down to work some time, though," Burnett suggested hopefully. "They won't have so much time for golf then."

"It would be a shame to let anything spoil their golf! She said, wide-eyed with indignation. "Their people have plenty of money! And there are any number of good businessmen and lawyers—and mighty few people who have a chance to win a championship!"

"That's so, of course," he admitted.

It was on a rainy afternoon in September, when a high wind was howling around the clubhouse, and the rain was coming down in sheets and the first touch of fall in the air had made Burnett's suggestion of a fire in the big fireplace a welcome one, that he actually nerved himself to the point of a proposal.

"Mary—I say—oh, Mary—" he began disjointedly. He went at it very much as he went at the task of driving a golf ball.

"What I mean is—Mary—I'd like to marry you."

She sat bolt upright in her chair and stared at him.

"Frank!" she said. "What on earth—Did you have some Scotch when you were downstairs?"

He was much too confused to be as angry as he had a perfect right to be.

"Not a drop!" he said earnestly. "Really, Mary, do you think we'd hit it off so badly? I know I'm a rotten golfer, but I'm improving—really I am! I had a chance for an eight at the tenth hole yesterday, but I putted right off the green and took twelve. Still . . ."

She began to laugh rather hysterically. And then she stopped. She had seen his eyes perhaps.

"This is so—so—" she said. "Oh, I can't help it! It is so—sudden! Frank, you ridiculous old dear! I'm crazy about you—I always have been! But I never dreamed about you that way! You oughtn't to go around springing proposals on girls like that. It isn't fair! You ought to give them a chance—to make up their minds."

He seized upon what wasn't the salient point of her speech at all.

"I don't go about doing anything of the sort," he said sullenly. "I never proposed to a girl before in my life!"

"I believe you!" she cried, and now she couldn't keep the hysterical note down at all. "Why, Frank, I'd have to start in knowing you all over again! I've always thought about you as if you were—oh, an awfully nice, jolly sort of uncle! I used to call you Frank before I went away just because I thought it was a nervy thing for me to do."

He wasn't really rational. He just seemed to be. And his years as a lawyer made him come back to the point doggedly and demand an answer to his question. He got up and began to treat her as he would have treated a recalcitrant witness in court.

"Yes or no, please," he said. "Are you going to marry me, Molly?"

"No!" she cried. "No and no and no! I'm not going to marry anyone for years and years!"

She too arose, and they stood looking at one another with the fire shining on their faces. It is easy to believe that she looked adorable and just barely possible to understand what happened—which was that old Burnett, the staid, the irreproachable, seized her with an incredible clumsiness and kissed her! He let her go almost at once, and, of course, she didn't scream or tell him to unhand her or do anything so silly. She did gasp; she was tremendously surprised.

"Frank!" she said. "Aren't you ashamed of yourself?"

"No," he said defiantly. "I'm not! Because you're all wrong! You *are* going to marry me! And I'm going to kiss you again too! Only—I'll do it better the next time!"

She drew away from him, and he laughed, but not at all in his usual nervous, embarrassed fashion.

"Oh, I don't mean now!" he said. "You'll want me to when I do!"

"You—you're ridiculous!" she said uncertainly. "I don't understand you at all, Frank."

"Of course you don't," he said cheerfully. "I'm coming to life, that's all! You wait!"

"I'm not going to marry you," she said experimentally. "I don't like you that way at all." And now she began to feel indignant. "You're perfectly shameless!" she said. "Do you suppose I let men kiss me whenever they feel like it?"

"I should hope not!" he said in a fine rage. "Just you let me catch anyone trying that on!"

"I guess they can kiss me if I want them to!" she said with a show of spirit. She stamped her foot too, because she wanted him to be impressed. But she was trying to hide her confusion really. The situation was a little too much for her. Clumsy boys had probably tried to kiss her in the past; it has been said that she was a pretty girl and hinted that she was the sort of pretty girl one does want to kiss. But this was different.

"You'd better look out—that's all!" said Burnett darkly and menacingly. "I'm not going to have any nonsense about this thing."

She began to be really angry then, and she felt like doing something desperate and a little melodramatic. But she couldn't very well. It kept right on raining, you see, and she had to get home. So he took her in his car. And that was so natural that even Mrs. Chapin, whose house they passed, didn't get excited.

Molly shied a little the next time she saw him, even though a lot of other people were about. But he behaved himself, and the only thing he did that was at all out of the way was to grin at her in a particularly irritating and proprietary fashion. No one noticed that—except Molly. And she couldn't do anything about it, of course.

Nothing at all happened for several days. Molly was virile; the open-air life she lived didn't furnish good soil for nervous maladies. But undeniably Burnett got upon her nerves. She was always expecting him to do some crazy thing—and not without reason, considering the one amazing performance that already stood to his credit. It was pretty trying for her, you know. She couldn't tell anyone about the way he had acted. That would have been silly; she couldn't admit that any man could act in such a fashion that she couldn't handle him. And no one would have believed her anyhow. So she had to let the old chap go on grinning idiotically every time he saw her. There was something beatific about that grin. And there was that square, determined look of his too. As if what she wanted didn't matter at all; as if the fact that his mind was made up was enough.

Most men, you know, after the sort of rebuff he had, would have made love to her; she hadn't when you come down to it, done anything to make him feel his case was hopeless. But he didn't know that. And he didn't know how to make love either in any of the recognized ways. He had a leaning to the primitive, an inclination toward neolithic methods.

It was Edgeburn's turn that year to hold about the last of the woman's tournaments; it was quite an important one too. Molly had been looking forward to it for some time. For one reason and another, she hadn't played much tournament golf in this first home summer, though she had a string of cups she had won abroad. Anyhow, she wanted to win this tournament; there had been a few catty remarks about her. Intimations, you know, that she was content to stand on her reputation, and didn't care about risking it. So, she was all primed when the day for the qualifying round came along.

Jimmy and Steve had gone back to college, but they both sent her telegrams, wishing her all the luck in the world. Old Burnett did better, though. He offered to be caddie for her, and because he did it on a Sunday afternoon, at tea time, the whole club sat up and took notice, and Mrs. Chapin looked happier than she had been for weeks. There was method in this mad self-betrayal, though. He reasoned that she wouldn't turn him down, with a lot of people about, no matter what the state of her feelings might be. He was right too. She told him he was very good.

There was a lot of amused comment about old Burnett's interest in this particular tournament. He volunteered for all sorts of odd jobs, and they jumped at the chance to put him on the committee. He attended to the drawings. And he stopped off, shamelessly, to tell Molly about the draw for the medal, the qualifying round.

"You're the odd one," he said. "You play alone."

"I don't mind," she said. "I ought to have the best score, you know, really."

"Of course you will," he assured her loyally.

Molly was the last one to drive off, and by that time no one was left to follow her around the course. It was raining, anyhow, and not much of a crowd turned out. Most of the spectators preferred to wait around the clubhouse. But this was to have been expected. A good many women players don't like a gallery anyhow, especially in a medal round.

Molly got a fine start. She drove a low, long ball that sailed right over the brook that was the first hazard, and it dropped dead, with a short pitch to the green for her, second shot.

"Mashie, please," she said curtly to Burnett. She had made up her mind to treat him just as she would an ordinary caddie. He handed her the club and stood back. The shot looked easy; she swung quickly and a little carelessly. The ball rose as the club head bit deep into the soggy turf. But it didn't drop on the green; it sailed off to the right at an amazing tangent and landed in a pit.

"For Heaven's sake!" said Molly, staring after her ball, the picture of dismay. "I haven't made a shot like that since I was fourteen!"

But she wasn't excited or dismayed. She climbed down into the pit and jammed the ball out with a vicious niblick shot that sent the wet sand flying all about her. She was on the edge of the green, and she shook her head when her long-approach putt was far from the line. She took two more, and her mouth was set in a hard little line when she walked off toward the second tee.

"Six!" she said. "And I had an easy three! Don't talk to me, please, Frank! They said I'd be nervous! I wonder if one can be nervous without knowing it?"

Some people had always insisted that Molly was a careless golfer. She did play in a dashing fashion that you don't often see. She wasted no time in thinking out her shots. Her method was to make up her mind as soon as she got near enough to her ball to see its lie, call for a club, and play the shot at once. And that was a method that had always served her well enough before. This was her Waterloo, that was all. There is no need to describe it in detail. Everything went wrong.

She took seven on the second hole, and the third scarred her card with another six—and the shortest hole at Edgeburn! By the time she drove from the fourth tee there could be no doubt she was nervous. She missed the ball altogether with her first swing and topped it, so that it rolled about fifty yards, when she finally did hit it. There were tears in her eyes by that time, and Burnett was shaking. He didn't say a word; even if he hadn't been beyond speech anyhow, he would have been afraid to open his mouth.

Molly gave it up after her second shot on the sixth hole. Her score for five holes was thirty-seven; her second on the sixth was a mid-iron that carried into the woods at the right of the fairway—a lost ball. She sat down under a tree that afforded small protection from the rain and began to howl.

"Molly—Molly—dear!" said Frank. "Don't—it's not serious enough for that—"

She lifted tragic, scornful eyes to his.

"That's all you know!" she said. "Frank—I'll never hear the last of this! They said I couldn't really play—that I just had a reputation I'd made on rotten courses against dubs! The people here know it isn't so—but how about the outsiders?"

"But—" he began.

"Oh, there isn't any but!" she wailed. "If I could just tear up my card and withdraw! But they'd know—"

"They needn't!" he said. She looked up at him, startled by the change in his tone. He looked bigger, too, somehow. "You can tear up your card—and you can have the best reason in the world for doing it too! Let's go back now—and tell 'em we're engaged! No one would expect a girl to get engaged and win a medal at the same time! Any girl would have a right to get excited—Molly—dear—won't you?"

He wasn't so awfully wise about girls even yet. But he saw something in her eyes this time. Anyhow he dropped right down on his knees in the silliest, most unromantic way you could imagine and kissed her—for the second time. And she did want to be kissed this time, too, just as he had told her she would. She—well, she kissed him too.

"Oh!" she said after a minute. "Oh! You—you do know things, Frank! Steve never would have thought of that! And—I meant to let you any-how—some time—"

"Come on!" he said deliriously, getting up and swinging her to her feet. He shouldered her clubs, and they walked back toward the club-house, holding hands. But when they came to a brook they stopped, and he tore up her card very solemnly and watched the pieces as they floated away.

Mrs. Chapin was the first one they told, and she smiled rather scorn-fully. She was very fond of Burnett.

"I wondered when you'd wake up, Molly!" she said.

Burnett clung to Molly's clubs. He told her he wanted to clean them himself, and she smiled at what seemed to be just an added proof of devotion. It wasn't, though. Old Burnett didn't look like a criminal, a conspirator dyed in the wool. But he was. What he wanted to do was to make very sure that Molly should never see the tiny bits of slivered chewing gum that he had stuck to one or two of her irons; tiny morsels, but big enough to make all the difference between a perfect shot and the sort of shot she had actually made.

He laid out her irons on a bench. And then his eyes grew round, and he stared at the shining irons incredulously. He knew which clubs he had treated; he had been careful not to overdo the thing. But they were inno-cent of all adornment now. He turned her bag upside down and shook it; he explored its inmost recesses with his hands. But there was no reward for his search.

Dazed, a little fearful, he wandered outside without knowing exactly what he was doing and moved about in the rain trying to solve the puzzle. But it was Molly who resolved his doubts and fears—which, to some extent at least, was to be her business in the future anyhow. He went to see her that evening, naturally, and they had the library and an open fire to themselves.

"Something ought to be done about the caddies," said Molly pensively. "Do you know that I found two or three bits of chewing gum—actually! chewing gum!—sticking to my irons this morning just before I started? And I had those clubs cleaned yesterday!"

Old Burnett mumbled something about speaking to the caddie master.

"Do you think it was quite honest not to admit that I made such a wretched fizzle this morning?" Molly asked him. "Just to let people think it was because—because you and I—?"

And then, before he could answer, she laughed.

"I don't care!" she said. "It was true anyway! I was so afraid I'd frightened you that other time! And it made me nervous to think of how much you wanted me to win—I couldn't have played decently today if the championship had depended on that round."

Burnett had the grace to blush. But it was all right, because Molly thought it was because they were so near the fire.

Golf on the Roof

Adele Howells

HAVING A HANKERING FOR AT LEAST NINE HOLES OF GOLF A DAY AND not living near a course, I attempted to satisfy this craving at home. After smashing the chandeliers of the living room and the hall. I was compelled by the gentle hints of my husband, who is *not* a golf "nut," to seek more suitable quarters for my daily game. I gazed from my window with longing at the alluring "fairways" of Riverside Park, but the sight of several policemen checked my wild ideas.

I spent an hour with a mashie in a deserted roadway under a viaduct near our house, pretending I was working out of the "rough," but it proved too horribly dusty. Finally, after haunting the golf departments of the big shops, I discovered the solution of my problem—a fiber mat, a rubber tee, a captive ball, and a little tin contrivance which is made for practice putting.

With this apparatus, I now betake myself to the roof of our apartment house before breakfast; lay down my mat; firmly place under it the spike to which my captive ball is attached with a long, strong cord; and then put down the little tin "hold" some distance away. Next I place my rubber tee on the mat, execute my favorite waggle several times in practice, and then "tee off." If I don't top the ball, slaff it, or miss it altogether, I get quite a decent drive down the "fairway," a narrow strip of roof marked on one side by the wall and a water pipe on the other, the ball sailing gaily into the air until pulled down by the attaching cord. I drive ten times, then make ten brassie shots. Ten midiron drives, ten diggings out of the rough with my niblick—merely precautionary practice in case

I should ever chance to get into the rough on the links, ten approach shots with my mashie, ten dexterously executed putts, and I have played my daily nine holes of golf.

Playing golf on the roof offers an advantage of which I was unaware when I embarked upon my adventure. It is bound to supply one with a gallery. And what is more essential in golf than practice in playing before a gallery? Not long after I began playing on the roof, the elevator boy who whizzes me up every morning kindly offered to carry my mat to the spot where I play. I declined his offer with thanks, but he insisted, for he had regarded me with the greatest curiosity not unmingled with suspicion and was evidently determined to discover what I was about. When we reached the place, I told him to put down the mat. He grinned from ear to ear and remarked, "I don't know much about this heah new-fangled game that everybody's getting crazy about."

"Thank you very much for carrying the mat. I shan't need you for anything else," I answered.

"Don't mention it," he replied quickly, "An' if you don't mind, I would like to watch you hit that ball."

There was nothing left for me to do but hit that ball.

Nor is the elevator boy all of my gallery. Every morning from the building that overlooks our roof, two young girls in pink negligees watch me from the front apartment, a thin, sallow-faced woman and a police dog look down from the next, while a fat man in vivid pajamas with purple and white stripes gazes intently from the adjoining window. I have a faint idea that the fat man is a "golf nut," too, for when I make a good drive, he wears a smile that won't come off; and yesterday morning I distinctly heard him say, "Damn!" as I felt the dull, sickening thud of a topped ball.

War and Golf

H. B. Martin

"In time of peace prepare for war." In time of war prepare for more war, or peace—which will you have it? Every golfer would prefer the quiet of a golf links to the excitement of war. Not that he is afraid to fight when the occasion demands, but war at its very best hardly equals the fascination of golf.

Golfers will not shirk their duty to their country, and in the enlistments that have been made so far, golfers were among the first to offer their services. But as the great majority of men who support the golf clubs are not available for the trenches or the ships, on account of their age, they are willing to do their bit, just the same, of whatever it may consist.

Just as soon as it was definitely settled that we were to have war, many golf clubs offered their courses to the government for training purposes. Some were even willing that their courses should be put under the plough. These were generous offers, but in neither case has it been necessary. What was asked of the golfers was that they cultivate a part of the links not needed for golfing purposes, and each member was requested to devote a small part of his time each week to raising vegetables.

The Dunwoodie Club of Yonkers put this suggestion up to the US Golf Association (USGA), which thought so well of it they asked the cooperation of all clubs in their jurisdiction. The clubs were only too glad of a chance to help in this way, and the result has been that all the spare ground around the various links is being put, or is to be put, to a practical use. Hereafter, when you slice or pull, the chances are that you will find your ball over in the vegetable garden among the cabbages and peas instead of in the long, rough grass.

The Dunwoodie plan was to have each member spend at least two hours a week in actual work. There was a small chance for escape, however, in the proviso that if he found that he was not suited for the job he could hire a boy to do his share.

Here is where the weakness of the whole plan comes in. There are a few golfers who would prefer weeding a garden to playing around the links, especially when they can hire a caddie to do this work for them for no more than he would charge for making a trip around the links. There are few caddies who would prefer carrying a large golf bag full of clubs to devoting the same amount of time hoeing vegetables. The problem seems to solve itself rather easily. The boy is happy because of a chance to make more money in his odd moments. The clubs are pleased over the amount of vegetables they are going to get for nothing, and the member is pleased over the fact that he will always be able to find a caddie on the links when he wants one, whether he is hoeing potatoes or waiting for a job to carry clubs.

The situation is not without its humor, after all, if you can imagine lining up a lot of duffers and sending them out to the cabbage patch. To begin with, most of them know as little about gardening or farming as they know about golf. Therefore it would be necessary to have a professional gardener on hand to teach them the proper stance and the proper grip on the hoe or spade. Some of them are no doubt qualified for digging, as this has been their principal pursuit for years. Digging up the soil is nothing new to the rank and file of duffers. If they are as expert at this sort of work as they are when there are no divots to replace, some of them will fit in very nicely.

The betting features of golf might easily enough be transferred to the potato field. For instance, a ball might be wagered on each hill or row hoed. Or a box of balls might be wagered on the most work done during the two hours. I'll venture to say that the golfer will get his fun out of it somehow.

The Coming Invasion

Francis Ouimet

AFTER SEVERAL YEARS OF LESSENED INTEREST DUE TO THE WAR, GOLF seems to have its greatest year awaiting it. As Kipling would say, "The lean years have passed." Certainly none will deny the fact that the past two years have been extremely lean ones as far as golfing tournaments are concerned, and they have been even leaner in England and Scotland for the past four years.

Now word comes from George Duncan, the brilliant English golfer, that Great Britain is planning an American invasion of the golf links the coming year. She is sending over her four brightest stars, and these stars, hungry after four years of non-competitive play, will be needing much watching. The quartet consists of Harry Vardon, whose name is a by-word among golfers; his far-hitting 1913 companion, Ted Ray; J. H. Taylor, the chubby man who won five British open championships, and James Braid who has done the same.

The game has been kept alive the past couple of years, as far as competitive golf is concerned, largely through the medium of exhibition golf matches, which assisted the game and humanity wondrously well, as most of these games were for Red Cross or other charity.

However, though these games called for a higher grade of golf than heretofore witnessed, they lacked much of the "zip" or spirit noticeable at championship meetings. These games were for the most part four-ball contests, at which the spectator sees much brilliancy exhibited but there is always lacking that conservatism, concentration, and "strain" that takes hold of the aspirant for the highest honors.

I cannot conceive of anything as exciting as the past five open championships. In 1912, John McDermott won out by two strokes, and it must be remembered that he came from behind with a rush and nosed out Tommy McNamara, though the latter had scored a phenomenal 69.

The year following, I had the good fortune to contribute to the excitement. At seventy-two holes I stood level with Harry Vardon and Ted Ray. Then in the play-off the "Goddess of Rain" made the going rather unpleasant for my opponents and I wallowed home in the mud and rain, a winner.

The year 1914 was one of intense excitement. The scene was Midlothian at Blue Island, Illinois. Walter Hagen, coming into his own, holed a fifteen-foot putt on the last green, for a grand total of 290. Directly behind him came the dashing Chick Evans. He needed a hole to chip shot from just off the green to tie Hagen. Of course no one expected him to hole it and he didn't, for his ball just missed the cup, leaving everybody trembling with excitement. Hagen won that year.

Then I can never forget "Jerry" Travers coming down those last four holes at Baltusrol. Thousands watched him play hole after hole with marvelous skill or extricate himself from real difficulty. Again Tommy McNamara came to the fore and, though he missed an easy six-foot putt on the last green, his total of 298 still looked good. "Jerry" carried on hole after hole and again Tommy was nosed out, this time by one shot. Tom has been a runner-up in 1909, 1912, and 1914.

The following year, Chick Evans came through at Minikahda, I think it was. Everybody was glad because Chick was due long before. However, it was nip and tuck all the way and Chick's 286 was two strokes better than Jock Hutchinson. Unless one has played in one of these contests I doubt if he appreciates fully the true spirit of competition. Red cross matches really do not give this.

Therefore, after two long years of idleness, competitions will come back. Every golfer who is conceited enough to think he can play the game will be looking forward to the spring and summer of 1919, when the championships and annual tournaments will in all probability be resumed. Only these, which call for individual play, provide the necessary excitement. Spectators love to see a player working out his own salvation and it also gives the onlooker the opportunity of studying the stars under fire.

And so, the anticipated visit of England's star professionals to this country next spring will afford the "Winter Leaguers" the opportunity of guessing just how the greatest of golfers will finish in America's blue-ribbon golfing event, the National open championship. I want to say that Harry Vardon is going to be a mighty difficult person to beat. I should not care to make him the favorite over the entire field, but I would select him against any three men in that field.

This will be Vardon's third attempt. His first visit was in 1900 when he came over with J. Henry Taylor and the pair finished one-two. That was eighteen years ago. He returned in 1913 when golf was vastly more popular than in 1900 and finished second. Harry Vardon today is fifty years or more old. In 1914, when he won the last British open championship, he was easily the best golfer alive.

Since that time he has played in no championships—because they had none—but he has engaged in numerous benefit games that certainly have kept him in good trim. The fact that he has had no other form of competitive golf other than the four-ball matches will make him a hard man to beat because all champions long for competition and any golfer in this frame of mind is bound to do well. He does well because he feels that at last the opportunity he has been waiting for—namely that of showing the fickle public that he is as good as ever—has come and he is ready to make the most of his opportunity.

Vardon's success heretofore has been due to the wonderful, machine-like soundness of his game. His putting has been poor, golfers will argue, but poor only in comparison to the rest of his play. He is not really a bad putter, but what one might call erratic. Chick Evans and he are alike in this respect.

At Brae-Burn, where the event will probably be staged, Vardon is going to find putting a most important factor. The great master will encounter no difficulty in either his tee shots or irons, which he has always played with uncanny perfection. He will need to play them well, but he usually does that, and his opponents never hope to gain strokes through Vardon's irons or woodens going astray. It is an occasional lapse upon the greens that they all look for. With the exception of five or six holes, I believe that the most difficult feature of Brae-Burn lies in the putting greens.

But, however badly Vardon may putt, he can be depended upon for the long putt. Unless it is Walter Travis, I do not know of any better approach putter. I saw him give a splendid exhibition of long putting at Prestwick in 1914. When we played against each other the previous year he putted splendidly and could not blame his defeat in the play-off upon poor putting, though I am told he missed many little ones that might have won for him without the play-off.

Harry Vardon can be depended upon to produce a sound and excellent game of golf, and if he is not successful—and mind you I am not prophesying he will win—it will be because the undulating, tricky Brae-Burn greens have lured his short putts from the hole. Three-, four-, or six-foot putts on the Brae-Burn greens are very difficult and they may prove to be Vardon's hoodoo. Nevertheless put him down as one of the big favorites.

There has been a bit of doubt in my mind as to whether Taylor or Braid should come next to Vardon in the matter of golf supremacy. Up to 1914 these two, along with Vardon, had each won five open championships and were known as the "triumvirate." Indeed, these fifteen titles that the "Big Three" won, covering a period of twenty years, is a most remarkable achievement. To think that with all the star golfers in England and Scotland these three collected fifteen out of twenty championships is wonderful.

But in writing of Taylor's chances in the coming championship, place his name next to Vardon's and ahead of Braid's because in 1914 he fought Vardon bitterly for the title that would break up the so-called triumvirate. Vardon won, but the glassy expression in his eyes told the story of what he had been through. I will wager it was the toughest fight he ever had for a golfing title. He won by two strokes. The year before, when McDermott and McNamara were the only Americans to qualify, Taylor won with a total of 304. Tom McNamara said it was one of the best performances he ever saw.

The famous Mid-Surrey "pro" is an elegant golfer and must be considered. In 1914 I had a hunch that Taylor would win the British title. I wrote friends telling them of my hunch, and but for a piece of bad luck he most certainly would have won in place of Vardon. Taylor will take to the Brae-Burn course readily and spectators will have the pleasure of seeing this fine chap in splendid action. He is a fighter all the way, and in this respect he is not unlike "Jerry" Travers.

His game, to those who have never seen him, is much like Tom McNamara's. He uses a very flat swing and is like Tom also in that he seldom goes off the course. He drives a longer ball than Tom and plays his mashie a tiny bit better, albeit Tom will out-putt Taylor or any other man.

Taylor is probably the greatest mashie player the world has ever known. He himself told me that he always tried to pitch the ball into the hole when playing a mashie. Maybe that is the reason why he is such an expert in using this club and will probably explain why his ball is usually so close to the pin.

He is not as easygoing as Vardon and gets more excited. This excitement, however, is of the sort that does not wreck his game but makes him more dangerous. I know lots of fellows who get so nervous they cannot speak to you, but to beat them is another job. J. Henry will take good care of himself in any company. You can put me on record now as saying I look to see Taylor proving himself more dangerous than any other British player.

The Curse of the Skirt

Marjorie R. S. Trumbull

WOMAN TODAY REFUSES TO REGARD HERSELF SOLELY AS A DECORATIVE feature. She has attained the ballot and discarded the bustle. She cavorts over the polo field in riding breeches and at college hangs up her record for the 100-yard dash in bloomers. In certain parts of the country, she has already appeared on the golf course in knickerbockers. Well, why shouldn't she? Only those who wear them can realize what a handicap skirts are to a woman when she goes in for sports.

Back in the dark ages, while her mate was out foraging breakfast for the kiddies, the woman who swung a mean club in defense of her cave home was not hampered by skirts. Her leopard-skin sport costume, fastening over the left shoulder, didn't hinder the follow through when she beaned the hungry mountain lion with a handy rock. The garment protected the vital parts of her body from sunburn and evening's chill and did not interfere with the agility of limb that gave her the right to survive. The cave woman was suitably clad for her environment. What more can one reasonably ask for in a garment?

One of the definitions of dress is "the suspension of foreign bodies from, or their attachment to, convenient portions of the body." It goes on academically to say that "it is chiefly from the waist ornaments that what is commonly considered clothing at the present day has climatically developed." And Anatole France, possibly the wisest gentleman of the twentieth century, claims that "one of the things that render women the terrible force they are today is civilization, which gave them draperies."

M. France is getting to be an old man and you may not agree with his cynicism, but up to a few generations ago there was a lot to be said for what he claimed. When woman no longer had strenuously to help out in the defense of the home, but became, indeed, an added object to be defended, she had a lot of spare hours left on her hands, and no better way to spend them than in making herself attractive to the defender. She certainly did become a pretty thorough, if charming, slacker.

WHAT J. CAESAR FOUND

When Julius Caesar led his cohorts northward, the Romans were amazed to find the barbarians, men and women alike, attired in trousers. But you can see that it didn't take the women many generations to become civilized enough to realize the value of clothes as opposed to a fifty-fifty labor union. The descendants of these hardy ones, slender and rotund alike, fell for the fashion set by their emaciated, long-waisted queen and pinched the waist into a narrow stomacher form that sprung a skirt so bouffant that the Elizabethan vamp looked as if she dressed over a barrel. A little later, hoops were so enormous that staircases in the smart London clubs were constructed with the balusters curved outward. Just picture a modern golf course dotted with ladies whose expanse of crinoline could cover an entire green!

Can't you remember your grandmother as she toasted her prunella slippers on the fender? She was awfully proud of her tiny feet and hands and waist. The slippers were never larger than sizes one and two. Everyone in the house ran on her errands, for she felt cold when she moved away from the fireplace, and it made her faint even to stoop to pick up a handkerchief. Can you picture her playing out of a trap?

Heaven alone knows why she allowed your mother to ride horseback. Perhaps it was because it was the one form of exercise that was considered "ladylike." Perhaps your mother just refused to give it up and go sit by the open fireplace. It made her feel so fine to have the blood coursing through her body when she finished her afternoon's ride. She began to like to walk, too, although her skirt of her "tailor-made suit" concealed the feet and she had to clutch it up behind with her left hand to avoid doing the street-cleaning department out of its job. It always kept her left hand a little lame. One day she resolutely had the skirt chipped off a daring four inches from the ground and revealed a number four shoe, while Grandma lamented and wondered what the younger generation was coming to. Eventually, she even achieved a regular plaid sport skirt lined with crimson silk.

Her daughter slashed the bottoms of all her skirts. She hasn't a long skirt in her closet—not even her dancing ones. Her sport shoes are rubber-soled and low-heeled, and she never dreams of camouflaging the fact that their size is five or six.

IN HORSEBACK RIDING

Far worse than that! They didn't have side saddles at the Oklahoma ranch where she visited her college roommate, and as there wasn't anything to do but ride, she borrowed brother Henry's riding breeches and had a bully time jumping her cow pony over sagebrush and rim rock in pursuit of the nimble jack rabbit. She gave her old riding skirt, with its curious bulging pouches, to the laundress's daughter and ordered knickerbockers to match her coat—also ones of tan and white linen.

Father was horrified when she appeared for her first home ride astride—told her to wait until all the other women were doing it so that she wouldn't be conspicuous. Conspicuous—and all the time her right hip was inches larger than the other from riding side saddle! He didn't think women had any business driving a motor car, either, and he still fusses over her knee-length bathing skirt and sleeveless jersey, although she is certainly in less danger when aqua-planing than when her swimming suit had bishop sleeves and baggy mohair bloomers to hinder her movements.

The war helped daughter a lot when it came to dressing for utility. She did a man's job then and her garments weren't allowed to hinder. After all, there's nothing beautiful about men's clothing. A man's suit is about as sadly ugly a sartorial creation as can be imagined, but you can't beat it for utility. When a daughter joined the motor corps she conceded the skirt for charity, but it wasn't long enough to hamper her, and beneath it she wore knickerbockers and leather putters on ambulance duty—she could always shed the skirt to do repairs beneath the car. The farmerette went into overalls. Goodness knows there is nothing fascinating about overalls—she willingly surrendered the allure of skirts for rows of extra plowing before sundown, just for the same reason that the Scotchman finds kilts better suited than trousers for walking through wet heather.

The soldier's uniform was designed for the maximum of utility. And when you remember the Battalion of Death and the women who rallied to the defense of Warsaw—to think of them as clothed in anything but the uniform of their country would be almost an insult their memory.

Altogether, it seems that Anatole France's epigram is a little sweeping. During the war, women didn't visualize a man when they wound a Red Cross bandage, drove ambulances, plowed a field. They did it to help. Older women forgot all about headache and nerves. The younger ones were amazed at the strength and endurance of the bodies that for generations they had been taught to consider fragile. The short skirts of the present fashion that so appall the conventional man are the direct result of the war. Women simply aren't going to be hampered by their clothing.

IN THE FIELD OF SPORT

Meanwhile, all that pep and endurance that women found during the war is now taking them onto the tennis courts—out to the golf courses. Any pro will tell you that they are working hard to improve their short game, lengthen their distance. Naturally, they aren't going to let their clothing interfere with their ambition. If they can chop a couple of strokes off their score by chopping a couple of inches off their skirts, they are going to do it. It's only in illustrations for funny papers now that you see women on the course in high-heeled shoes, picture hats, and floating draperies.

On one of the championship courses, a fine, but slender golfer was questioned the other day as to why he wore anything so unbecoming as knickerbockers. He answered that the knickerbockers actually saved him, as well as he could estimate, at least a stroke a round. If it is true that knickerbockers give you that advantage over trousers, think what an edge they give you over skirts!

If women do take to knickerbockers on the links, they certainly should be given credit for the desire to improve their golf. None of them can be charged with believing that it will improve their looks. When they come out attired in those garments they will have to stand for a lot of criticism. Their male relatives will have many a word to say on the matter.

Man consistently flatters himself that attracting men is all there is in life for women. He resents any encroachment by her on what he considers his prerogatives. Under no circumstances does he wish her to adopt his style of dress. The usual argument he falls back upon is modesty. And yet in the abstract even he will admit that modesty is conventional rather than reasonable.

In Tahiti you may discard all your clothing, but you must be tattooed; Mahommedan women may unclothe all but the face, in Sumatra the knee, in Asia the fingertips. When you consider our own ball gown you have to allow that we moderns have strange conventions about dress. Anatole was right when he inferred that clothing was not developed for the sake of modesty.

If knickerbockers do replace skirts on the links, mixed foursomes may become more harmonious. At least the husband will lose one alibi for not playing with his wife. He can no longer complain that the flattering and flapping of her skirt on a windy day interfere with his putting. Of course, many men will stubbornly content to the last that feminine apparel is no handicap to the golfer. Well, we'd just like to see Chick Evans in skirts consent to meet Alexa Stirling in knickerbockers.

Hit the Ball

Eddie Loos

A GOOD MANY YEARS AGO, I HAD A PUPIL WHO WORRIED ME. HE COULD swing perfectly without a ball. In practice, he would hit 50 percent of his shots with a surety that made your heart rejoice. But in actual play, he was the most erratic performer who ever topped his approach, missed his putt, sliced his drive, or dubbed an iron shot.

The more lessons I gave him, the worse his performance got. And the worst of it was, I liked him personally, so my feelings as well as my pride as an instructor were at stake.

He laughed—I guess he liked me too—I was an earnest if not a fully competent boy—and he told me something like this: "It isn't your fault, Eddie. I've been to some of the best instructors in the country before I came to you, and while you haven't helped me, my game isn't any worse than it was before you took hold."

This was scant consolation for a young fellow who really wanted to help his pupils and who laid awake nights trying to figure out how—if you can imagine such a thing in golf.

I talked to some of the older pros. Outside of the fact that they were not much interested—in my problems, at least—the best I got was: "It's mental . . ."

I studied and I pondered and I questioned, but the more I questioned them on this "mental" thing, the closer I came to the conclusion that they had read it somewhere—didn't know what it meant.

My pupil himself gave me the clue—unwittingly. He came out one day, to take another lesson, and with the courage born of desperation, I told him the truth. "It isn't any use taking any more lessons. I just simply can't teach you anything and I don't want to take pay without giving something in return." And I needed the money, too.

He laughed and told me not to worry about that side of it, then he asked me a question. "Eddie, what do you think of when you hit a golf ball?"

I had never considered the question before, so I stopped and thought carefully, and when I answered, I told him truthfully, "I just think of hitting the ball."

My answer, incidentally, with a slight addition would be the same today. And then, on the spur of the moment, I impulsively asked him the same question. "What do you think of when you hit a golf ball?

He looked at me, and then he replied, "Well, I think of my grip and my stance and keeping my head still and swinging back slowly and maintaining the correct arc and rolling my forearms as I come into the ball, and not swaying . . . and following through . . ."

I stopped him—I was astounded. "Do you mean to say you think of all those things when you hit at a ball?"

"I try to . . ." he said slowly.

And then it dawned on me that I couldn't hit a ball myself if I tried to keep my mind on anything besides actually hitting it, let alone a dozen things—the swing is too fast to permit of consecutive thinking, although I didn't argue it out that way then.

He took a practice swing as I stood thinking. It looked fine—the arc was true—his wrists worked properly—everything coordinated perfectly.

I had an idea, and made a beginning. "I'm going to give you a lesson after all," I said, and teed up a ball, "but," I added, "I'm going to learn more than you do, and you've got to do just what I say."

He laughed and agreed.

"Now," I said slowly, trying to get my idea clear, "I want you to step up to that ball and look at it. Then I want you to make a swing without an idea in your head except to hit the ball—hit through it."

He did—and since this isn't a fairy story, I'll have to admit that he tightened—and the ball was badly topped.

I scratched my head. "What did you think of?" I asked.

"Hitting the ball," he answered.

"Anything else?" I asked.

"Well," he grinned a little, "I guess I thought of hitting it—hard."

"Let's try it again," I said, and teed up another ball.

"I want you to hit this ball a hundred yards—only a hundred yards— do it by swinging easily not by trying to shorten your swing," I told him.

"Hit it a hundred yards," he repeated and then stepped up to the ball.

Out it sailed—two hundred and ten yards—the longest ball he had ever hit in his life. He reached for another ball without a word, started his club back, and stopped.

"Getting ready to slug it," he explained. "Guess I'd better try again."

He did and the next ball went around two hundred.

I pulled the driver from his hands and gave him a mashie. We were both learning something.

At the end of that lesson, he had hit more perfect balls than ever before in his life at one sitting—or standing.

And from that time on, I gave that man lessons by simply reminding him to hit the ball. His swing was all right except when he spoiled it by thinking about it or by tightening up to try and slug the ball.

When he realized that clean hitting brought distance, the tightening disappeared—and when he got the knack of thinking about hitting the ball, his handicap inside of one season went from 25 to 14—no miracle, but a splendid improvement.

And that was the beginning of my realization of something that has been of immense value to me in my teaching ever since. In my own mind, I make a distinct differential between teaching the swing and hitting the ball. In spite of the fact that practice swings mean nothing, a man with patience can better learn to play golf without a ball than he can with one—simply because every time he dubs or slices, or hooks or tops, he begins to make a change in his swing and thereby defeats any possibility of really developing skill in the swing.

There are two sides to golf—the mechanical and the mental. And it's mighty simple and a sure recipe for improvement, if you'll let it sink into your system.

The mechanical side is the swing—when you have learned the correct swing, that part of your game should be behind you. It is a tool you have acquired, and its use is in hitting the ball.

And the mental side of golf is not intense, wrinkle-browed concentration—it's simply stepping up to the ball with the determination to hit it where you want to go, or "hit through it," whichever expression you prefer—with no other thought in your mind—none whatever.

When I step up to the ball, no matter where it lies, I look at it—I determine the path it is going to take and suddenly I find my club has snapped it into space right in the direction pre-determined. When I try to think of anything else, my shot is spoiled.

No thought of turning wrists or top of swing or anything else—just hit the ball where you want it to go. Even people with ugly swings who have this knack can secure surprising results.

We all know men whose swings look like nothing this side of the nether regions, yet they shoot good golf. Their minds are on hitting the ball where they want it to go.

It's far better fun to play golf with a good swing than with a bad one, but the man with his mind on hitting the ball, no matter what his form is, is going to play better golf than the fellow with splendid form who is trying in a fraction of a second the golf swing takes to think of sixteen different parts of his anatomy.

I have talked with hundreds of professionals. They all tell me the same thing—when they're frank—their thoughts are on hitting the ball.

Their analysis of the swing for teaching purposes is the result of observation. Their swings are not consciously executed. Their instructions to you are the things they have noticed in their own swings when they studied them for tuition purposes. This plus the mouth to mouth methods of transmitting golf lore that have always been prevalent in professional ranks.

Golf is no more difficult than driving a nail or swinging an axe. True, the planes in golf are a little confusing to the beginner, but the most difficult part of golf is the part that we inject into it by making a mental thing of something that should be mechanical.

Try this experiment.

Go out and make a few practice swings without a ball—make sure your clubhead grazes the ground and comes through on a straight line for a few inches before and after the spot where the ball ought to be.

When this comes easily and naturally, lay down a ball. Fix the direction you want to go and step up to the ball in the same mental state that you would start to swing an axe. Think of the objective, not the physical motions necessary to attain it. Step up to hit that ball straight and true—never mind distance—just as you would drive a nail or chop a tree.

You may surprise yourself.

Now, of course, a good many people will feel that by taking this attitude, I am discounting the value of professional instruction, but this could hardly be true, considering the fact that I earn my living in that particular manner.

Professional instruction develops the ideal swing—the "good form" with which every ambitious man wants to play golf. And for that reason alone, professional coaching will always be in demand.

But the man who is going to play a good game of golf, with or without professional coaching, must make up his mind to divorce the mechanical and the mental sides of golf.

He will learn to swing so his control over his club is exercised without any more thought than he uses a hammer or an axe or reaches for a glass of water.

And then, when he plays, he will forget his swing—put the mechanical part of it behind him. His mind will be on hitting the ball the distance he wants to go. His attention will be concentrated on that little flight path that starts a few inches before the ball and ends several inches past it pointing in the desired direction.

And with his mind and his attention concentrated right at the bottom of the swing where it belongs, he will find that handicaps go down and balls fly straight and true.

I firmly believe that a clear understanding of this principle will do wonders for any golfer.

And just as a last word—a confession, I have observed that when a shot fails to come off to my satisfaction, that my mind was elsewhere than on hitting the ball.

The danger of the amateur lies in filling his mind with so many things that he can't center on hitting the ball.

The danger of the professional is that his certainty is so great and his swing so true that he may let his mind wander entirely off the golf course.

And the fact that even when he does this, he brings off a good shot most times, shows that a good swing—a formed habit—is well worth cultivating.

Women Handicapped by Men's Courses

Alexa W. Stirling

WHAT WOULD HAPPEN TO THE BOLD MEMBER, WHO AT A MEETING OF the executive committee of the US Golf Association (USGA), might be foolish enough to propose that the men's tournaments should henceforth be played over courses some 7,500 yards long, trapped without reference to the science of their game and with a par well over 80? And yet he would be proposing just such a set of conditions for the men as have hitherto generally applied to the golf of women.

Even in these days of female munitions workers, farm laborers, car conductors, aviators and deep-sea divers, the most militant suffragette must admit that physically women are at a disadvantage, and that this applies in golf as in nearly every other form of exercise. There hardly can be any need to discuss the matter—it is a fact that cannot be seriously questioned. And it is just as true that the best golf courses have been laid out without reference to women's play, but scientifically to suit the distance of the men's shots, which their superior strength enables them to make much longer than women's. Men have the advantage of adding to their own power that which lies in long and heavy clubs and heavy balls, while their superior height and acknowledged strength of body, arm, and wrist enable them to take the turf for iron shots with less difficulty.

I am here trying to explain the apparent inferiority of women's golf when compared to that of men, and the apparent remedy, of course, is to set forward the tees for women.

I do not believe, however, that such an action can ever make out of a first-class course for men, one of equal quality for women, because it will upset to a great extent the system upon which the hazards have been placed. All the best courses laid out in recent years have been constructed on the most scientific lines, and as is natural, have been designed for men. Consequently, all distances, traps, bunkers, and greens have been measured for men alone.

The good modern course laid out for men, is as a rule built with four one-shot holes, that is, one shot from tee to green, with a par of 3; two or three three-shot holes with a par of 5, and the remainder two-shot holes with a par of 4. It has come to be a generally recognized fact that a two-shot hole requiring a drive and a full iron shot to the green is the greatest and truest test of a good golfer's ability. Two-shot holes may, however, vary a great deal in length so that one will be a drive and a mashie, another a drive and an iron, and still another a drive and a cleik, and so on.

Par for such a course as I have mentioned, will range anywhere from 71 to 74, and it will as a rule, be from 6,300 to 6,500 yards long, which is recognized as the ideal distance, provided, also, that the topography of the country is suitable. However, no matter how good the "lay of the land" may be, a course cannot be considered at its best unless every shot has its special interest and possible penalty, and the approaches to the greens are specially guarded. A green to which the approach would be made with a mashie, is very severely trapped, as a good exponent of the mashie is expected to be able to stop his ball within a limited area. The green that is approached by a full iron shot is not trapped so severely because it is a recognized fact that it is hard to drop a full iron shot within a limited area, and have the ball stay there. A green that can be reached only with a wooden club is left still more open. The traps on the sides of the course and in the fairways also play a most important part and must of course be scientifically placed so as to catch bad shots and let good ones escape.

All this is done for the game of men. When we put a woman on a man's course, this scientific, well-thought-out construction is in all probability found to be inappropriate to her and I shall try to state here in greater detail, some of the evils of the present system.

If we consider, for example, any ordinary two-shot hole, properly and well guarded by hazards of some description, a good male golfer will have no difficulty in negotiating such a hole under ordinary circumstances, because it was built for him. But, put a woman on the same hole and let her use the same clubs as the man, and she will nearly always fall short of the green and not improbably into a trap. At any rate she requires a third shot to get to the green. I believe it is the general opinion amongst experienced golfers that the worst and most unfair type of hole is that which cannot quite be reached in two shots but requires a short chip shot to get on the green after two full shots. It is on such occasions that a hole is "nobody's 4 and everybody's 5." This means that on such holes the good player is unfairly handicapped, and the poor player unduly benefited, because while the distance to the green is too great for two shots for either player, the third is so short and easy even for the indifferent player, that his previous bad shots are not properly penalized with the result that the scores of the two players probably will be equal.

Yet this is the type of hole women constantly have to play, producing, for instance, a series of 5s that should be 4s. This gives their play an apparent inferiority that, in reality, it does not possess.

In comparing men's and women's golf, it should always be borne in mind that when one player is perfectly free to choose his clubs, he has a distinct advantage over an opponent who, in order to get sufficient distance, is forced to press his shot or to use a club that is less advantageous for the particular lie. This disadvantage is constantly apt to fall to the lot of women in playing over a course scientifically constructed for men. Men are expected to play par 3 for any distance under 225 yards, and women to play par 3 for any distance under 175 yards. Yes there are par 3 holes for both men and women from 100 yards upward in which it may be easy for a man to use a mashie and therefore make his ball lie snugly on the green, where a woman would have to use a less advantageous club. Therefore, I think, to have an actually fair test for women, mashie holes for men should be so shortened for women as to become mashie holes for them also. Men and women ought to be able to use the same club for any particular shot in order to make their par play equal.

Let us compare women's golf with men's over an average 550-yard hole with a par of 5, and trapped in an ordinary manner, both playing from the same tee. The object of the first hazard is to catch balls of insufficient carry. Still farther down may be some ditch, stream, or artificial hazard to catch short, hooked, or sliced balls, while close on the green is a series of traps shutting it off more or less completely according to the nature of the club with which the third shot ought to be made if the two previous shots have been played with the accuracy and distance the plan of the hole necessitates for par golf.

When a woman plays from the men's tee, it is natural that she should either fall short of the first hazards, be mixed up in them, or so press her drive that she pulls or slices into the rough beyond. Even if it safely passes the traps on the fairway, an excessive effort on the second shot will be needed to place the ball in the same position as the man's for the all-important third shot, which is to lay it and keep it on the green. The man will use his mashie or niblick, the woman may have to use an interior club. A woman playing a man's distance is therefore continuously pressing or running foul of the rough or hazards.

The average man's drive ranges anywhere from 200 to 235 yards, with an average of about 220 yards when the ground is not exceptionally hard. His second with a wooden club will be about the same or perhaps a little less. Taking the average distance, it will be found that in two shots he covers about 435 yards. The remaining distance is convenient for a mashie pitch with cut, or a pitch and run, or a run-up shot, according to the way in which the hole is constructed.

The average woman's drive ranges anywhere from 175 to 210 yards, with an average of about 190 yards, under the same weather conditions as those stated for the men, and her second will be just about the same length, but perhaps a little less. Again taking the average distance, her two shots cover only 375 yards, she is then left with 175 yards to go. A shot as long as 175 yards for a woman necessitates a full iron, and in some cases a full wooden club shot. Neither of these has enough cut on it to count, and this has a most important effect upon her score. That is how she is handicapped on a full-length course.

It is doubtful also, as has already been said, whether a man's course can ever be made exactly suitable for women, because the mere advancement of the tees does not remove all disadvantages. She is still penalized, as the man is not, where the course is scientifically constructed for his game. For instance, in the case of a par 5 hole for men according to the figures of the Women's Western Association, it will be noticed that the women's tee should be set forward nearly 150 yards. The effect of this upon the first shot would be that the first traps would be of no use for the purposes for which they were played. If their object is to catch a badly topped ball, they would catch it too soon, or not at all because the women's tee would be close upon and even beyond them. If they are to catch a long ball, but with just insufficient carry, the women's tees would be so close that the hazards would be too easily negotiated. The women's second shot, according to the Women's Western figures, would put her ball about fifty yards ahead of the position mapped out for the finish of a man's shot. The trapping therefore, for the second shot would be unsuitable for the women, and the third accordingly would be correspondingly out of gear with the man's third shot.

The same sort of argument applies to par 4 holes, and there are many one-shot holes where the topography is such that it is impossible to shorten the hole for women so as to make the shot for them correspondingly difficult or easy, as compared to the man's shot, because the tee and the green are frequently separated by deep depressions or irregularities of the surface, which, if used for tees, would change the character of the hole.

As has already been said, the object to be aimed at is to give women on any individual hole, the same type of shot as that intended for men. As it is not practicable to move the greens, and so shorten the holes from both ends, the moving of the tees seems to be the only way to minimize the difference between men's and women's golf.

Why I Quit Gambling on Golf

Anonymous

WHEN I TOOK UP GOLF, I DID IT MUCH AFTER THE MANNER IN WHICH I take a pill. The idea wasn't exactly pleasant, but I thought it would do me good.

Entirely customary conclusions compelled me to the step. My work as a bank official made some outdoors hours absolutely necessary. The fact that most of my friends and business associates had already taken up the game made it the obvious method of attaining my end.

I had no intention of going into the sport with any serious ambition. Like every other neophyte, I felt I would be entirely contented with an ability to play the game on about the same footing as others of my age, habits, and business environment.

After going through the throes and woes of the beginner, of course, the game took hold. I found a most congenial atmosphere in a foursome of a minor manufacturer, an attorney of growing reputation, and the head of a brokerage house. We were about of an age and ambitious—golf and otherwise.

We became regular weekenders, and whenever else opportunity—which we frequently created—occurred, found us battling over the course. Our competition was keen, but its spirit was fine. We observed all the ethics, all the rules, and all the courtesies of the game. Personally, I was content to go on golfing forever in the even tenor of this way.

Finally, the realization dawned that there were lots of the regular players getting more out of the sport than we were. It's true their games were stronger—that possibly might explain the difference between their competitive attitude and ours. On the other hand, as our games improved, as we consulted the pro more and more each week, as we spent more hours in practice, I noticed that our competition still lacked the fire of any number of golfing inseparables at our club.

Their conduct on the course was less parliamentary than our own. They moved off the greens slower than we did. I noted that our cards were marked at the end of each hole in about half the time required by the more combative players. There seemed to be more causes for golfing debate and the tones employed in these discussions were frequently more of the forum than an ethically quiet course.

Locker room conversations didn't lack spirit, but they did seem to be almost without the spirit of sportsmanship that has made Scotia's pastime. Compliments paid rival players were few and far between. Their good shots were attributed to luck. There was no sympathy for bad play. It was generally laughed at, and the laughs didn't have much mirth and certainly small camaraderie.

Checkbooks were displayed a whole lot more than cards to be signed for play at the good old nineteenth hole—for, alas! those were the days before vandals destroyed that venerable institution. Tickets were daily signed for enough golf balls to last the ordinary player a lifetime.

One Saturday afternoon, a member of our foursome suggested: "Let's try a modest syndicate—say a ball a hole."

We all accepted gladly. I don't mean to say that the game had lost any of its charm for any of us, but the bare suggestion of having something tangible to stand for your honest belief in your own golfing superiority and your personal willingness to stand by that belief, threw a new zest into the game—a zest that not one of us had known before.

Soon after we drove off the first tee, I realized my game had changed. I took my stance more carefully. I addressed the ball with a grimmer determination to do things to it than my golfing spirit had ever shown before. I was charged with a desire to do everything exactly as I had been instructed, everything that golf reading and authoritative information had brought my golfing knowledge.

It wasn't hard to discover my three companions were inspired by the same spirit. Unquestionably our games showed an immediate response to it. I had a glowing satisfaction when I won my first syndicate, which I don't know I had felt at any moment in a lifetime that had reached the middle years.

When we reached the clubhouse, we found out we had finished practically on even terms. No one's golf ball supply had been materially increased. No one was hurt. But what new joy we got in going over our cards again and again after we came out from the showers. We joked each other merrily on our several shortcomings. We spoke with a laugh on uncanny luck that had attended our games. We returned to the city like schoolboys from a picnic. Every one of us candidly believed we had found the thing to give the crowning touch to the game in which we were already hopelessly fascinated.

That spirit kept on for weeks and all that time we were getting new thrills as the syndicate grew to individual bets of increasing proportions. We soon found ourselves not only betting on every hole, but betting between each individual on every hole, the match, medal score, and on a whole lot of the hundred odd opportunities to wager that the game offers.

Still, there was no harm done. We were all men of perhaps more than moderate means. Our losses were never more than our finances could readily stand, though I admit that on occasions I would have been loathe to inform my wife just exactly what a day's golfing had cost me. Our games were about evenly strong—or weak, as you choose. Our temperaments weren't far out of line. Golfing luck will always practically even up among men who play together constantly.

But that gay companionship that had marked our early golfing days had now disappeared. Golf is proverbially a dour game, but no one has ever accused it of being a sour game. And that was the mental condition in which we finally found ourselves.

Unconsciously, we began to regard each other with a savage rivalry. We began to watch each other a bit too closely as an opponent played out of a hazard. Our discussion on rules became fervid. More than once, there were covert hints that several members of the foursome had had mental or mathematical lapses when it came to totaling strokes.

The condition had become almost unbearable when it was relieved by a fortunate incident that approached tragic at the time.

We had inspired our caddies with the gambling spirit. They began to follow our example with just as much avidity if the stakes were not as high as marked our sport.

It was a caddie who finally brought us to our senses. One of my companions had sliced for the tee to what was apparently a bad lie. His caddie had a bet of what was to him mammoth proportions on that very hole. When my companion reached his ball, he found that the caddie's surreptitiously moved toe had put him in beautiful position to play a brassie to the green.

Another of the players had seen the caddies' move. That savagery that had marked the play of each one of us during the last few months temporarily got the better of his judgment and his innate gentility. He openly charged his fellow player with collusion with the caddie.

The accused player—of course innocent—responded to primordial impulse. He launched a blow with his club at his companion that, had it landed, would have caused a funeral. It missed by a fraction of an inch. Fortunately, we were near enough at hand to rush up and prevent casualties.

But certainly nothing more unseemly was ever seen on a course. Further golfing was out of the question. I immediately called a caucus of our foursome in the clubhouse, asking the combatants to put aside prejudice until we could straighten out this tangle as became gentlemen.

The incident had given me some very illuminating ideas on the process that had destroyed as fine a foursome as ever dubbed over a course.

I spoke those ideas when we reached the clubhouse. "We fellows in the past few months," I explained, "have absolutely deprived ourselves of a perfect pleasure that we had attained in life at a period and during an age when pleasures are few and far between.

"And we've done it for exactly nothing in the world. Do you realize that recently we have been playing golf in exactly the same spirit as is shown in a cut-throat stud game in a professional home? And what for? I doubt if there is a man here more than $100 ahead or $100 behind on the whole period in which we've been thinking of each other in terms of the underworld while we have been playing what is essentially a gentlemen's game.

"The whole answer is that we have not been playing golf. We have simply been using the game of golf as a method for gambling. Now I found out early in life that I could give up gambling and I have also found out a bit late in life that I can't give up golf. I don't propose to, so I'm going to give up gambling."

And not only I did, but so did the rest of the foursome, and we are back playing our old game and having the same old good time.

The Americanization of Archie

Hugh S. Fullerton

Archie MacNichol's farm straggled along the side of Charity Knob, Ohio. Worn and washed land it was, clay that yielded sparse crops, a straggling beechwood at one boundary, but mostly bleak fields, half concealed in sparse grass, with great gullies gouged through the hillsides where the rains washed. His cornfield always was straggling and uneven, his little garden plot, in spite of his diligence and care, usually yielded a poor crop. Over the 180 acres of hillside farm, his little band of sheep roved, picking a sparse living from the bunch grass and dry growths. His chief crops, according to the neighbors whose prosperous farms spread in the creek valleys that lay on three sides of Charity Knob, were rabbits and blackberries.

Archie was a little old man, bandy of leg, shaggy of hair, and whiskered. Whether bachelor or widower none was certain, but he lived alone in the little house by the spring just below the crest of the knob, and around the house were a few old apple trees, gnarled from neglect. His dooryard was near, and a row of old-fashioned flowers grew along the unnecessary front fence. He was a silent, dour fellow, wasting few words on his neighbors, and unsociable, repelling, perhaps without intent, their efforts at the neighborly kindnesses that were characteristic of the scattered community. Each Sunday he drove into town, attended the services at the Presbyterian church, declined curtly and without thanks invitations to remain to dinner, and drove home.

Our farm was in the creek valley, a mile from Archie's little house on the hill. One corner of our farm adjoined his where a little angle of woodland extended up the hill. Through these clumps of oak and maple flowed Archie's spring branch to join the waters of the creek. The bit of woodland was my playground, just below where the spring branch emptied into the creek was the swimming hole, and in the cool shade of the tiny forest I played cowboys and Indians and dug the bandit cave.

Through the woodland, as I grew older, I made sallies into the blackberry thicket on Archie's land, a favorite hiding place of rabbits in the fall, and there, in the shade of the woods, the berries grew largest in summer. Archie forbade trespassing, which in the nature of things made adventures into his domain more tempting. Many times I fled bearing treasure, at the sound of his voice in angry scoldings. Later I learned that Archie did not care, but feared reckless shooting might wound his sheep.

At evening, especially during the fall months, when the berry bushes turned waxen red and the oaks and maples were aflame with color, when the smoke haze and the odor of burning brush hung over the land, Archie sat at the door of his house and played upon his pipes and, on quiet evenings, when distance permitted the tune to emerge from the clashing skirl of the pibroch, we could roll in the grass under the trees of our dooryard and listen to the brave lilt of the "Campbells are Coming," or the clashing defiance of the MacGregor hymn, and once, only once, I recall the plaintive wail of "Lochaber Nae Mair."

Afterward, when the ministers preached about "One crying in the wilderness," I always thought of Archie alone with his sheep and his ancient collie, sitting there in the twilight pouring the death wail of a lost nation into the pipes.

He was a harsh, unsociable man, and not liked. Even Annie, the gentlest of souls, said he was dirt and smelled of sheep.

I was sixteen, I remember, when I became Archie's friend. I had always stood rather in fear of him. There were tales among us little boys of how Archie once caught a boy stealing apples in his orchard and had cut his ears off. Somehow my ears always felt uncomfortable when he was near. When I became big enough to work and to plough in the big bottom at the foot of his hill, my curiosity was aroused by some peculiar actions on his part. For up the rain-rutted side of the bleak hill, he would stand and presently he would strike something with a stick and follow it and strike again, and after a time he would start off in another direction, still swinging a stick and hitting something that was on the ground, and after he had gone all the way around his house, first downhill, then uphill, then over the crest, he would cease striking and attend to his work.

At first I believed he was killing some reptile or animal, but afterward I discovered he was playing a game.

One day, when I was sixteen, I went out of the cornfield and up into the little wooded corner to get a cool drink at the spring branch, and, at the side of the paths that led up the hill, I found a curious, hard, round object. Its surface was chipped and cut, and I wondered what it might be. I took it to the house with me that evening and Charlie, the hired man, said it was "Auld A-a-a-rchie's" ball with which he played his game. Charlie always referred to him as "Auld A-a-a-rchie," rolling the name inimitably. So in the evening I walked up the lane and took the ball to its owner.

Archie's joy at recovering the ball was overwhelming. He seized upon it as if recovering a treasure and regarded me as if in doubt whether to charge me with stealing the ball or thank me for returning it.

"Ye'r nae sae bad a boy, after a,'" he decided finally. "I'll nae forbid that ye shall shoot the wee hares, gin ye nae shoot night the sheep."

The magnificence of his offer left me dumb. To be the only boy in the neighborhood who could hunt rabbits on Archie's berry fields was not a distinction lightly to be regarded. He told me he had lost the ball "fower" days ago, and had searched the entire hillside, and was grieving because he must wait an entire week before he could secure another one "frae Jock MacIndoo, in Nae York," and asked where I had found the ball. I described the spot and he swelled with pride.

"Nae sae bad," he decided. "Two hunnerd and saxty yards, aboot, and fair direction. Ma drivin' is improving, thos' maybe I'm a wee bit slicing."

I inquired of him about the game he played and instantly he regarded me indignantly.

"And ye're a Soct?" he said. "A Scot and nae ken gowf? 'Tis an oncevalized land and a gener-a-a-tion of triflers. Tell yer faither 'tis as weel nae tae baptize a Scotch bairn a snae tae teach him gowf."

After that, I got along famously with the old man. I used to go up the Knob to his farm in the evenings and sit with him in his doorway while he played upon his pipes and I learned to join him, when, at the height of his evening concert, he arose and, marching with the pipes and both thumping the floor hard with our feet, played and sang:

"The great Argye went on before."

He told me about the game of "gowf" and showed me the little rough, three-hole course laid out in a triangle around his house, and for my instruction played around several times and allowed me to examine his bag of clubs that had come from Scotland with him.

A year or so later I went away from the farm. On the rare occasions when I revisited the old place, I went up to call on Archie. He was getting older and a bit more garrulous. When I told him I had learned "gowf" and was playing over a wonderful course in the East he was delighted and insisted upon giving me instruction as to shots. He made me describe the course and, after studying the matter for a few minutes, remarked: "Nae sae bad for an onceevalized country. But of course tes nae Sent Anders."

For that I sent him a box of golf balls when my vacation was over and received a note of thanks.

It was five years later that the home folks in the town near which we lived decided to have a golf club. The country is beautifully rolling and rough in spots, well wooded and watered, and ideal for golfing. The boys asked me to find an architect who would do the work and I managed to persuade one of the best to undertake the task. Very properly they decided to start modestly, preferring nine well-laid-out and well-kept holes to eighteen mediocre ones, and the bit of countryside they chose enabled them to have a perfect little gem of a course. They wrote and asked me to be home for the opening and I went.

The evening before the formal opening of the club we had a gay little gathering in the clubhouse—a preliminary to the formal dinner and dance for the next evening. I had kidnapped one of the foremost players in the country and dragged him home with me to attend the celebration. And during that informal gathering before the wood fire in the huge fireplace of the clubhouse I told them the story of Archie and his golf course on Charity Knob. Some of the fellows knew Archie.

"We must get the old fellow to come in to the opening," someone exclaimed. "Why, he's the father of golf in this part of the country."

The proposal met with enthusiastic seconds. So early the following morning, the famous golfer and I, with two others of the fellows, drove out to Charity Knob. We found Archie, older, a little more bent, a little more grizzled, a great deal more greasy, tending his sheep. I told him that a famous golfer, who had played all the courses in Scotland, was visiting me and that he had asked to see him and talk golf.

"And sae ye've played Sent Anders? Archie asked after the introduction. "D'yre mind the saxteeenth? I tik a sax on it, forty-sax years agone. I should ha had a fower, but the ba' found the trap to the right, d'ye min?"

In spite of his mild protests, we arrayed him in golfing clothes we had brought and carried him off in triumph, taking his ancient war bag of clubs and his pipes. He never had ridden in an automobile before but scorned to show nervousness.

That afternoon, leading the field, he drove off against the famous player. I am not accusing anyone of deliberately losing a golf match, but the fact that Archie came in glowing, and the one up on one of the greatest golfers in the world, looks suspicious.

And that evening Archie, with a wee dram more than necessary to give him courage, stepped out bravely with his pipes and led the march down the great lounging room and around the table while our feet pounded the floor and men and women joined in the brave words:

"The great Argyle went on before
To make the guns and the cannon roar.
Sound of trumpets and pipes and drum
And banners waving in the sun."

And then, when the Campbells were Coming, we roared the chorus until even the shrill of the pibroch was drowned.

In the wee hours of the morning, when the famous player and I helped a slightly befuddled but wholly happy old man out of an automobile on the top of Charity Knob, he said:

"Ye're gude lads. 'Tis happy I've been the day as I na hoped ta he in this life. 'Tis nae sae onceevalized a country after a.'"

Excerpt from *Babbitt*

Sinclair Lewis

I

All the way home from Maine, Babbitt was certain he was a changed man. He was converted to serenity. He was going to cease worrying about business. He was going to have more "interests"—theaters, public affairs, reading. And suddenly, as he finished an especially heavy cigar, he was going to stop smoking.

He invented a new and perfect method. He would buy no tobacco; he would depend on borrowing it; and, of course, he would be ashamed to borrow often. In a spasm of righteousness he flung his cigar case out of the smoking compartment window. He went back and was kind to his wife about nothing in particular; he admired his own purity, and decided, "Absolutely simple. Just a matter of will-power." He started a magazine serial about a scientific detective. Ten miles on, he was conscious that he desired to smoke. He ducked his head, like a turtle going into its shell; he appeared uneasy; he skipped two pages in his story and didn't know it. Five miles later, he leaped up and sought the porter. "Say, uh, George, have you got a—" The porter looked patient. "Have you got a timetable?" Babbitt finished. At the next stop he went out and bought a cigar. Since it was to be his last before he reached Zenith, he finished it down to an inch stub.

Four days later, he again remembered that he had stopped smoking, but he was too busy catching up with his office work to keep it remembered.

II

Baseball, he determined, would be an excellent hobby. "No sense a man's working his fool head off. I'm going out to the game three times a week. Besides, fellow ought to support the home team."

He did go and support the team, and enhance the glory of Zenith, by yelling "Attaboy!" and "Rotten!" He performed the rite scrupulously. He wore a cotton handkerchief about his collar; he became sweaty; he opened his mouth in a wide loose grin; and drank lemon soda out of a bottle. He went to the game three times a week, for one week. Then he compromised on watching the Advocate-Times bulletin board. He stood in the thickest and steamiest of the crowd, and as the boy up on the lofty platform recorded the achievements of Big Bill Bostwick, the pitcher, Babbitt remarked to complete strangers, "Pretty nice! Good work!" and hastened back to the office.

He honestly believed he loved baseball. It is true he hadn't, in twenty-five years, himself played any baseball except back-lot catch with Ted—very gentle, and strictly limited to ten minutes. But the game was a custom of his clan, and it gave outlet for the homicidal and sides-taking instincts that Babbitt called "patriotism" and "love of sport."

As he approached the office he walked faster and faster, muttering, "Guess better hustle." All about him the city was hustling, for hustling's sake. Men in motors were hustling to pass one another in the hustling traffic. Men were hustling to catch trolleys, with another trolley a minute behind, and to leap from the trolleys, to gallop across the sidewalk, to hurl themselves into buildings, into hustling express elevators. Men in dairy lunches were hustling to gulp down the food cooks had hustled to fry. Men in barber shops were snapping, "Jus' shave me once over. Gotta hustle." Men were feverishly getting rid of visitors in offices adorned with the signs, "This Is My Busy Day" and "The Lord Created the World in Six Days—You Can Spiel All You Got to Say in Six Minutes." Men who had made five thousand, year before last, and ten thousand last year, were urging on nerve-yelping bodies and parched brains so that they might make twenty thousand this year; and the men who had broken down immediately after making their twenty thousand dollars were hustling to catch trains, to hustle through the vacations the hustling doctors had ordered.

Among them Babbitt hustled back to his office, to sit down with nothing much to do except see that the staff looked as though they were hustling.

III

Every Saturday afternoon he hustled out to his country club and hustled through nine holes of golf as a rest after the week's hustle.

In Zenith it was as necessary for a successful man to belong to a country club as it was to wear a linen collar. Babbitt's was the Outing Golf and Country Club, a pleasant gray-shingled building with a broad porch, on a daisy-starred cliff above Lake Kennepoose. There was another, the Tonawanda Country Club, to which belonged Charles McKelvey, Horace Updike, and the other rich men who lunched not at the Athletic but at the Union Club. Babbitt explained with frequency, "You couldn't hire me to join the Tonawanda, even if I did have a hundred and eighty bucks to throw away on the initiation fee. At the Outing we've got a bunch of real human fellows, and the finest lot of little women in town— just as good at joshing as the men—but at the Tonawanda there's nothing but these would-bes in New York getups, drinking tea! Too much dog altogether. Why, I wouldn't join the Tonawanda even if they—I wouldn't join it on a bet!"

When he had played four or five holes, he relaxed a bit, his tobacco-fluttering heartbeat more normally, and his voice slowed to the drawling of his hundred generations of peasant ancestors.

Forty Miles from Nowhere

George Ade

WITHOUT AN UNDUE SLATHERING OF THE FIRST-PERSON SINGULAR, LET it be recorded that the original plans for the amusement park and golf corral now known as Hazelden provided for a mere shack where a buffeted author might find desk room. No need to explain how and why the house became elongated and the garage grew a second story and the icehouse was followed by the residence for cows and the swimming pond and the cottage and the dancing pavilion and the greenhouse and the water tower and various other non-productive departments until our sylvan retreat began to look like a suburban development.

I had such a spread of country place that I couldn't afford any other residence in the summer months. Therefore, I lived at home. The environment was all that any back-to-the-soil advocate might prescribe for one who had tarried along between the high walls and under the blanket of smoke. Venerable oak trees, whistling birds, pathways bordered by flowers, much food that never had ridden on the ears. The mornings were great for uninterrupted work. The afternoons were yawning vacancies. Motoring across the flat cornlands is mighty monotonous. Woodland rambles have a tameness and sameness after one or two days. Tennis proved a bit violent and tantalizing, and besides, who wants to do a day's work in thirty minutes?

Games were invented to provide excitement for the inmates and their visitors. One was a sort of outdoor "squash" played with tennis racquets and balls, with the plastered wall of the water tower as the receiving surface of the open courts, the ball to be returned back to an area marked out on the turf. A good game for one who is not sufficiently nimble to do all the jumping-jack stuff required by tennis. A good game, yes—but only good for a little while at a time.

BOWLING GOLF

Did you ever hear of bowling golf? Another local invention and the best one we ever worked out. It is a simple elaboration of the old English game of "bowls." Instead of remaining on one green, the balls are rolled toward fixed marks and each mark becomes the tee or starting point for another mark beyond. The numbers were affixed to trees and stakes. Heavy composition roque balls of different colors were used for the bowling. The pathways or alley leading toward each numbered tree or stake was rather closely mowed down and also swept with a lawn sweeper. The first bowl was from the south doorway of the house toward a sundial stump out on the lawn. The ball placed nearest the objective won the first count. Any number of players up to eight could bowl in one match and sometimes the scoring was based upon the position of balls near the mark, the same as in quoits. The team winning the first roll took the honor and tried to place the balls near No. 2, which was a linden tree at the corner of the garage and about thirty yards distant. The course worked out into a total of twenty-seven numbers, with distances ranging from fifteen yards to fifty. Most of the playing was in the shade of the big trees. The beginner was about as good as the expert. No special costuming was necessary. No one became overheated. The spirit of competition always ran high, even if a description of the game does sound like nothing whatsoever. Each contestant walked a full half mile in each round, did a useful "home exercise" twenty-seven times in picking up his ball, and simply had to limber up in order to execute the long spinning shots across the award. I have grabbed a little valuable space in Grantland Rice's new weekly to tell about this inane game of "tree golf" because it is like symbolic music, a good deal better than it sounds.

THE NERVE WRECKER

For years, we made out with tennis and squash and bowling golf and some horseback riding and desultory target practice with small rifles. Even these piffling pastimes had their interesting moments.

For instance, can you sense the dramatic importance of the following situation: It is Saturday afternoon, and the dusty weekender has just alighted from the awful "accommodation." The day is warm. The guest is shown a tall mint julep, frosted on the outside and canopied with the lush green of nature's favorite vegetable grown, hereafter to be used only in conjunction with spring lamb. He steps out of the Saint Anthony division and reaches for the life-saving decoction. He is restrained. The drink shall be his, but a certain preliminary is necessary. A time-honored ceremony will have to be observed. He is led outdoors and a small rifle loaded to the stem with spit-fire cartridges is given to him. He is shown an iron target on an oak tree fifty yards away. In the center of the target is a small open bull's-eye. He is told that a bell will ring as soon as a bullet enters the bull's-eye. When the bell rings, he will receive the mint julep.

Admitting that the proposition sounds like cruelty to the city trade, can't you see the entertainment possibilities? William Tell going after the apple and the Sergeant York piling up the Germans in front of him had nothing much on the grim and determined guest who was trying to make that bell ring.

THE TROUBLE BEGINS

Hazeldon was a sort of a place before a certain epoch-marking morning, but our diversions had to be pumped about by main force. The actual trouble began when we hauled forth a bagful of dusty clubs, left over from Exmour and South Shore and Palm Beach and French Lick, and began trying pitch shots toward imaginary cups in the lawn. In order to make the mark definite, a tomato-can was sunk. A pocket handkerchief area around the cup was clipped and rolled and it became almost a putting green. Then spoke the tempter as follows: "Instead of playing for the same silly old cup all the time, why not lay out a conservative course of nine holes with hazards and everything?

The house was on a gentle knoll in a ten-acre enclosure that had an ample growth of oak, hickory, wild crab, hawthorn, hazel brush, elder, blackberry, and grapevines. The native copses were impenetrably thick and there were all sorts of sporty, gateways to guard the small greens in the open. So, we laid out a nine-hole course. The first hole was one hundred yards, and the player could take his choice of a run-up under the spreading branches of a big oak or a bold mashie right over the top of the tree. The shortest hole was twenty-eight yards. The largest green was only about forty feet in diameter.

Before going into detail as to the evolution of the toy course, let me give you the "lay of the land." Hazelden is on the main pike two mile east of Brook, Indiana, which has a population of 1,200 or so. The next nearest town is Goodland, nine miles to the south and just about the same size as Brook. Thirteen miles to the southwest is Kentland, the county seat. As I was born in Kentland, I will give it a population of 1,500 no matter what the census returns may indicate. These three towns are mentioned because they have provided the membership of the Hazelden Golf Club, except for a small and important contingent who live out on their own farms.

Hazelden is far from any settlement that can label itself a "city." Kankakee, beloved of the paragraphers, is across the Illinois line and forty miles to the north. Danville, Illinois, home of "Uncle Joe" Cannon, is forty miles to the southwest, La Fayette is fifty miles toward Indianapolis. These geographical data are given so that you may know how easy it is to start away out in the country, far removed from what we have come to regard as a golfing population.

GREEN IN LEFT FIELD
Some of the younger business- and professional men of the three nearby towns had become snarled up in a "soft ball" tournament being played off at Hazelden. When they came out one Wednesday, they discovered a putting green in left field and they gathered around it and gazed at it and derived much entertainment from the first low-comedy attempts at putting. Not one of them had played. Some of them had caught glimpses of it from railway trains and motor cars. They were pleasantly skeptical

about the merits of the game, not contemptuous but merely uninformed. They took turns about with the few clubs available, and the virus did the rest. "Soft ball" went into the discard, and I sent a hurry-up call to some of my friends in Chicago to let me have all of the mashies, jiggers, approach cleiks, and putters that have been retired from service. The response was a veritable "shower" of clubs suitable for the short game. Within a month, thirty or forty devotees were fighting the little nine-hole course.

The Hazelden Golf Club had been formally christened. A row of lockers had been installed in the dancing pavilion near the first tee. The maniacal cackle of the winner and the sepulchral alibi of the loser were now heard in the land, and those who were supposed to be normal began to show evidence of temperament on the putting greens, and there were shrill disputes as to the rules. The best traditions of the game were being observed, although our members had never heard of these traditions.

We had a couple of annual tournaments with big dinners and cups and no end of excitement and rivalry, all generated from the dinky nine-hole affair.

CITY FOLKS ARRIVE

City folks who came out were especially enthusiastic over the little course. They could go out and play a round while waiting, or luncheon, and all of them said they needed practice on the short game. To make some of the open holes more sporty, barriers interlaced with green boughs were set up as hazards.

It was fore-ordained that we would not remain content with mere approaching and putting. Several of us began to play cross-country holes. We would walk south to the main farm buildings a half mile away and play back to the green immediately south of the house—through the woods, across the pastures, past the garden, and over the hedges, winter rules governing. I think an average for this half-mile hole was about thirteen.

Often we discussed the possibility of going in for a regular nine-hole course and learning to play for distance from the tee. The inducements were in evidence, a sixty-acre pasture just east of the house, heavily turfed and rolling away gently toward the south to a wandering drainage ditch that had taken on the aspects of a natural brook.

The decision came in 1913 after a winter at Belleair and orders from the physician to remain near home. It became evident that the only way to get a golf course was to go right out and steal a lot of land from the farm and fence it off and peg out our holes and begin to play. The elbow-shaped tract suggested by Tom Bendelow took up almost forty acres. The old turf was too valuable to be sacrificed, but it was full of bumps and hammocks.

We burned and hand-raked and top-dressed but we never got a fairway surface until we sent for a huge road roller and put it to work after a heavy rain. The ground was spongy, and the steam roller certainly did iron it out. Of course the fairways were as hard as pavements the first year and the dub who topped his ball could get two hundred yards, but the grass survived and after one winter of freezing and thawing a springy surface was restored. The fairways have always been excellent.

The course we laid out and over which our happy band has been disporting itself for several years is not constructed for the paying of regular golf, and we know it. But it provides plenty of excitement and gives us a chance to try all kinds of shots. Here are the holes and the distances:

No. 1 .... 420 yards

No. 2 .... 210 yards

No. 3 .... 300 yards

No. 4 .... 105 yards

No. 5 .... 230 yards

No. 6 .... 310 yards

No. 7 .... 340 yards

No. 8 .... 165 yards

No. 9 .... 425 yards

We have two corking good holes, the short No. 4 is a mashie pitch to a plateau beyond the brook, with trouble on all sides, No. 5, commonly called "The Kaiser" because it was a tough proposition to overcome, is guarded from tee to green by a wide brook and must be played as a dogleg by one who is not sure of distance and direction.

THE CLUB GROWS

Year by year, the club has grown until now we have seventy members and could easily increase the total to one hundred. Until last year the annual dues were fifteen dollars, but now the sustaining members insist on paying fifty dollars a year, so we may improve the course and buy new equipment. We have two classes of members. Sustaining members may vote at meetings and have clubhouse privileges for their relatives and friends. Playing memberships are based yearly at twenty dollars.

In 1917 we dedicated a clubhouse, set in the hickory grove just across the pike from No. 1 tee. It was built entirely of white oak logs and was meant to last forever, for the foundations are of stone and the cypress-shingled roof is guttered with lead. The building is ninety feet long, with two screened porches; a living room, twenty-eight by eighteen; a restroom for women; a locker for men; and the necessary showers and toilets. There are also a small work bench and equipment for cleaning and repairing clubs and an electric range for cooking. City visitors are especially taken with our unique little clubhouse. The members have all sorts of parties at the house during the season and especially in the autumn after the big fireplace can be set to roaring.

It is true that the Hazelden club started as a private course and that the club members who first came were, in a way, unruly guests of the owner. Now they insist upon taking over the financial responsibilities. These not heavy. During the season, two men are kept at work on the course. Each was paid last year eighteen dollars a week. We find that a horse-drawn, three-unit mower is needed on the course an average of two days a week. If the man and horse had to be hired from the outside, the weekly payroll would be nearly $50, counting the occasional extra help needed for night sprinkling. Our whole staff at Hazelden is accustomed to going out and fussing with the golf course, and so it is rather difficult to gauge the real cost of labor, but I think fifteen hundred dollars would cover the annual payroll of an average nine-hole course.

The most important problem to be solved by a suburban or country golf club involves water to the greens. At first we laid down small pipes and depended upon gravity pressure from the tower. When the terrible drought came last year, we could not get enough water to the green (which we were constantly enlarging) and they burned to a crisp. Last fall we put in an underground tank and laid new and larger pipes and now we can flood three greens at one time with a forty-pound pressure and we feel sure our greens will come back and be as good as they used to be, which was pretty good.

We have no kitchen. Members bring their picnic baskets and often prepare warm coffee or heat coffee at the electric range. The caretaker serves a Sunday dinner at his cottage to all who notify him in advance.

THE BIG DAY

Sunday is the big day. We have tournament play for prizes every Sunday afternoon. We were thundered at for awhile from some of the local pulpits, but now our church-going members seem to have arrived at a friendly understanding with the pastors. The boys pass the contribution boxes in the morning and cuss their mashie shots in the afternoon. The average number of players on Sunday is about forty. The average number on weekdays, except Saturday, is about eighteen to twenty. No one comes on Saturday except the weekenders from the large towns.

The course record is held by Chick Evans, who on two different occasions has played the nine holes in 30. Also, he holds the record for the best two consecutive rounds—63.

In September 1918, the Hazelden Club held a Red Cross tournament, which was a proud day for our little organization, as we cleared over two thousand one hundred dollars. No club in Indiana raised one-third of that amount. The players were Chick Evans and Ken Edwards against Jock Hutchinson and Bob McDonald. We had Walter Hagen on hand ready for substitute. A gallery of 1,500 followed the players. We had an overhead parade by twelve airplanes. It was a lovely day, and we had all of our flags out.

When a golfing event can be made such a terrible success in what might be classed as a rural community, miles and miles from any good-sized town, doesn't it prove that the whole of America is ripe territory simply waiting for the invasion of the grand old Scottish game?

THE SMALL TOWN BOOM

There are thousands and thousands of small towns in which the business- and professional men, the lawyers and doctors, and merchants and grain buyers and bankers, find open time on their hands during the long summer afternoons. Every one of these men is a candidate for golf. He needs golf if he is to escape becoming pot-bellied and lazy and slow of movement. It is a cinch that no other game will ever hold and claim his interest.

Riding around in a Ford car at twilight isn't going to speed up his circulation or eliminate the toxins. Golf was simply made for this lad and if it is put within his reach, he will go to it. He will go to it with a vim and a never-subsiding enthusiasm. The fifty-year-olders will be set back to thirty-five, and the retired farmer will have something to live for, for the first time in history.

A successful golf course can be established on any clean open site in the middle west that has five thousand population within twenty miles of the first tee. The hard roads and the superabundance of moderate-priced cars have eliminated the distance. The daily papers and popular magazines have given the entire population a preliminary introduction to the game and aroused in them a pleasant curiosity regarding it. Our experience out at Hazelden has been that everyone within riding distance of the course has expressed a desire to "try" the game. You know what happens to the fellow who experimentally sniffs cocaine or begins taking small doses of opium, just in a spirit of fun.

OFF THE BABY COURSE

I forgot to say that our local membership refused to play the baby course after we opened the longer holes. For a time we maintained an eighteen-hole course, the nine short holes in the home grounds and No. 10 to be the first of the long holes in the open. Our ambitious talent always played off at No. 10, so we abandoned the toy nine, much to the regret of the pilgrims from the city.

Although our golfers are pretty much self-taught, I suppose that twenty of the thirty regulars have shot the course under forty and a couple have done as well as thirty-four. They can hold their own with players from larger and more important clubs. Even with the increase of annual dues and the greater cost of supplies, the game has laid no particular burden on the member of moderate means.

In view of what has happened in our neighborhood and because golf interest becomes contagious whenever it finds lodgment, it may be predicted with confidence that hundreds of nine-hole courses are going to plant their cherry little banners on the plains and hillsides of inland America within the next few years. In each community there will have to be a few courageous promoters, but the game will take care of itself wherever properly planted.

Youth Is Served Again When Gene Sarazen Lays Low Golf's Wizards and Wins the Open

Damon Runyon

Skokie Country Club, Glencoe, Illinois, July 15—Gene Sarazen, who is the "dead spit" of Rodolpho Valentino, as Mr. Valentino appeared doing his stuff in "The Four Horsemen," grabbed the American golf championship this afternoon.

In accomplishing this feat, Sarazen ruined a lot of excellent thoughts that many newspaper gentlemen, including the writer, were all set to put on paper if Johnny Black of California came through, about age triumphing over youth. Age, as represented by Johnny Black, did its absolute darndest, but the years became a heavy load on a man's back in this sporting life when youth lays up alongside and looks you in the eye.

Puffing at a villainous old dudeen, Johnny plodded and plugged and pegged away down what you might call the homestretch, and at the finish he was one stroke behind Gene.

One stroke in golf is just the same as a mile in the final reckoning. It was a game finish for age, at that, and the middle ages did not feel despondent.

Sarazen is just twenty-one and looks it. He is an Italian, born at Rye, New York, and a few years ago he was a caddie at the Apawamis Club, toting a sack of sticks around on his immature back for the golfing great.

Now he has caddie of his own and splits the golfing honors of the world with Walter Hagen, the holder of the British title. He saw the new

American champion standing beside the British champion this evening. They looked like a horse and a colt. Walter and Gene are the same deep bay color from the sun and Gene wears his hair slicked back the same way as Walter. Gene is about four hands shorter than Walter.

At this time Gene is the professional at the Highlands Club of Pittsburgh. The reader will note that we seem to have considerable information about Gene now in view of the fact that his name has not hitherto appeared in these columns. We can explain this paucity of mention in a few words. We candidly admit that we are one of the many who did not know Gene was in the tournament.

We saw him go past this morning, little and brown and kiddish-looking, with Johnny Farrell, who used to be a caddie contemporaneous with Gene and we confess his passing left us quite cold. No palpitating gallery of spectators followed Gene and Johnny, just, their scorer and club bearers.

Bobby was playing every shot very carefully. He looks something like Willie Hoppe, the one-time boy wonder of billiards. Perhaps it is the way he parts his hair. He played with all the discretion of Hoppe on tough shots, too.

When his ball was on the green, near the hole, Bobby would squat down and look things over at length. He would inspect the grass between his ball and the hole, then he would get away back behind the ball and squint his eye over the situation.

Duncan plays golf like Alfred De Oro plays pool, continuing the simile between golf and its distant relative.

The Scotchman is a fast man. He steps up to the pill, gives the layout one brief scrutiny, then wham! The shot is made. Some golf experts say Duncan would be a better golfer if he would take more time. He is rough on the spectators, too.

Johnny Black was paired with long Jim Barnes today and they were among the last to start this morning. A big gallery was lined up waiting for them.

The Pacific Coast professional had a pipe in his mouth. It is one of the oldest and most odorous pipes the world has ever seen. It is a good scheme to keep up the wind from Johnny when he has the old stove going or you may be gassed by the fumes.

Johnny wore a cap, a brown sweater, and a pair of loose flannel trousers. John and Jim were about the only golfers on the course wearing "stacks" or long trousers.

One not acquainted with golf felt that these two kids, whoever they were, ought to leave off practicing when such an important tournament was being decided, with so many important golfing personages requiring the use of the course.

No one paid much attention when Gene turned in a score of 75 for the morning. If anyone should have happened to mention it you would have said absently; "Is that so, well, what did Black do?" All of the folks couldn't even pronounce Gene's name this morning. Now they roll it off their tongues glibly.

When Gene came home in the afternoon with his faithful companion, Johnny Farrell, a big gallery was collected about the last hole, and some politely inquired the identity of the young man, while looking over their heads to see if any of the big chaps were in the offing.

Then when Gene plunked the ball in everybody suddenly awoke to the fact that here was a championship possibility. They gathered about the dark little fellow slapping him on the back and cheering wildly. Gene grinned amiably.

"There's two or three still out there that have a chance to get 288, too," we suggested timidly to young Sarazen as he stood posing for the moving picture operators after rounding out that score.

"I know," said the brown-skinned youth, gazing into the distance where his competitors were still struggling along. "They've got a chance to get it—but I've got mine!"

Bobby Jones of Atlanta, another "kid" in the tournament, made a finish as valiant as that of Johnny Black. The Georgia boy finished with the same score as Black, 289. It was the final hours of the tournament that gave one some idea of the real thrill in golf, when half a dozen were coming in neck and neck, so to speak. Furthermore, there was something of the dramatic in the dark youth suddenly bobbing up right out of the haze, unknown, as fresh as paint, and topping all the men whose names are bywords throughout the world of golf.

About 39,000 feet patterned about the lovely but somewhat heated Skokie meadow today, allowing two feet to every person with the exception of a one-legged man. This man was the most fortunate of all the spectators. He had only one foot to get sore.

A small but select assemblage was at the hopping-off point at 9 o'clock when Frank Sprogell of Memphis and George Martin of Santa Barbara tuned up. From that time on, the folks were coming through the gates in big bunches.

It was another great day, a perfect meteorological frame for the gathering of lovely ladies in their most freely colored dresses, and the gents in their sports clothes.

The ladies present had much more endurance than the men. We followed one girl who wore extremely high-heeled shoes for two miles to watch her collapse, but we collapsed first.

To view properly the big golfers at play, one should have had a pair of stilts.

The players shoved off again today in pairs, as usual, but they did not all have the partners they had on other days. The committee switched them around some. This struck as an inconvenience, especially to those golfers who drew no galleries but wandered about over hill and dale all alone.

Each pair still had their caddies, and scorer, of course. The scorer in some cases was really unnecessary. The golfers could have been trusted to turn in their correct marks. From the shade of an old crab apple tree, we watched a couple of them shoot and we know they wouldn't have dared lie much.

Before noon the Skokie meadow teemed, as you might say, with humanity. Distinguished-looking citizens and citizenesses were flat-footing hither and yon, especially yon.

You could locate the big golfers from afar by the size of the galleries. Yonder went Hagen and Chick Evans with several thousand folks panting behind them. Over there, by the trees were George Duncan and Bobby Jones. These two pairs had fat galleries from start to finish. In Jones's following, one heard the accents of dear old southland, indicating that Bobby had some admirers from home.

Scott Hudson, the old-time harness horse driver, was among them. Rugged and red-looking, Scott trailed the whole town all the way.

They must have been a jolly pair.

Neither spoke a word, and their expressions were exquisitely mournful. Not all the spectators followed the golfers about the course. Thousands banked themselves on camp chairs at the start, and at the last hole in front of the Skokie clubhouse.

Though we have no knowledge of Who's Who in Chicago society, we feel sure that this society was strongly represented in the gathering. Chiropodus, the patron saint of golf, probably frowned on their inactivity, however. His disciples will do no business among them.

Many hot sports from the region of the loop were seen on the lawn.

These casual visitors heard with interest that there are speculative phases to golfing. A pool is held before these big tournaments, and you can buy in a player the same as you buy a number in pool aboard ship.

For instance, Hagen's chances of winning may bring a thousand dollars, this money going into the general pool and the total amount going to the buyer of the winning player. After the more prominent golfers have been sold off, the lesser lights are bunched and sold as the field.

Visions of the possibilities of "fixing" a golf tournament may immediately unroll themselves in the minds of some of our Broadway readers, but we assure you such a thing would be considered a "faux pas" in the best golfing circles.

The Tantalus Loving-Cup

W. G. Van Tassel Sutphen

IT WAS ROBINSON BROWN WHO MADE THE DISCOVERY THAT GRAEME Elphinstone had never won any kind of a golf prize, although he had been a member of the Marion County Club for more than twenty years. It was astonishingly incredible, but after the Executive Committee had taken the matter up and gone carefully over the prize list from the very first page, it was seen that Brown was right—the name of Graeme Elphinstone was conspicuously absent from that roll of immortal fame. When this painful task was ended, the members of the Executive Committee leaned back in their chairs and exchanged glances of sorrowful dismay. What were they to do in the face of a situation so unparalleled? How was it possible that Elphinstone had escaped?

"But he has," growled Montague, "and that argues a defect in the system somewhere. Once again, what are we going to do about it?"

"It's something of a distinction in itself, isn't it?" suggested Alderson. "Might we not award him some kind of a cup in recognition . . . er . . . of his extraordinary career as a non-prize winner?"

"Golf is not charity," quoted the Fiend, austerely.

"Of course not," laughed Robinson Brown, "but it's a pretty fair business. Now I'm not much of a player, but I did very well last season for a man without any definite occupation in life. I entered every one of the seventy-six competitions and cleared a trifle over eight thousand dollars in plate. Really, gentlemen, I don't know how I should ever have got through the hard winter of 1905 if the department stores had not offered me a very generous rate of exchange in the matter of flannels and groceries. I actually lived for three months upon the proceeds of the Grand Challenge Cross for Class M players, and Robinson Brown, Jr., would not be at Princeton now if it were not for that blessed Lackawanna Cup and your kindness, gentlemen, in keeping my handicap at fifty-four." And Brown pulled out a big bandanna handkerchief and proceeded to fleck away an imaginary fly on his nose.

I think we were all more or less affected as we remembered what a brave fight dear old Brown had made against a veritable sea of troubles—wrong stance, impossible grip, golf elbow, and I don't know what all. Of course we had helped him out, for that was the way we did things at Lauriston. When a member fell into pecuniary difficulties, we did not insult him by passing around a subscription paper or by doling out soup tickets; not at all; we simply raised his handicap allowance and increased our orders at the medal factory.

"But Elphinstone is well off," objected Montague. "He doesn't need assistance."

"That's not the question," retorted Bob Challis, impatiently. "He has never won a prize of any description, and the fact is a reflection upon the club that must be removed at any cost. We have a tournament tomorrow, at medal play, for the famous Punch-bowl Pewter, and Elphinstone's present handicap is minus four. I move that it be raised to plus eighteen." The motion was adopted, nem con, and the committee rose.

Well, the blind handicap for the Punch-bowl Pewter came off, and Elphinstone's gross score of 82 was an easy winner when reduced by the liberal allowance of eighteen strokes. We all pressed forward to congratulate him upon his accession to the noble army of cup winners, but he waved aside our outstretched hands and demanded an immediate audience of the Green Committee. Upon its being accorded, Elphinstone confessed that he had tried a few practice putts upon the fourth green the morning of the match, and was consequently disqualified. There was no getting around this, and the Pewter went to the Fiend, 104–72–32.

We were all very sorry for Elphinstone, and the committee tried in several ways to give him another chance at the prize barrel, but without success. Something always happened at the last moment to knock out the unlucky Elphinstone, and finally he refused altogether to hand in his cards, alleging as an excuse that his ill fortune was too persistent to be overcome. Too bad! For by this time his handicap was away up in double figures, and on one occasion he might have won Marion County Mug, No. 1318, in the remarkable score of four strokes net, had he not torn up his scorecard at the very last hole simply because he had failed to hole an eighteen-foot putt.

There was just one more chance during this present season, and that was the regular autumn tournament, conducted under medal and match rules for the possession of the Tantalus Loving-Cup, an ornate piece of massive plate that took two men to carry, and whose cost was about equal to the annual salary of a bank president. It was certainly worth winning, and it was hinted (unofficially of course) that it was to go to Elphinstone, and that it would be as much as a man's membership was worth to win it over the poor fellow's head.

Well, through the luck of the draw, Elphinstone was obliged to dispose in succession of every crack player in the club, and Robinson Brown, of all men, was left in with him for the finals. The contest would hardly be worth much from the golfing point of view, seeing that Elphinstone could easily give Brown two strokes a hole, but the gallery nevertheless turned out in force. Everybody wanted to see for the last time the man who had never won a prize in twenty years of play at the Marion County Golf Club.

It was a bright, glorious October morning, and Robinson Brown was on the ground at an early hour, practicing brassie shots and running up short approaches. Elphinstone still remained in the seclusion of his humble home a short distance away, and I fancy that few among that brilliant gallery that was assembling around the first tee would have recognized the favorite of the day in the wan-faced, sad-eyed man sitting in a darkened room, and nervously awaiting the fatal stroke of ten. But perhaps it is just as well that our ordinary human eyes are as yet unprovided with the X-ray appliance. No member of the Marion County Club could have fathomed the meaning of that piteous spectacle—a strong man in his agony.

"It's of no use, Mary," said Elphinstone, sadly, to his devoted wife, in answer to the mute appeal in her eyes. "I've fought against this thing for twenty years, and now the end has come. I can't put up a bad enough game to let Robinson Brown beat me, a man who possesses a heaven-born genius for foozling. And yet it is hard—hard to be obliged to win a prize after all these years of falsifying scores, slyly kicking my ball into unplayable lies, and negotiating short putts with my eyes shut. And we were so happy in our humble way of living, our little income just sufficient for our needs, and not even the care of a solitary claret jug to weigh upon our minds." His voice broke, and his breast heaved with a dry, choking sob.

"But we must be brave," continued Graeme Elphinstone, with a mighty effort. "We will take turns in sitting up nights to guard that accursed piece of plate and perhaps by the first of next month I may be able to set enough aside from my slender salary to hire a safe deposit vault. But I fear that Johnny will have to leave school, and Ellen must give up her piano lessons. You know as well as I do that the Tantalus Loving-Cup is but the beginning of the deluge. We are lost!"

"Graeme," said Mrs. Elphinstone, with a resolute ring in her voice, "I can't tell why I know it, but I feel sure, absolutely sure, that there is yet some way out of this miserable business. See how nicely I have oiled the grips of your clubs; it is almost impossible to hold them at all. Now go; it wants but five minutes of the hour. Heaven will not desert our just, though humble, cause while a bunker remains upon the Marion County course."

"Amen!" echoed Elphinstone, fervently and with bowed head. Then straightening up, and with a new light in his eyes: "You have given me new faith, new courage; I believe the opportunity will present itself, that the way of escape will open. We have not worked and suffered all these years that our imitation oak—finished sideboard should groan beneath the weight of a sixteen-thousand-dollar golf cup. I can cheerfully slave and toil for you, Mary dear, and for our beloved children, but I will not spend my very lifeblood in paying storage and insurance charges upon an inartistic monstrosity that is neither food, drink, nor good clothes to wear." And Graeme Elphinstone brought his mighty fist down upon the family Badminton with a crash that fairly dislocated the photographic reproduction of Mr. Hutchinson's famous full swing. (Poor, simple-minded

Elphinstone! He knew naught of Mr. Robinson Brown's advantageous contract with the department stores.)

"Colonel Bogey will surely protect his own," murmured Mrs. Elphinstone as she watched her husband's tall form striding rapidly down the road to the clubhouse. "Let me not forget in my prayers that lost ball is lost hole."

It was to be expected that Elphinstone would outclass Robinson Brown, but no one had supposed that the latter could be actually seventeen holes down at the ending of the first round. Elphinstone had played badly enough, but Brown's foozling had been something super human. He played as though inspired (as, indeed, he was by a hint from the Executive Committee), and Elphinstone could not have lost a hole if he had played with his eyes shut. The home hole was halved by the pure accident of a long putt, and the morning play ended with Elphinstone seventeen up and eighteen to go. Elphinstone was as white as a sheet when we went into the clubhouse for luncheon, but we put it down to nervous excitement at the prospect of winning the magnificent Tantalus Loving-Cup. We tried to encourage him by assurances that he could not possibly lose, but he refused to be comforted, and lunched in gloomy seclusion upon a biscuit and a soda lemonade. Brown, on the contrary, was the center of an uproarious circle who drank champagne at his expense, and chaffingly offered odds of a hundred thousand to one against him. And Brown took all the bets.

Now it is an unwritten law of the club that the principals in the last round of an important match shall wear all the medals, crosses, and similar small insignia they may have won in previous contests. The custom is a picturesque one, and Brown was certainly a resplendent spectacle as he stepped to the tee in response to the referee's call of time. Eighty-nine medals, stars, and crosses, by actual count, were displayed upon his ample person; he was simply incrusted with gold and glitter and looked for all the world like an idol out for a holiday call upon some neighboring deity. But his chief pride and glory was one enormous gold medal, about the size of a soup plate, which he wore suspended from a chain around his neck. This medal had been awarded to Brown for his remarkable record in holing the long course in sixty-nine minutes actual time—number of strokes not given. Brown had a way of alluding to this record without mentioning the word minutes, and this omission led literal-minded persons into forming erroneous conclusions as to Mr. Brown's standing in the world of golf. However, we all have our weaknesses, and no one could be deceived who had ever seen Brown play.

Elphinstone had made a poor tee shot, and it was Brown's turn to play. As he addressed his ball, the full force of the sun caught the polished surface of the big medal, and the sudden dazzle seemed to disconcert him. He stood there apparently forgetful of his surroundings, his podgy white hands mechanically waggling the club and his mild blue eyes fixed in a curious glassy stare. What could be the matter with the man?

Elphinstone had been watching his adversary intently, and now, as though moved by a sudden impulse, he stepped forward and whispered a few words in Brown's ear. The latter nodded an assent, and then drove what any golfing reporter would have described as a clean two-hundred-yard raker. As a matter of fact, it did carry the green, one hundred and forty-seven yards away, and the hole was his in two. Elphinstone sixteen up and seventeen to play.

After Brown had won fourteen straight holes by the most machine-like and perfect of golf, Alderson, of the Executive Committee, managed to get him to one side and remonstrated with him. Brown declared, with every show of sincerity, that he had been doing his utmost to play off, but that the ball *would* find its way into the hole. "I'm going to press every shot after this," he concluded, timidly, "That ought to do the business, don't you think?"

"Be sure that it does," returned Alderson, with cold severity. "Understand clearly, Brown, that there must be no more trifling in this matter. It is some five years since you began feeding at the public crib, and as the Fiend has well said, 'Golf is not charity.' If Elphinstone doesn't win, look out for squalls."

Well, Brown did the next four holes each in a stroke below par, and the score stood all square, with one hole to play. Brown had the honor, of course, at the eighteenth tee, and he looked as though he were about to collapse as he prepared to drive.

"Top it into the pond," admonished Alderson, in a loud stage whisper. "You've done it often enough when it wasn't necessary."

The wretched man gasped, shut his eyes tight, and literally threw his club at the patiently waiting "gutty." It was beautiful to see the ball cleave the air as straight and hard as though shot out of a rifle barrel—there! It had carried the green—it was rolling true for the cup—down in one!

Shame!

The "gallery" shouted the execration as one man, and Brown opened his eyes only long enough to see what he had done and to cower beneath the lightning scorn that flamed upon him from every quarter. Then he fell down in a fit and was carried off to the horse trough by two of the grooms.

Jove! But it was fine, the plucky way in which Elphinstone took his defeat. He was very quiet, but curiously cheerful, and he even insisted on shaking hands with Robinson Brown when that scoundrelly hypocrite, very wet and very penitent, presented himself at the back door of the club and tried to explain away his abominable conduct. The Tantalus Loving-Cup was hastily handed over without any of the usual jollification and speech making, and then Alderson compassionately bundled him into a cab and sent him home, while a meeting of the full board was immediately called to consider the question of his expulsion from the club. It was a serious situation, for you recall the wagers that Brown had taken against himself at the ridiculous odds of one hundred thousand to one. He had won no less than eighty million dollars by his trickery, and bankruptcy stared us all in the face.

It is six months later, and I add a postscript. Robinson Brown is still a member of the club, but Graeme Elphinstone has resigned, and is now living somewhere out west. It was the week after he went away that we received his explanation in a letter to Alderson. It seems that Brown had involuntarily hypnotized himself while admiring the glittering radiance of his big gold medal, and Elphinstone had grasped the situation and had taken advantage of it. Poor Brown had been but a puppet in his hands for the whole of that remarkable final round, and of course was perfectly innocent of any sharp practice. In making this amazing communication, Elphinstone expressed no regret for his extraordinary course of action except by way of apology to Brown, and when we came to think it over, there really seemed to be no tenable ground of offence. It was not as though Elphinstone had won the Tantalus Loving-Cup by his psychological coup; it simply remained a mystery.

Of course, Brown was reinstalled with all the honors. We settled the bets by giving him our I.O.U.'s for the several amounts, and Brown used them as fuel wherewith to cook a chafing-dish of oysters à la Chamberlin. They were delicious; it is not often that one has a chance at a chafing dish supper that cost $80,000.

It was at this supper that Brown read some extracts from another letter he had just received from Elphinstone.

"He sends lots of love, and says he is very happy," said Brown, glancing over the pages. "They have organized a golf club, and it must be an odd one. Just listen:

"⊠No clubhouse—simply an old stone barn, with a big fireplace at one end and the club-maker's bench at the other.

"⊠No society functions, nor afternoon tea. There isn't a red coat nearer than a thousand miles, and the only refreshment allowed is Scotch and soda.

"⊠No handicap prizes.

"⊠No prizes of any kinds, except a spring and autumn medal (value, fifty cents), and one challenge cup, which must be won ninety-nine consecutive times to become anyone's absolute property. We call it THE CUP.'"

"Gracious Bogie!" gasped Montague. "No clubhouse, no society, no tea, no handicaps. What do they have, then?"

"Just golf," put in the Silent Member, with an emphasis that made everybody jump.

"What rot!" ejaculated the Fiend, recovering himself. "Come, you fellows, and help unpack the spring prizes; I see the express wagons have just driven up. By the way, Brown, it's your turn to win the May Scratch event. Which would you rather have, a silver cleik with gold mountings or a house and lot?"

But Robinson Brown answered never a word; he was staring absent-mindedly into the fire.

"Just golf!" he murmured, under his breath. "What an idea!"

The Joy of Golf

Alvin R. Springer

IS IT POSSIBLE THAT, IN THE EFFORT WE MAKE TO PLAY GOLF AND TO play it correctly and accurately and precisely and according to "form" that we do not take the time nor the perspective to really enjoy and appreciate the grandeur and beauty of the game itself?

Is all of golf and golf pleasure in the skill and science of the game well played? To have the best of clubs; a good, new ball; to take the proper stance; secure the orthodox grip; execute the proper upswing and to duplicate it coming back; to hit the ball just right and in the proper place and at the correct time; and to see the ball sail away for its fair two hundred yards or more over a lovely blue-grass lawn: These things are certainly productive of ample pleasure and gratification for any mortal man, it occurs to me, and yet I find there is vastly more to golf than the perfection of play that we strive so grimly for and so seldom attain.

For instance, take a fine summer morning, the day promising hot, the languid air from the sunny south giving every evidence of the scorching you will get at noonday. Who has not felt and appreciated the very love of life as he mounts the familiar tee box at number one, received a sweet kiss on the south cheek from that morning breeze and a sharp slap in the eye by that bright morning sun, as he tees up for his first drive with a good friend to fight and a good field for the combat? I say the man who has missed all these sensations, has missed a good round portion of the joys allotted to man.

Or, on another day in fall. The afternoon sun comes slanting across from the southwest. The wind has taken a furlough for the day. The leaves on the distant trees have lost the summer luster of various greens and in lieu thereof, have donned robes of every hue. The grass, too, has begun to lay plans for winter, hugging the ground so closely, hiding here and there under fallen leaves and preparing its setting for the long and bitter struggle that approaches so rapidly and whose coming is accentuated by the frost of every morning. The wilder grass has already browned. The rough is forbidding as it has never been before. The bunkers are presenting bare fronts and somber guard to the unwary. It is then that the golfer enjoys the middle of his round the more.

The brassie begins to give way for the sterner irons. The firm, hard ground renders its assistance if perchance (and perish the thought) the mighty effort with the midiron should prove a dub.

By the way now, where does that name come from? The DUB. No other word so completely fills the bill. If the shot was half as good as the name, well, the term might be used elsewhere. But golf has laid hold of that short and ugly word and appears to have it forever enslaved. But listen; the dubs on that fall round may be numberless and innumerable. They may take a large toll on every hole and work havoc on every tee box. But all things may end. You are 180 yards away from the home green. You are in rough and rocky terrain. The bunkers loom up before you, gaunt and forbidding. The lie is unfavorable indeed. Your trusty old clubs have all proved faithless this day.

Your midiron is poised aslant your right ear, its polished blade glistens in the evening sunlight, your eye is riveted on that charmed spot just behind your well-worn pellet, and with a mighty sweep of trusty club and arms of knotted muscles, you lay against that old ball the accumulated wrath of one whole afternoon of unrequited toil. How sweet the feel of contact as steel meets ground and ball, just shaving off the wild growth of withered grass. How charming in its shock you feel that ball take every ounce and fraction thereof encompassed in your mighty co-ordination of mind and muscle. There is nothing for beauty, wonder, magnificence, or sublime that equals the flight of a golf ball well played, especially if you are the player. That ball sails away on wings invisible, it hangs poised in its journey for a fragment of a second just over the green, then, having spent its force, having fought its way against air and the laws of gravitation, that ball, your ball, the ball you struck yourself, succumbs to the immutable laws of nature and, without struggle, drops quietly and serenely on the green. Oh, the exhilaration of red blood coursing through your veins. You march proudly to the haven called home, and note with some slight satisfaction your opponent has run afoul of that element of shot or number of shots that we have heretofore and herein classified by the three letter term.

Here lies your ball, cold, still, silent, just fifteen inches from the cup. You are down for a "birdie" on that grand old hole. And now, gone are the ill-made drives, gone forever the memory of brassies topped and midirons of mostly earth. Gone are the mashie hooks and short putts. Gone forever all the dubs of that day's play and into the forgotten abyss of the past—in one second of time the true golfer is able to cast all the losses, littleness, unhappy things, untimely and ungraceful occurrences of the day. What wonderful compensations one good shot will make. What vast realm of psychology is opened up when you play such a game of mystery? Inexplicable indeed, and yet a vastly pleasant and real and human game is this.

The poet has wisely said, "Of him who in the love of nature holds communion with her visible forms, she speaks a various language." And what is golf but a happy coordination of the laws of nature with the human being? Is golf a scientific test of muscle, a study of skill, or is it a product of a healthy love for everything that is lovely, clean, beautiful, and magnificent in this wonderful world of ours?

The Magic of Golf

Reinette Douglas

No MORE DELECTABLE STATE OF MIND COULD BE DESIRED THAN THAT resulting from having sent a golf ball arching through the air with surpassing grace and unexpected ease; nor is any species of achievement more satisfying to one's vanity. A secret thrill runs through a man—or even a woman—but not for worlds will he show it. He prefers to remain unmoved by the "Ah's" of approval from the clubhouse, struts to his bag, and flips his driver thereinto with an admirable nonchalance.

Since Adam, the animal, has chosen to appear scornful of praise justly earned, no matter how obviously he may have striven for that very commendation in the past. Within each atomic mortal there dwells a chronic pride; we wish to forget past failures as perfect as at the moment of our success.

Just so the golfer. When he has momentarily glorified himself in the eyes of the gallery, he suddenly becomes the finished artist and sees himself a master of the game. His smile is beatific as he acknowledges those direct approbations that reach his modest ears; his irrelevant remark about the "sand being pretty dry" is a masterpiece of careless ease.

Glory proves itself short-lived all too soon, and visions fade ironically with the second shot. I have stood with patronage in my soul and condescension in my manner, waiting for those less skilled players ahead of me to move off the green. I have gazed across the vast checkerboard of sunburned turf and vivid putting green with uptilted nose, a benign complacence and the lightest of heads, when the caddie's "Fore" has impersonally and hence reverentially announced that I might drive if I so desired. I have turned and addressed the ball with the most luxuriant leisure. In my mind's eye, I have seen myself a vision of perfect stroke, my ball a foot from the cup. I have taken a new grip an eighth of an inch shorter—changed back to the old one. At last I have been ready, and have gracefully indulged in a full wide swing. A plumy bit of cloud has crossed my sight. My perfect second is dancing merrily down the hill with topped speed in a direct line for the worst trap on the course!

For every bump of conceit unceremoniously punctured on one side, there arises a tender bump of wisdom on the other side of the head, so to speak. The rule: "Keep your eye on the ball" comes ruefully slinking back to mind at the same instant that the ball slips over the edge and out of sight. A sadder and wiser man, I have approached my third shot.

On the green, if the first long putt is short of the hole, and we are justly peeved, it only makes the joy of sinking the short one the greater. But, if the second fails to click, metallically from our line of vision, Necessity lays hands on us and says, "That ball must go down!" For, in those unwritten catalogs of the game, the man who habitually takes three putts is a hopeless dubber, and he who takes more than three is merely playing the game for his health.

Speaking of health, oddly enough, he who starts out by playing golf for his health is usually the one who has to be restricted to twenty-seven holes a day to keep him from killing himself. Physically speaking, one's ability or disability is not an excuse for one's presence on the links. A man plays golf for *golf*; he mows the lawn for his health.

I have kept the gender masculine throughout; it is with sorrow in my heart that I am forced to admit the foregoing principles do not apply universally to women. Too often, the subtler sex play for an excuse to wear barbarous combinations of color, and to hide comfort under the title "fashion" with regard to woolen hose. A dashing helmet-hat will send the average feminine follower of the game out on the fairway much more rapidly than the most perfect golfing day. And alas! It seldom makes much difference to her if she makes the first hole—a bogie five—in twelve or fourteen. In fact, she often neglects to count, and, as a matter of course, jots down a neat little "6" with the silver pencil hung around her neck on a jeweled silver chain.

But even the average woman, if fortune favors her with appreciation of the game, forgets herself and leaves the silver chain at home. Finding that its absence is an advantage, she abandons it entirely, as well as picture hats and lorgnettes, and becomes a feminine golfer a trifle above the average. What woman is not more attractive with glowing cheek and sparkling eye and golfing sense—which, after all, is very little different from the common sense—than with languid air and the latest of sport costumes, if she cannot put said costume to proper use?

So, amateur or professional, dub or champion, the fascination of the game grips us and winds itself about our lives. We may start the finest of novels, but, even in the brief intermission of a turning page, the lure is upon us, tripping us up on our way along the path to the state of being well read. Sport summons us with a carefree fling of the arm; Chance taunts us with a flirting wink—we have left the novel behind, face down and weeping in the stuffy pillows, and are swinging along the country road to a more alluring playground.

Each round is a story in itself; each match an adventure with true Romance a companion by my side. Exultation takes me by the hand when my long, low ball cuts over the bunker with only an inch to spare. Triumph claps me soundly on the back, when it has traveled a good two hundred yards, defying the mid-summer gale. Self-Disgust stands by with lashing tongue and sullen eye when I forget that primer rule. Despair, this this—as in the Great Game, when countless efforts seem of no avail—hovers low, with black batwings and enveloping cloak, threatening to smother all zest for the game.

I have sliced a dozen balls, each attempted remedy has been void of result—tossed into the discard with a sigh. Life's darkest moment! Then the "pro" passing me on the fairway grins at my dejected mien—drops a hint. And Hope comes singing through the fog, swift as a shaft of light. Impatience spurs me on—then Joy stands beside me, her hand in mine, when the next time the club head sweeps through it meets the ball with clean and sound impact! Castles appear just above the haze of the horizon hills, and silver loving cups are visible through the marble portals. Caution tweaks my ear, and I plod off the tee in pensive contemplation on the miracle of golf.

Luck may vary with each passing shot, our scores may fluctuate with an astonishing range of digits, but the charm remains unmoved, magnetic, compelling. Dubbers we be—yet ridicule cannot turn us aside. Our heels may be run down, our gloves full of holes, yet the money continues to flow in exchange for lessons, clubs, and small white spheres as easily as wine has flowed on the Christmas Eves of years gone by. Sometimes we profit; sometimes we pay for a reservoir of flattery and false hope; but we go on. Some of us wax childish and petulantly break clubs and memorize great awe-inspiring vocabularies for use when occasion demands. Some of us wax foolish and organize "Dawn to Dew" clubs. And some of us even overstep these bounds—I recall a member of my own family putting one night at 10:30 with the aid of the head-lights of a car run on the fairway for that purpose. Some of us take it too seriously—some of us not seriously enough; but we go on playing the grand old game; becoming more irrevocably entwined with each finished round, following the tacit master with dog-like devotion.

Any broad stretch of sod, smoothed and flattened across the acres, dented with traps, glistening with water hazards, ruffled and dotted with bunkers and "chocolate drops," is a fair section of that Big Stage on which we all are players. Out of bounds, the balance of power may change from nation to nation; inside the fence, hopes may soar aloft—and topple back into oblivion. In the world, prosperity may exist side by side with the dinginess of penury; on the green, glory of achievement may sing in the heart of one man, the hopelessness of failure submerges the heart of his companion.

On number eighteen, Walters, the broker who cleared fifty thousand on the morning's speculation, is facing his putter before his ball; if he sinks it, he will tie the course record. He bends over to carefully remove a dry leaf from the line to the hole, straightens and refaces his putter. He has the line—a caddie sneezes—he has the distance—moves the putter back of the ball—a clear, faint "fore" floats lazily across the course—he looses his wrists—the putter pendulum swings in his hands—

From number ten green, not fifty yards away, ring shouts of laughter, Judge Henderson, who heard and sentenced a man to prison not four hours since, has sunk a "birdie." His companions' mirth bursts forth boisterously, for the judge has the highest handicap in the club. "Well I'll be dad-gummed!"—"Hay! No fair sinkin' 'em over twenty feet!"—"Your syndicate all right, you old hypocrite"—"Hand over your dines, boys"— while up on number eighteen, the ball has stopped just an inch from the cup, just an inch from the course record, just an inch from fame, "By golly! That was a good try"—"Tough luck, old man, you should have had it"—"Well, come on, boys. Let's go 'round again."

So the game goes on continually. We stop at sunset, but somewhere, on the other side of the glove, other devotees are "going 'round again," losing dimes, gaining skill, sinking putts, missing drives, breaking records, breaking clubs, forgetting weight of wordly things, losing themselves in the maze of green plain and infinite sky.

From a tee on the summit of a hill, very nearly the whole course is stretched before the eye. Over the hill comes the familiar warning and a singing ball whirs past, strikes earth, and bounds along to gradual rest like a frightened rabbit.

We walk hundreds of miles and drive a good many dollars into some unoffending farmer's woods. You say they are wasted—these miles— these dollars? You say you are fools and ridiculous in the bargain? To the uninitiated, I must admit it would seem incongruous for a number of large, fat men to follow a number of small, white balls over hill and dale, from early morning down through the heat of the day to sunset. And the money spent to pay a very small boy to carry a very large bag, filled with a dozen, more or less, meaningless-looking clubs, may seem a criminal waste.

But there is a purely sensuous delight in "coming through," every muscle working in harmony, not one taut, not one wholly unused. You, who gave not gainsay the joy of lofting one out clean from the heavy sands of a trap. If we are fools—we are happy fools. If we are ridiculous— may you grow fat on the laugh you enjoy at our expense.

The winds from the great open spaces of Scotland blow away the malice in human nature: We do not decide your ignorance; we rather pity you in the fun you are missing. But it is you who turn derisively away and poke a jeering thumb back at us over a bigotedly shrugged shoulder. Very well—and we turn back to our game.

Winter Dreams

F. Scott Fitzgerald

I

Some of the caddies were poor as sin and lived in one-room houses with a neurasthenic cow in the front yard, but Dexter Green's father owned the second-best grocery store in Black Bear—the best one was "The Hub," patronized by the wealthy people from Sherry Island—and Dexter caddied only for pocket money.

In the fall when the days became crisp and gray, and the long Minnesota winter shut down like the white lid of a box, Dexter's skis moved over the snow that hid the fairways of the golf course. At these times the country gave him a feeling of profound melancholy—it offended him that the links should lie in enforced fallowness, haunted by ragged sparrows for the long season. It was dreary, too, that on the tees where the gay colors fluttered in summer there were now only the desolate sandboxes knee-deep in crusted ice. When he crossed the hills, the wind blew cold as misery and, if the sun was out, he tramped with his eyes squinted up against the hard dimensionless glare.

In April the winter ceased abruptly. The snow ran down into Black Bear Lake scarcely tarrying for the early golfers to brave the season with red and black balls. Without elation, without an interval of moist glory, the cold was gone.

Dexter knew there was something dismal about this northern spring, just as he knew there was something gorgeous about the fall. Fall made him clinch his hands and tremble and repeat idiotic sentences to himself, and make brisk abrupt gestures of command to imaginary audiences and armies. October filled him with hope that November raised to a sort of ecstatic triumph, and in this mood the fleeting brilliant impressions of the summer at Sherry Island were ready grist to his mill. He became a golf champion and defeated Mr. T. A. Hedrick in a marvelous match played a hundred times over the fairways of his imagination, a match each detail of which he changed about untiringly—sometimes he won with almost laughable ease, sometimes he came up magnificently from behind. Again, stepping from a Pierce-Arrow automobile, like Mr. Mortimer Jones, he strolled frigidly into the lounge of the Sherry Island Golf Club—or perhaps, surrounded by an admiring crowd, he gave an exhibition of fancy diving from the springboard of the club raft. . . . Among those who watched him in open-mouthed wonder was Mr. Mortimer Jones.

And one day it came to pass that Mr. Jones—himself and not his ghost—came up to Dexter with tears in his eyes and said that Dexter was the damned best caddie in the club, and wouldn't he decide not to quit if Mr. Jones made it worth his while, because every other damn caddie in the club lost one ball a hole for him—regularly.

"No, sir," said Dexter decisively. "I don't want to caddie anymore." Then, after a pause: "I'm too old."

"You're not more than fourteen. Why the devil did you decide just this morning that you wanted to quit? You promised that next week you'd go over to the state tournament with me."

"I decided I was too old."

Dexter handed in his "A Class" badge, collected what money was due him from the caddie master, and walked home to Black Bear Village.

"The best damned caddie I ever saw," shouted Mr. Mortimer Jones over a drink that afternoon. "Never lost a ball! Willing! Intelligent! Quiet! Honest! Grateful!"

The little girl who had done this was eleven—beautifully ugly as little girls are apt to be who are destined after a few years to be inexpressibly lovely and bring no end of misery to a great number of men. The spark, however, was perceptible. There was a general ungodliness in the way her lips twisted down at the corners when she smiled, and in the—Heaven help us!—in the almost passionate quality of her eyes. Vitality is born in such women. It was utterly in evidence now, shining through her thin frame in a sort of glow.

She had come eagerly out on to the course at nine o'clock with a white linen nurse and five small new golf clubs in a white canvas bag the nurse was carrying. When Dexter first saw her, she was standing by the caddie house, rather ill at ease and trying to conceal the fact by engaging her nurse in an obviously unnatural conversation graced by startling and irrelevant grimaces from herself.

"Well, it's certainly a nice day, Hilda," Dexter heard her say. She drew down the corners of her mouth, smiled, and glanced furtively around, her eyes in transit falling for an instant on Dexter.

Then to the nurse: "Well, I guess there aren't very many people out here this morning, are there?"

The smile again—radiant, blatantly artificial—convincing.

"I don't know what we're supposed to do now," said the nurse, looking nowhere in particular.

"Oh, that's all right. I'll fix it up."

Dexter stood perfectly still, his mouth slightly ajar. He knew if he moved forward a step, his stare would be in her line of vision—if he moved backward he would lose his full view of her face. For a moment he had not realized how young she was. Now he remembered having seen her several times the year before—in bloomers.

Suddenly, involuntarily, he laughed, a short abrupt laugh—then, startled by himself, he turned and began to walk quickly away.

"Boy!"

Dexter stopped.

"Boy—"

Beyond question he was addressed. Not only that, but he was treated to that absurd smile, that preposterous smile—the memory of which at least a dozen men were to carry into middle age.

"Boy, do you know where the golf teacher is?"

"He's giving a lesson."

"Well, do you know where the caddie master is?"

"He isn't here yet this morning."

"Oh." For a moment this baffled her. She stood alternately on her right and left foot.

"We'd like to get a caddie," said the nurse. "Mrs. Mortimer Jones sent us out to play golf, and we don't know how without we get a caddie."

Here she was stopped by an ominous glance from Miss Jones, followed immediately by the smile.

"There aren't any caddies here except me," said Dexter to the nurse, "and I got to stay here in charge until the caddie master gets here."

"Oh."

Miss Jones and her retinue now withdrew, and at a proper distance from Dexter became involved in a heated conversation, which was concluded by Miss Jones taking one of the clubs and hitting it on the ground with violence. For further emphasis she raised it again and was about to bring it down smartly upon the nurse's bosom, when the nurse seized the club and twisted it from her hands.

"You damn little mean old thing!" cried Miss Jones wildly.

Another argument ensued. Realizing that the elements of the comedy were implied in the scene, Dexter several times began to laugh, but each time restrained the laugh before it reached audibility. He could not resist the monstrous conviction that the little girl was justified in beating the nurse.

The situation was resolved by the fortuitous appearance of the caddie master, who was appealed to immediately by the nurse.

"Miss Jones is to have a little caddie, and this one says he can't go."

"Mr. McKenna said I was to wait here till you came," said Dexter quickly.

"Well, he's here now." Miss Jones smiled cheerfully at the caddie master. Then she dropped her bag and set off at a haughty mince toward the first tee.

"Well?" The caddie master turned to Dexter. "What you standing there like a dummy for? Go pick up the young lady's clubs."

"I don't think I'll go out today," said Dexter.

"You don't—"

"I think I'll quit."

The enormity of his decision frightened him. He was a favorite caddie, and the thirty dollars a month he earned through the summer were not to be made elsewhere around the lake. But he had received a strong emotional shock, and his perturbation required a violent and immediate outlet.

It is not so simple as that, either. As so frequently would be the case in the future, Dexter was unconsciously dictated to by his winter dreams.

II

Now, of course, the quality and the seasonability of these winter dreams varied, but the stuff of them remained. They persuaded Dexter several years later to pass up a business course at the state university—his father, prospering now, would have paid his way—for the precarious advantage of attending an older and more famous university in the East, where he was bothered by his scanty funds. But do not get the impression, because his winter dreams happened to be concerned at first with musings on the rich, that there was anything merely snobbish in the boy. He wanted not association with glittering things and glittering people—he wanted the glittering things themselves. Often he reached out for the best without knowing why he wanted it—and sometimes he ran up against the mysterious denials and prohibitions in which life indulges. It is with one of those denials and not with his career as a whole that this story deals.

He made money. It was rather amazing. After college he went to the city from which Black Bear Lake draws its wealthy patrons. When he was only twenty-three and had been there not quite two years, there were already people who liked to say: "Now there's a boy—" All about him rich men's sons were peddling bonds precariously, or investing patrimonies precariously, or plodding through the two dozen volumes of the "George Washington Commercial Course," but Dexter borrowed a thousand dollars on his college degree and his confident mouth, and bought a partnership in a laundry.

It was a small laundry when he went into it, but Dexter made a specialty of learning how the English washed fine woolen golf stockings without shrinking them, and within a year he was catering to the trade that wore knickerbockers. Men were insisting that their Shetland hose and sweaters go to his laundry, just as they had insisted on a caddie who could find golf balls. A little later he was doing their wives' lingerie as well—and running five branches in different parts of the city. Before he was twenty-seven he owned the largest string of laundries in his section of the country. It was then that he sold out and went to New York. But the part of his story that concerns us goes back to the days when he was making his first big success.

When he was twenty-three Mr. Hart—one of the gray-haired men who like to say, "Now there's a boy"—gave him a guest card to the Sherry Island Golf Club for a weekend. So he signed his name one day on the register, and that afternoon played golf in a foursome with Mr. Hart and Mr. Sandwood and Mr. T. A. Hedrick. He did not consider it necessary to remark that he had once carried Mr. Hart's bag over this same links, and that he knew every trap and gully with his eyes shut—but he found himself glancing at the four caddies who trailed them, trying to catch a gleam or gesture that would remind him of himself, that would lessen the gap that lay between his present and his past.

It was a curious day, slashed abruptly with fleeting, familiar impressions. One minute he had the sense of being a trespasser—in the next he was impressed by the tremendous superiority he felt toward Mr. T. A. Hedrick, who was a bore and not even a good golfer anymore.

Then, because of a ball Mr. Hart lost near the fifteenth green, an enormous thing happened. While they were searching the stiff grasses of the rough there was a clear call of "Fore!" from behind a hill in their rear. And as they all turned abruptly from their search a bright new ball sliced abruptly over the hill and caught Mr. T. A. Hedrick in the abdomen.

"By Gad!" cried Mr. T. A. Hedrick, "they ought to put some of these crazy women off the course. It's getting to be outrageous."

A head and a voice came up together over the hill:

"Do you mind if we go through?"

"You hit me in the stomach!" declared Mr. Hedrick wildly.

"Did I?" The girl approached the group of men. "I'm sorry. I yelled, 'Fore!'"

Her glance fell casually on each of the men—then scanned the fairway for her ball.

"Did I bounce into the rough?"

It was impossible to determine whether this question was ingenuous or malicious. In a moment, however, she left no doubt, for as her partner came up over the hill she called cheerfully:

"Here I am! I'd have gone on the green except that I hit something."

As she took her stance for a short mashie shot, Dexter looked at her closely. She wore a blue gingham dress, rimmed at throat and shoulders with a white edging that accentuated her tan. The quality of exaggeration, of thinness, which had made her passionate eyes and down-turning mouth absurd at eleven, was gone now. She was arrestingly beautiful. The color in her cheeks was centered like the color in a picture—it was not a "high" color, but a sort of fluctuating and feverish warmth, so shaded that it seemed at any moment it would recede and disappear. This color and the mobility of her mouth gave a continual impression of flux, of intense life, of passionate vitality—balanced only partially by the sad luxury of her eyes.

She swung her mashie impatiently and without interest, pitching the ball into a sand pit on the other side of the green. With a quick, insincere smile and a careless "Thank you!" she went on after it.

"That Judy Jones!" remarked Mr. Hedrick on the next tee, as they waited—some moments—for her to play on ahead. "All she needs is to be turned up and spanked for six months and then to be married off to an old-fashioned cavalry captain."

"My God, she's good looking!" said Mr. Sandwood, who was just over thirty.

"Good looking!" cried Mr. Hedrick contemptuously. "She always looks as if she wanted to be kissed! Turning those big cow eyes on every calf in town!"

It was doubtful if Mr. Hedrick intended a reference to the maternal instinct.

"She'd play pretty good golf if she'd try," said Mr. Sandwood.

"She has no form," said Mr. Hedrick solemnly.

"She has a nice figure," said Mr. Sandwood.

"Better thank the Lord she doesn't drive a swifter ball," said Mr. Hart, winking at Dexter.

Later in the afternoon the sun went down with a swirl of gold and varying blues and scarlets, and left the dry, rustling night of western summer. Dexter watched from the veranda of the golf club, watched the even overlap of the waters in the little wind, silver molasses under the harvest moon. Then the moon held a finger to her lips and the lake became a clear pool, pale and quiet. Dexter put on his bathing suit and swam out to the farthest raft, where he stretched dripping on the wet canvas of the springboard.

There was a fish jumping and a star shining and the lights around the lake were gleaming. Over on a dark peninsula, a piano was playing the songs of last summer and of summers before that—songs from "Chin-Chin" and "The Count of Luxembourg" and "The Chocolate Soldier"—and because the sound of a piano over a stretch of water had always seemed beautiful to Dexter he lay perfectly quiet and listened.

The tune the piano was playing at that moment had been gay and new five years before when Dexter was a sophomore at college. They had played it at a prom once when he could not afford the luxury of proms, and he had stood outside the gymnasium and listened. The sound of the tune precipitated in him a sort of ecstasy and it was with that ecstasy he viewed what happened to him now. It was a mood of intense appreciation, a sense that, for once, he was magnificently attuned to life and that everything about him was radiating a brightness and a glamor he might never know again.

A low, pale oblong detached itself suddenly from the darkness of the island, spitting forth the reverberate sound of a racing motorboat. Two white streamers of cleft water rolled themselves out behind it and almost immediately the boat was beside him, drowning out the hot tinkle of the piano in the drone of its spray. Dexter raising himself on his arms was aware of a figure standing at the wheel, of two dark eyes regarding him over the lengthening space of water—then the boat had gone by and was sweeping in an immense and purposeless circle of spray round and round in the middle of the lake. With equal eccentricity one of the circles flattened out and headed back toward the raft.

"Who's that?" she called, shutting off her motor. She was so near now that Dexter could see her bathing suit, which consisted apparently of pink rompers.

The nose of the boat bumped the raft, and as the latter tilted rakishly, he was precipitated toward her. With different degrees of interest they recognized each other.

"Aren't you one of those men we played through this afternoon?" she demanded.

He was.

"Well, do you know how to drive a motorboat? Because if you do I wish you'd drive this one so I can ride on the surfboard behind. My name is Judy Jones"—she favored him with an absurd smirk—rather, what tried to be a smirk, for, twist her mouth as she might, it was not grotesque, it was merely beautiful—"and I live in a house over there on the island, and in that house there is a man waiting for me. When he drove up at the door I drove out of the dock because he says I'm his ideal."

There was a fish jumping and a star shining and the lights around the lake were gleaming. Dexter sat beside Judy Jones and she explained how her boat was driven. Then she was in the water, swimming to the floating surfboard with a sinuous crawl. Watching her was without effort to the eye, watching a branch waving or a seagull flying. Her arms, burned to butternut, moved sinuously among the dull platinum ripples, elbow appearing first, casting the forearm back with a cadence of falling water, then reaching out and down, stabbing a path ahead.

They moved out into the lake: turning, Dexter saw that she was kneeling on the low rear of the now uptilted surfboard.

"Go faster," she called, "fast as it'll go."

Obediently he jammed the lever forward and the white spray mounted at the bow. When he looked around again the girl was standing up on the rushing board, her arms spread wide, her eyes lifted toward the moon.

"It's awful cold," she shouted. "What's your name?"

He told her.

"Well, why don't you come to dinner tomorrow night?"

His heart turned over like the flywheel of the boat, and, for the second time, her casual whim gave a new direction to his life.

III

Next evening while he waited for her to come downstairs, Dexter peopled the soft deep summer room and the sun porch that opened from it with the men who had already loved Judy Jones. He knew the sort of men they were—the men who when he first went to college had entered from the great prep schools with graceful clothes and the deep tan of healthy summers. He had seen that, in one sense, he was better than these men. He was newer and stronger. Yet in acknowledging to himself that he wished his children to be like them he was admitting that he was but the rough, strong stuff from which they eternally sprang.

When the time had come for him to wear good clothes, he had known who were the best tailors in America, and the best tailors in America had made him the suit he wore this evening. He had acquired that particular reserve peculiar to his university, that set it off from other universities. He recognized the value to him of such a mannerism and he had adopted it; he knew that to be careless in dress and manner required more confidence than to be careful. But carelessness was for his children. His mother's name had been Krimplich. She was a Bohemian of the peasant class and she had talked broken English to the end of her days. Her son must keep to the set patterns.

At a little after seven, Judy Jones came downstairs. She wore a blue silk afternoon dress, and he was disappointed at first that she had not put on something more elaborate. This feeling was accentuated when, after a brief greeting, she went to the door of a butler's pantry and pushing it open called: "You can serve dinner, Martha." He had rather expected that a butler would announce dinner, that there would be a cocktail. Then he put these thoughts behind him as they sat down, side by side on a lounge and looked at each other.

"Father and mother won't be here," she said thoughtfully.

He remembered the last time he had seen her father, and he was glad the parents were not to be here tonight—they might wonder who he was. He had been born in Keeble, a Minnesota village fifty miles farther north, and he always gave Keeble as his home instead of Black Bear Village. Country towns were well enough to come from if they weren't inconveniently in sight and used as footstools by fashionable lakes.

They talked of his university, which she had visited frequently during the past two years, and of the nearby city that supplied Sherry Island with its patrons, and whither Dexter would return next day to his prospering laundries.

During dinner she slipped into a moody depression that gave Dexter a feeling of uneasiness. Whatever petulance she uttered in her throaty voice worried him. Whatever she smiled at—at him, at a chicken liver, at nothing—it disturbed him that her smile could have no root in mirth, or even in amusement. When the scarlet corners of her lips curved down, it was less a smile than an invitation to a kiss.

Then, after dinner, she led him out on the dark sun porch and deliberately changed the atmosphere.

"Do you mind if I weep a little?" she said.

"I'm afraid I'm boring you," he responded quickly.

"You're not. I like you. But I've just had a terrible afternoon. There was a man I cared about, and this afternoon he told me out of a clear sky that he was poor as a church mouse. He'd never even hinted it before. Does this sound horribly mundane?"

"Perhaps he was afraid to tell you."

"Suppose he was," she answered. "He didn't start right. You see, if I'd thought of him as poor—well, I've been mad about loads of poor men, and fully intended to marry them all. But in this case, I hadn't thought of him that way, and my interest in him wasn't strong enough to survive the shock. As if a girl calmly informed her fiancé that she was a widow. He might not object to widows, but—

"Let's start right," she interrupted herself suddenly. "Who are you, anyhow?"

For a moment Dexter hesitated. Then: "I'm nobody," he announced. "My career is largely a matter of futures."

"Are you poor?"

"No," he said frankly, "I'm probably making more money than any man my age in the northwest. I know that's an obnoxious remark, but you advised me to start right."

There was a pause. Then she smiled and the corners of her mouth drooped and an almost imperceptible sway brought her closer to him, looking up into his eyes. A lump rose in Dexter's throat, and he waited breathless for the experiment, facing the unpredictable compound that would form mysteriously from the elements of their lips. Then he saw— she communicated her excitement to him, lavishly, deeply, with kisses that were not a promise but a fulfilment. They aroused in him not hunger demanding renewal but surfeit that would demand more surfeit . . . kisses that were like charity, creating want by holding back nothing at all.

It did not take him many hours to decide that he had wanted Judy Jones ever since he was a proud, desirous little boy.

IV

It began like that—and continued, with varying shades of intensity, on such a note right up to the dénouement. Dexter surrendered a part of himself to the most direct and unprincipled personality with which he had ever come in contact. Whatever Judy wanted, she went after with the full pressure of her charm. There was no divergence of method, no jockeying for position or premeditation of effects—there was a very little mental side to any of her affairs. She simply made men conscious to the highest degree of her physical loveliness. Dexter had no desire to change her. Her deficiencies were knit up with a passionate energy that transcended and justified them.

When, as Judy's head lay against his shoulder that first night, she whispered, "I don't know what's the matter with me. Last night I thought I was in love with a man and tonight I think I'm in love with you—" It seemed to him a beautiful and romantic thing to say. It was the exquisite excitability that for the moment he controlled and owned. But a week later he was compelled to view this same quality in a different light. She took him in her roadster to a picnic supper, and after supper she disappeared, likewise in her roadster, with another man. Dexter became enormously upset and was scarcely able to be decently civil to the other people present. When she assured him that she had not kissed the other man, he knew she was lying—yet he was glad that she had taken the trouble to lie to him.

He was, as he found before the summer ended, one of a varying dozen who circulated about her. Each of them had at one time been favored above all others—about half of them still basked in the solace of occasional sentimental revivals. Whenever one showed signs of dropping out through long neglect, she granted him a brief honeyed hour, which encouraged him to tag along for a year or so longer. Judy made these forays upon the helpless and defeated without malice, indeed half unconscious that there was anything mischievous in what she did.

When a new man came to town everyone dropped out—dates were automatically canceled. The helpless part of trying to do anything about it was that she did it all herself. She was not a girl who could be "won" in the kinetic sense—she was proof against cleverness, she was proof against charm: if any of these assailed her too strongly she would immediately resolve the affair to a physical basis, and under the magic of her physical splendor the strong as well as the brilliant played her game and not their own. She was entertained only by the gratification of her desires and by the direct exercise of her own charm. Perhaps from so much youthful love, so many youthful lovers, she had come, in self-defense, to nourish herself wholly from within.

Succeeding Dexter's first exhilaration came restlessness and dissatisfaction. The helpless ecstasy of losing himself in her was opiate rather than tonic. It was fortunate for his work during the winter that those moments of ecstasy came infrequently. Early in their acquaintance it had seemed for a while that there was a deep and spontaneous mutual attraction—that first August, for example—three days of long evenings on her dusky veranda, of strange wan kisses through the late afternoon, in shadowy alcoves or behind the protecting trellises of the garden arbors, of mornings when she was fresh as a dream and almost shy at meeting him in the clarity of the rising day. There was all the ecstasy of an engagement about it, sharpened by his realization that there was no engagement. It was during those three days that, for the first time, he had asked her to marry him. She said, "Maybe someday." She said, "Kiss me." She said, "I'd like to marry you." She said, "I love you"—she said—nothing.

The three days were interrupted by the arrival of a New York man who visited at her house for half September. To Dexter's agony, rumor engaged them. The man was the son of the president of a great trust company. But at the end of a month, it was reported that Judy was yawning. At a dance one night she sat all evening in a motorboat with a local beau, while the New Yorker searched the club for her frantically. She told the local beau that she was bored with her visitor, and two days later he left. She was seen with him at the station, and it was reported that he looked very mournful indeed.

On this note the summer ended. Dexter was twenty-four, and he found himself increasingly in a position to do as he wished. He joined two clubs in the city and lived at one of them. Though he was by no means an integral part of the stag lines at these clubs, he managed to be on hand at dances where Judy Jones was likely to appear. He could have gone out socially as much as he liked—he was an eligible young man, now, and popular with downtown fathers. His confessed devotion to Judy Jones had rather solidified his position. But he had no social aspirations and rather despised the dancing men who were always on tap for the Thursday or Saturday parties and who filled in at dinners with the younger married set. Already he was playing with the idea of going east to New York. He wanted to take Judy Jones with him. No disillusion as to the world in which she had grown up could cure his illusion as to her desirability.

Remember that—for only in the light of it can what he did for her be understood.

Eighteen months after he first met Judy Jones, he became engaged to another girl. Her name was Irene Scheerer, and her father was one of the men who had always believed in Dexter. Irene was light-haired and sweet and honorable, and a little stout, and she had two suitors whom she pleasantly relinquished when Dexter formally asked her to marry him.

Summer, fall, winter, spring, another summer, another fall—so much he had given of his active life to the incorrigible lips of Judy Jones. She had treated him with interest, with encouragement, with malice, with indifference, with contempt. She had inflicted on him the innumerable little slights and indignities possible in such a case—as if in revenge for having ever cared for him at all. She had beckoned him and yawned at him and beckoned him again and he had responded often with bitterness and narrowed eyes. She had brought him ecstatic happiness and intolerable agony of spirit. She had caused him untold inconvenience and not a little trouble. She had insulted him, and she had ridden over him, and she had played his interest in her against his interest in his work—for fun. She had done everything to him except to criticize him—this she had not done—it seemed to him only because it might have sullied the utter indifference she manifested and sincerely felt toward him.

When autumn had come and gone again it occurred to him that he could not have Judy Jones. He had to beat this into his mind, but he convinced himself at last. He lay awake at night for a while and argued it over. He told himself the trouble and the pain she had caused him, he enumerated her glaring deficiencies as a wife. Then he said to himself that he loved her, and after a while he fell asleep. For a week, lest he imagined her husky voice over the telephone or her eyes opposite him at lunch, he worked hard and late, and at night he went to his office and plotted out his years.

At the end of a week, he went to a dance and cut in on her once. For almost the first time since they had met he did not ask her to sit out with him or tell her that she was lovely. It hurt him that she did not miss these things—that was all. He was not jealous when he saw that there was a new man tonight. He had been hardened against jealousy long before.

He stayed late at the dance. He sat for an hour with Irene Scheerer and talked about books and about music. He knew very little about either. But he was beginning to be master of his own time now, and he had a rather priggish notion that he—the young and already fabulously successful Dexter Green—should know more about such things.

That was in October, when he was twenty-five. In January, Dexter and Irene became engaged. It was to be announced in June, and they were to be married three months later.

The Minnesota winter prolonged itself interminably, and it was almost May when the winds came soft and the snow ran down into Black

Bear Lake at last. For the first time in over a year, Dexter was enjoying a certain tranquility of spirit. Judy Jones had been in Florida, and afterward in Hot Springs, and somewhere she had been engaged, and somewhere she had broken it off. At first, when Dexter had definitely given her up, it had made him sad that people still linked them together and asked for news of her, but when he began to be placed at dinner next to Irene Scheerer, people didn't ask him about her anymore—they told him about her. He ceased to be an authority on her.

May at last. Dexter walked the streets at night when the darkness was damp as rain, wondering that so soon, with so little done, so much of ecstasy had gone from him. May one year back had been marked by Judy's poignant, unforgivable, yet forgiven turbulence—it had been one of those rare times when he fancied she had grown to care for him. That old penny's worth of happiness he had spent for this bushel of content. He knew that Irene would be no more than a curtain spread behind him, a hand moving among gleaming teacups, a voice calling to children . . . fire and loveliness were gone, the magic of nights and the wonder of the varying hours and seasons . . . slender lips, downturning, dropping to his lips and bearing him up into a heaven of eyes. . . . The thing was deep in him. He was too strong and alive for it to die lightly.

In the middle of May when the weather balanced for a few days on the thin bridge that led to deep summer, he turned in one night at Irene's house. Their engagement was to be announced in a week now—no one would be surprised at it. And tonight they would sit together on the lounge at the University Club and look on for an hour at the dancers. It gave him a sense of solidity to go with her—she was so sturdily popular, so intensely "great."

He mounted the steps of the brownstone house and stepped inside. "Irene," he called.

Mrs. Scheerer came out of the living room to meet him.

"Dexter," she said. "Irene's gone upstairs with a splitting headache. She wanted to go with you, but I made her go to bed."

"Nothing serious, I—"

"Oh, no. She's going to play golf with you in the morning. You can spare her for just one night, can't you, Dexter?"

Her smile was kind. She and Dexter liked each other. In the living room he talked for a moment before he said good night.

Returning to the University Club, where he had rooms, he stood in the doorway for a moment and watched the dancers. He leaned against the door post, nodded at a man or two—yawned.

"Hello, darling."

The familiar voice at his elbow startled him. Judy Jones had left a man and crossed the room to him—Judy Jones, a slender enameled doll in cloth of gold: gold in a band at her head, gold in two slipper points at her dress's hem. The fragile glow of her face seemed to blossom as she smiled at him. A breeze of warmth and light blew through the room. His hands in the pockets of his dinner jacket tightened spasmodically. He was filled with a sudden excitement.

"When did you get back?" he asked casually.

"Come here and I'll tell you about it."

She turned and he followed her. She had been away—he could have wept at the wonder of her return. She had passed through enchanted streets, doing things that were like provocative music. All mysterious happenings, all fresh and quickening hopes, had gone away with her, come back with her now.

She turned in the doorway.

"Have you a car here? If you haven't, I have."

"I have a coupe."

In then, with a rustle of golden cloth. He slammed the door. Into so many cars she had stepped—like this—like that—her back against the leather, so—her elbow resting on the door—waiting. She would have been soiled long since had there been anything to soil her—except herself—but this was her own self outpouring.

With an effort he forced himself to start the car and back into the street. This was nothing, he must remember. She had done this before, and he had put her behind him, as he would have crossed a bad account from his books.

He drove slowly downtown and, affecting abstraction, traversed the deserted streets of the business section, peopled here and there where a movie was giving out its crowd or where consumptive or pugilistic youth lounged in front of pool halls. The clink of glasses and the slap of hands on the bars issued from saloons, cloisters of glazed glass and dirty yellow light.

She was watching him closely and the silence was embarrassing, yet in this crisis he could find no casual word with which to profane the hour. At a convenient turning he began to zigzag back toward the University Club.

"Have you missed me?" she asked suddenly.

"Everybody missed you."

He wondered if she knew of Irene Scheerer. She had been back only a day—her absence had been almost contemporaneous with his engagement.

"What a remark!" Judy laughed sadly—without sadness. She looked at him searchingly. He became absorbed in the dashboard.

"You're handsomer than you used to be," she said thoughtfully. "Dexter, you have the most rememberable eyes."

He could have laughed at this, but he did not laugh. It was the sort of thing that was said to sophomores. Yet it stabbed at him.

"I'm awfully tired of everything, Darling." She called everyone darling, endowing the endearment with careless, individual camaraderie. "I wish you'd marry me."

The directness of this confused him. He should have told her now that he was going to marry another girl, but he could not tell her. He could as easily have sworn that he had never loved her.

"I think we'd get along," she continued on the same note, "unless probably you've forgotten me and fallen in love with another girl."

Her confidence was obviously enormous. She had said, in effect, that she found such a thing impossible to believe, that if it were true, he had merely committed a childish indiscretion—and probably to show off. She would forgive him, because it was not a matter of any moment but rather something to be brushed aside lightly.

"Of course you could never love anybody but me," she continued. "I like the way you love me. Oh, Dexter, have you forgotten last year?"

"No, I haven't forgotten."

"Neither have I!"

Was she sincerely moved—or was she carried along by the wave of her own acting?

"I wish we could be like that again," she said, and he forced himself to answer:

"I don't think we can."

"I suppose not. . . . I hear you're giving Irene Scheerer a violent rush."

There was not the faintest emphasis on the name, yet Dexter was suddenly ashamed.

"Oh, take me home," cried Judy suddenly: "I don't want to go back to that idiotic dance—with those children."

Then, as he turned up the street that led to the residence district, Judy began to cry quietly to herself. He had never seen her cry before.

The dark street lightened, the dwellings of the rich loomed up around them, he stopped his coupe in front of the great white bulk of the Mortimer Joneses' house, somnolent, gorgeous, drenched with the splendor of the damp moonlight. Its solidity startled him. The strong walls, the steel of the girders, the breadth and beam and pomp of it were there only to bring out the contrast with the young beauty beside him. It was sturdy to accentuate her slightness—as if to show what a breeze could be generated by a butterfly's wing.

He sat perfectly quiet, his nerves in wild clamor, afraid that if he moved, he would find her irresistibly in his arms. Two tears had rolled down her wet face and trembled on her upper lip.

"I'm more beautiful than anybody else," she said brokenly. "Why can't I be happy?" Her moist eyes tore at his stability—her mouth turned slowly downward with an exquisite sadness: "I'd like to marry you if you'll have me, Dexter. I suppose you think I'm not worth having, but I'll be so beautiful for you, Dexter."

A million phrases of anger, pride, passion, hatred, tenderness fought on his lips. Then a perfect wave of emotion washed over him, carrying off with it a sediment of wisdom, of convention, of doubt, of honor. This was his girl who was speaking, his own, his beautiful, his pride.

"Won't you come in?" He heard her draw in her breath sharply.

Waiting.

"All right," his voice was trembling. "I'll come in."

V

It was strange that neither when it was over nor a long time afterward did he regret that night. Looking at it from the perspective of ten years, the fact that Judy's flare for him endured just one month seemed of little importance. Nor did it matter that by his yielding he subjected himself to a deeper agony in the end and gave serious hurt to Irene Scheerer and to Irene's parents, who had befriended him. There was nothing sufficiently pictorial about Irene's grief to stamp itself on his mind.

Dexter was at bottom hard-minded. The attitude of the city on his action was of no importance to him, not because he was going to leave the city, but because any outside attitude on the situation seemed superficial. He was completely indifferent to popular opinion. Nor, when he had seen that it was no use, that he did not possess in himself the power to move fundamentally or to hold Judy Jones, did he bear any malice toward her. He loved her, and he would love her until the day he was too old for loving, but he could not have her. So he tasted the deep pain that is reserved only for the strong, just as he had tasted for a little while the deep happiness.

Even the ultimate falsity of the grounds upon which Judy terminated the engagement that she did not want to "take him away" from Irene—Judy who had wanted nothing else—did not revolt him. He was beyond any revulsion or any amusement.

He went east in February with the intention of selling out his laundries and settling in New York—but the war came to America in March and changed his plans. He returned to the west, handed over the management of the business to his partner, and went into the first officers' training camp in late April. He was one of those young thousands who greeted the war with a certain amount of relief, welcoming the liberation from webs of tangled emotion.

VI

This story is not his biography, remember, although things creep into it that have nothing to do with those dreams he had when he was young. We are almost done with them and with him now. There is only one more incident to be related here, and it happens seven years farther on.

It took place in New York, where he had done well—so well that there were no barriers too high for him. He was thirty-two years old, and, except for one flying trip immediately after the war, he had not been west in seven years. A man named Devlin from Detroit came into his office to see him in a business way, and then and there this incident occurred, and closed out, so to speak, this particular side of his life.

"So you're from the middle west," said the man Devlin with careless curiosity. "That's funny—I thought men like you were probably born and raised on Wall Street. You know—wife of one of my best friends in Detroit came from your city. I was an usher at the wedding."

Dexter waited with no apprehension of what was coming.

"Judy Simms," said Devlin with no particular interest: "Judy Jones she was once."

"Yes, I knew her." A dull impatience spread over him. He had heard, of course, that she was married—perhaps deliberately he had heard no more.

"Awfully nice girl," brooded Devlin meaninglessly, "I'm sort of sorry for her."

"Why?" Something in Dexter was alert, receptive, at once.

"Oh, Lud Simms has gone to pieces in a way. I don't mean he ill-uses her, but he drinks and runs around—"

"Doesn't she run around?"

"No. Stays at home with her kids."

"Oh."

"She's a little too old for him," said Devlin.

"Too old!" cried Dexter. "Why, man, she's only twenty-seven."

He was possessed with a wild notion of rushing out into the streets and taking a train to Detroit. He rose to his feet spasmodically.

"I guess you're busy," Devlin apologized quickly. "I didn't realize—"

"No, I'm not busy," said Dexter, steadying his voice. "I'm not busy at all. Not busy at all. Did you say she was—twenty-seven? No, I said she was twenty-seven."

"Yes, you did," agreed Devlin dryly.

"Go on, then. Go on."

"What do you mean?"

"About Judy Jones."

Devlin looked at him helplessly.

"Well, that's—I told you all there is to it. He treats her like the devil. Oh, they're not going to get divorced or anything. When he's particularly outrageous she forgives him. In fact, I'm inclined to think she loves him. She was a pretty girl when she first came to Detroit."

A pretty girl! The phrase struck Dexter as ludicrous.

"Isn't she—a pretty girl, anymore?"

"Oh, she's all right."

"Look here," said Dexter, sitting down suddenly. "I don't understand. You say she was a 'pretty girl' and now you say she's 'all right.' I don't understand what you mean—Judy Jones wasn't a pretty girl, at all. She was a great beauty. Why, I knew her. I knew her. She was—"

Devlin laughed pleasantly.

"I'm not trying to start a row," he said. "I think Judy's a nice girl and I like her. I can't understand how a man like Lud Simms could fall madly in love with her, but he did." Then he added: "Most of the women like her."

Dexter looked closely at Devlin, thinking wildly that there must be a reason for this, some insensitivity in the man or some private malice.

"Lots of women fade just like that," Devlin snapped his fingers. "You must have seen it happen. Perhaps I've forgotten how pretty she was at her wedding. I've seen her so much since then, you see. She has nice eyes."

A sort of dullness settled down upon Dexter. For the first time in his life, he felt like getting very drunk. He knew he was laughing loudly at something Devlin had said, but he did not know what it was or why it was funny. When, in a few minutes, Devlin went, he lay down on his lounge and looked out the window at the New York skyline into which the sun was sinking in dull lovely shades of pink and gold.

He had thought that having nothing else to lose, he was invulnerable at last—but he knew that he had just lost something more, as surely as if he had married Judy Jones and seen her fade away before his eyes.

The dream was gone. Something had been taken from him. In a sort of panic he pushed the palms of his hands into his eyes and tried to bring up a picture of the waters lapping on Sherry Island and the moonlit veranda, and gingham on the golf links and the dry sun and the gold color of her neck's soft down. And her mouth damp to his kisses and her eyes plaintive with melancholy and her freshness like new fine linen in the morning. Why, these things were no longer in the world! They had existed and they existed no longer.

For the first time in years, the tears were streaming down his face. But they were for himself now. He did not care about mouth and eyes and moving hands. He wanted to care, and he could not care. For he had gone away, and he could never go back anymore. The gates were closed, the sun was gone down, and there was no beauty but the gray beauty of steel that withstands all time. Even the grief he could have borne was left behind in the country of illusion, of youth, of the richness of life, where somnolent his winter dreams had flourished.

"Long ago," he said, "long ago, there was something in me, but now that thing is gone. Now that thing is gone, that thing is gone. I cannot cry. I cannot care. That thing will come back no more."

Golf in Hades

John Kendrick Bangs

"Jim," said I to Boswell one morning as the typewriter began to work, "perhaps you can enlighten me on a point concerning which a great many people have questioned me recently. Has golf taken hold of Hades yet? You referred to it some time ago, and I've been wondering ever since if it had become a fad with you."

"Has it?" laughed my visitor; "well, I should rather say it had. The fact is, it has been a great boon to the country. You remember my telling you of the projected revolution led by Cromwell, and Caesar, and the others?"

"I do, very well," said I, "and I have been intending to ask you how it came out."

"Oh, everything's as fine and sweet as can be now," rejoined Boswell, somewhat gleefully, "and all because of golf. We are all quiet along the Styx now. All animosities are buried in the general love of golf, and every one of us, high or low, autocrat and revolutionist, is hobnobbing away in peace and happiness on the links. Why, only six weeks ago, Apollyon was for cooking Bonaparte on a waffle iron, and yesterday the two went out to the Cimmerian links together and played a mixed foursome, Bonaparte and Medusa playing against Apollyon and Deliliah."

"Dear me! Really?" I cried. "That must have been an interesting match."

"It was, and up to the very last it was nip-and-tuck between 'em," said Boswell. "Apollyon and Delilah won it with one hole up, and they got that on the putt. They'd have halved the hole if Medusa's back hair hadn't wiggled loose and bitten her caddie just as she was holing out."

"It is a remarkable game," said I. "There is no sensation in the world quite equal to that which comes to a man's soul when he has hit the ball a solid clip and sees it sail off through the air toward the green, whizzing musically along like a very bird."

"True," said Boswell, "but I'm rather of the opinion that it's a safer game for shades than for you purely material persons."

"I don't see why," I answered.

"It is easy to understand," returned Boswell. "For instance, with us there is no resistance when by a mischance we come into unexpected contact with the ball. Take the experience of Diogenes and Solomon at the Saint Jonah's Links week before last. The Wiseman's Handicap was on. Diogenes and Simple Simon were playing just ahead of Solomon and Montaigne. Solomon was driving in great form. For the first time in his life he seemed able to keep his eye on the ball, and the way he sent it flying through the air was a caution. Diogenes and Simple Simon had both had their second stroke and Solomon drove off. His ball sailed straight ahead like a missile from a catapult, flew in the bee line for Diogenes, struck him at the base of his brain, continued on through, and landed on the edge of the green."

"Mercy!" I cried. "Didn't it kill him?"

"Of course not," retorted Boswell. "You can't kill a shade. Diogenes didn't know he'd been hit, but if that had happened to one of you material golfers there'd have been a sickening end to that tournament."

"There would, indeed," said I. "There isn't much fun in being hit by a golf ball. I can testify to that because I have had the experience," and I called to mind the day at Saint Peterkin's when I unconsciously stymied with my material self the celebrated Willie McGuffin, the Demon Driver from the Hootmon Links, Scotland. McGuffin made his mark that day if he never did before, and I bear the evidence thereof even now, although the incident took place two years ago, when I did not know enough to keep out of the way of the player who plays so well that he thinks he has a perpetual right of way everywhere.

"What kind of clubs do you Stygians use?" I asked.

"Oh, very much the same kind that you chaps do," returned Boswell. "Everybody experiments with new fads, too, just as you do. Old Peter

Stuyvesant, for instance, always drives with his wooden leg, and never uses anything else unless he gets a lie where he's got to."

"His wooden leg?" I roared, with a laugh. "How on earth does he do that?"

"He screws the small end of it into a square block shod like a brassie," explained Boswell, "tees up his ball, goes back ten yards, makes a run at it, and kicks the ball pretty nearly out of sight. He can putt with it too, like a dream, swinging it sideways."

"But he doesn't call that golf, does he?" I cried.

"What is it?" demanded Boswell.

"I should call it football," I said.

"Not at all," said Boswell. "Not a bit of it. He hasn't any foot on that leg, and he has a golf-club head with a shaft to it. There isn't any rule that says the shaft shall not look like an inverted nine-pin, nor do any of the accepted authorities require the club shall be manipulated by the arms. I admit it's bad form the way he plays, but, as Stuyvesant himself says, he never did travel on his shape."

"Suppose he gets a cuppy lie?" I asked, very much interested at the first news from Hades of the famous old Dutchman.

"Oh, he does one of two things," said Boswell. "He stubs it out with his toe or goes back and plays two more. Munchausen plays a good game too. He beat the colonel forty-seven straight holes last Wednesday, and all Hades has been talking about it ever since."

"Who is the colonel?" I asked, innocently.

"Bogie," returned Boswell. "Didn't you ever hear of Colonel Bogey?"

"Of course," I replied, "but I always supposed Bogey was an imaginary opponent, not a real one."

"So he is," said Boswell.

"Then you mean—"

"I mean that Munchausen beat him forty-seven up," said Boswell.

"Were there any witnesses?" I demanded, for I had little faith in Munchausen's regard for the eternal verities, among which a golf card must be numbered if the game is to survive.

"Yes, a hundred," said Boswell. "There was only one trouble with 'em." Here the great biographer laughed. "They were all imaginary, like the colonel."

"And Munchausen's score?" I queried.

"The same, naturally. But it makes him kingpin in golf circles just the same because nobody can go back on his logic," said Boswell. "Munchausen reasoned it out very logically indeed, and largely, he said, to protect his own reputation. Here is an imaginary warrior, said he, who makes a bully, but wholly imaginary, score at golf. He sends me an imaginary challenge to play him forty-seven holes. I accept, not so much because I consider myself a golfer as because I am an imaginer—if there is such a word."

"Ask Dr. Johnson," said I, a little sarcastically. I always grow sarcastic when golf is mentioned.

"Dr. Johnson be—" began Boswell.

"Boswell!" I remonstrated.

"Dr. Johnson be it, I was about to say," clicked the typewriter, suavely; but the ink was thick and inclined to spread. "Munchausen felt that Bogey was encroaching on his preserves as a man with an imagination."

"I have always considered Colonel Bogey a liar," said I. "He joins all clubs and puts up an ideal score before he has played over the links."

"That isn't the point at all," said Boswell. "Golfers don't lie. Realists don't lie. Nobody in polite—or say, rather accepted—society lies. They all imagine. Munchausen realizes he has only one claim to recognition, and that is based entirely upon his imagination. So when the imaginary Colonel Bogey sent him an imaginary challenge to play his forty-seven holes at golf—"

"Why forty-seven?" I asked.

"An imaginary number," explained Boswell. "Don't interrupt. As I say, when the imaginary colonel—"

"I must interrupt," said I. "What was he colonel of?"

"A regiment of perfect caddies," said Boswell.

"Ah, I see," I replied. "Imaginary in his command. There isn't one perfect caddie, much less a regiment of the little reprobates."

"You are wrong there," said Boswell. "You don't know how to produce a good caddie—but good caddies can be made."

"How?" I cried, for I have suffered. "I'll have the plan patented."

"Take a flexible brassie, and at the ninth hole, if they deserve it, give them eighteen strokes across the legs with all your strength," said Boswell. "But, as I said before, don't interrupt. I haven't much time left to talk with you."

"But I must ask one more question," I put in, for I was growing excited over a new idea. "You say give them eighteen strokes across the legs. Across whose legs?"

"Yours," replied Boswell. "Just take your caddie up, place him across your knees, and spank him with your brassie. Spank isn't a good golf term, but it is good enough for the average caddie; in fact, it will do him good."

"Go on," said I, with a mental resolve to adopt his prescription.

"Well," said Boswell, "Munchausen, having received an imaginary challenge from an imaginary opponent, accepted. He went out to the links with an imaginary ball, an imaginary bagful of fanciful clubs, and licked the imaginary life out of the colonel."

"Still, I don't see," said I, somewhat jealously, perhaps, "how that makes him a kingpin in golf circles. Where did he play?"

"On imaginary links," said Boswell.

"Poh!" I ejaculated.

"Don't sneer," said Boswell. "You know yourself that the links you imagine are far better than any others."

"What is Munchausen's strongest point?" I asked, seeing that there was no arguing with the man—"driving, approaching, or putting?"

"None of the three. He cannot putt, he foozles every drive, and at approaching he's a consummate ass," said Boswell.

"Then what can he do?" I cried.

"Count," said Boswell. "Haven't you learned that yet? You can spend hours learning how to drive, weeks to approach, and months to putt. But if you want to win you must know how to count."

I was silent, and for the first time in my life I realized that Munchausen was not so very different from certain golfers I have met in my short day as a golfiac, and then Boswell put in: "You see, it isn't lofting or driving that wins," he continued. "Cups aren't won on putting or approaching. It's the man who puts in the best card who becomes the champion."

"I am afraid you are right," I said, sadly, "but I am sorry to find that Hades is as badly off as we mortals in that matter."

"Golf, Sir," retorted Boswell, sententiously, "is the same everywhere, and that which is done in our world is directly in line with what is developed in yours."

"I'm sorry for Hades," said I; "but to continue about golf—do the ladies play much on your links?"

"Well, rather," returned Boswell, "and it's rather amusing to watch them at it, too. Xanthippe with her Greek clothes finds it rather difficult; but for rare sport you ought to see Queen Elizabeth trying to keep her eye on the ball over her ruff! It is really one of the finest spectacles you ever saw."

"But why don't they dress properly?"

"Ah," signed Boswell, "that is one of the things about Hades that destroys all the charm of life there. We are but shades."

"Granted," said I, "but your garments can—"

"Through all eternity we shades of our former selves are doomed to wear the shadows of our former clothes."

"Then what the devil does a poor dressmaker do who goes to Hades?" I cried.

"She makes over the things she made before," said Boswell. "That's why, my dear fellow," the biographer added, becoming confidential—"that's why some people confound Hades with—ah—the other place, don't you know."

"Still, there's golf!" I said; "and that's a panacea for all ills. You enjoy it, don't you?"

"Me?" cried Boswell. "Me enjoy it? Not on all the lives in Christendom. It is the direst drudgery for me."

"Drudgery?" I said. "Bah! Nonsense, Boswell!"

"You forget? It must be you who forget, if you call golf drudgery."

"No," sighed the genial spirit. "No I don't forger. I remember."

"Remember what?" I demanded.

"That I am Dr. Johnson's caddie!" was the answer. And then came a heart-rending sign, and from that time on all was silence. I repeatedly put questions to the machine, made observations to it, derided it, insulted it, but there was no response.

It has so continued to this day, and I can only conclude the story of my Enchanted Typewriter by saying that I presume golf has taken the same hold upon Hades that it has upon this world, and that I need not hope to hear more from that attractive region until the game has relaxed its grip, which I know can never be.

Hence let me say to those who have been good enough to follow me through the realms of the Styx that I bid them an affectionate farewell and thank them for their kind attention to my chronicles. They are all truthful; but now that the source of supply is cut off, I cannot prove it. I can only hope that for one and all the future may hold as much of pleasure as the place of departed spirits has held for me.

Sources

"Golf" by Rudyard Kipling. From *The Alamanac of Sports*, 1897.

"The Other Lure of Golf" by Grantland Rice. From *The American Golfer*, 1920.

"Golf for Women" by Charles Quincy Turner (writing as "Albion"). From *Outing*, 1890.

"The "Super-Sensitive Golf Ball" by Edwin L. Sabin. From *Golf: The Bulletin of the United States Golf Association*, 1901.

"The Humorous Side of Golf" by A. W. Tillinghast. From *Country Club Life*, 1914.

"Advice To a Young Golfer" by Max Behr. From *Golf Illustrated*, 1915.

"Dormie One" by Holworthy Hall. From *Everybody's Magazine*, 1917.

"The Revenge That Went Astray" by A. E. Thomas. From *Golf: The Bulletin of the United States Golf Association*, 1902.

"The Greatest Golf Finish I Ever Saw" by John G. Anderson. From *The American Golfer*, 1921.

"Hypothetically Golf" by Richard Florance. From *The Smart Set*, 1915.

"Playing Alone" by Marrion Wilcox. From *Golf: The Bulletin of the United States Golf Association*, 1901.

"When You Play on Public Links" by Walt Lantz. From *The American Golfer*, 1922.

"The Golden Rules of Golf" by O. B. Keeler. From *The American Golfer*, 1921.

"Foursomes" by John Montgomery Ward. From *The American Golfer*, 1908.

"Golf at the White House" by Heywood Broun. From *Vanity Fair*, 1921.

"Justice Harlan and the Game of Golf" by Richard Harlan. From *Scribner's Magazine*, 1917.

"Cowboy Golf" by Zane Grey. Excerpted from *Light of the Western Stars*, 1914.

"Shush!!!" by Ring Lardner. From *The American Golfer*, 1921.

"Do We Play for Pleasure?" by R. L. (Rube) Goldberg. From *The American Golfer*, 1920.

"Gentlemen, You Can't Go Through!" by Charles E. Van Loan. From the *Saturday Evening Post*, 1917.

"Winning the Double Crown" by Chick Evans. Excerpted from *Chick Evans's Golf Book*, 1921.

"Boy Golfer Falls Before Champion." From the *New York Times*, 1916.

"Homebred and Foreign Pros Compared" by Walter Hagen. From *Golf Illustrated*, 1917.

"The Rub of the Green" by William Almon Wolff. From *Collier's*, 1916.

"Golf on the Roof" by Adele Howells. From *The American Golfer*, 1921.

SOURCES

"War and Golf" by H. B. Martin. From *Golf: The Bulletin of the United States Golf Association*, 1917.
"The Coming Invasion" by Francis Ouimet. From *Golfer's Magazine*, 1919.
"The 'Curse of the Skirt'" by Marjorie R. S. Trumbull. From *The American Golfer*, 1920.
"Hit the Ball" by Eddie Loos. From *The American Golfer*, 1922.
"Women Handicapped by Men's Courses" by Alexa Stirling. From *Golf Illustrated*, 1917.
"Why I Quit Gambling." From *The American Golfer*, 1820.
"The Americanization of Archie" by Hugh Fullerton. From *The American Golfer*, 1920.
Excerpt from *Babbitt* by Sinclair Lewis, 1922.
"Forty Miles from Nowhere" by George Ade. From *The American Golfer*, 1920.
"Youth Is Served Again" by Damon Runyon from *Universal Services*, 1922.
"The Tantalus Loving-Cup" by W. G. Van Tassel Sutphen. From *Harper's Magazine*, 1898.
"The Joy of Golf" by Alvin R. Springer. From *Golfer's Magazine*, 1918.
"The Magic of Golf" by Reinette Douglas. From *The American Golfer*, 1922.
"Winter Dreams" by F. Scott Fitzgerald. From *Metropolitan Magazine*, 1922.
"Golf in Hades" by John Kendrick Bangs. Excerpted from *The Enchanted Type-Writer*, 1899.

About the Author

A former columnist for the *Los Angeles Herald Examiner*, Jeff Silverman has written regularly for such publications as the *New York Times* and *Sports Illustrated*. As an editor, his anthologies include *The Greatest Baseball Stories Ever Told*, *The Greatest Boxing Stories Ever Told*, and *Bernard Darwin on Golf*. *Great American Golf Stories* is his fifteenth book. His twelfth—*Merion: The Championship Story*—received the USGA's Herbert Warren Wind Award.